LUCKY GIRL GOODBYE

and its sequel

A BIT OF TIME

Renate Greenshields

With best wishes
Renate Greenshields

LUCKY GIRL GOODBYE

First published 1988
Second edition 1995
Third edition 2002
Fourth edition 2006

A BIT OF TIME

ISBN 0-9553655-0-3

Published by Renate Greenshields, Hawkchurch, Devon
Printed by Creeds the Printers, Broadoak, Bridport, DT6 5NL

GERMANY

1928 - 1946

The Rectory Lehrte

Drawing by Tom Greenshields

*For my husband, Tom,
my children,
Anne, Jane, Tim, George and Maria,
and my brother,
Georg-Wilhelm.*

It would not be a good idea to go back after all these long years and look at the place where I spent my childhood - my happy unforgettable childhood - and my youth, some of it happy, some sad.

I should love to see the old timber-framed house once again, but I know that would spoil my memory of its dear and welcoming, slightly wrinkled face. I am told that it has had a face-lift, that its kind eyes - the windows - which told the truthful age of the house, have been replaced with modern ones. Instead of the pinkish yellow and slightly crumbling plaster, which at the same time was rather appealing, it stands dressed in a coat of brilliant white.

I was born in the early hours of 20th September 1928. When my father received the news on a golden September morning, he jumped onto his bike and cycled to the nearest station to catch the train to Osnabrueck. When he entered the Maternity Hospital he heard several babies crying, but one voice was especially loud and forceful. When he remarked upon it, he was told by the nurse, "That is our little Parson's daughter."

Mother recovered slowly after my birth. My Godmother, who lived in the same village, moved in and looked after us. I was christened on my father's birthday in his study by my paternal grandfather, as mother was still too weak to walk the short distance to the Church. My father was at that time the rector of a small Westphalian village and my grandfather, semi-retired at the age of seventy, still looked after his own parish near Gottingen. I was given six names: Renate Frida Emma Margarete Arnoldine Ethelinde.

The name Renate was not well known in Germany, and father explained the meaning of it to me when I was old enough to understand. It came from the Latin word natare, which means 'to be born', but the Re was the important part of the name, meaning 'again'. So I was called 'born again'.

The winter of 1930 was a very severe one. The Parsonage became almost uninhabitable. In spite of all the love and care, I developed double pneumonia and for weeks was dangerously ill. My parents decided that the sea air would do my lungs good and a large party consisting of my parents, my brother Gewi (short for Georg Wilhelm), maternal grandmother and my Godmother set off to Langeoog, one of the North Sea islands, for six long weeks in the early summer.

Numerous photographs showed the happy party in large wicker chairs, whose backs ended in a roof above so as to provide shelter from both sun and wind. Or they showed me, plump and happy in a small basin of water, or my brother standing forlorn in the sand dunes looking out to sea. The funniest ones were of my parents in striped swimming costumes reaching as far as the knees and with little short sleeves. The only way to get to these islands then was by a horse-drawn carriage at low tide when the sea went out for miles.

The holiday was a great success and everybody returned home well. And my lungs have never given me any trouble again.

In the following autumn my brother had a severe accident. It happened on a warm sunny October afternoon while my parents were having tea in the garden. I was sitting in my pram beside them and my brother was playing ball somewhere in the garden. Suddenly they heard the screeching of brakes. My brother had opened the gate and run into the road to retrieve the ball. A car hit him and dragged him along several metres. He suffered severe concussion, and for another winter my mother had to look after a sick child. Under her constant care and love and through her efficiency, he recovered completely.

After two more years father decided to move to a larger town for two reasons; firstly, he did not want his children to leave home for school, as he never forgot the misery he suffered when he had to leave home at the early age of eight to go to a school twenty kilometres away. Secondly, his voice gave him trouble. The church was an enormous Gothic building with a chancel five metres high, the acoustics being bad and after every sermon his voice went. Thereafter, he found it difficult to speak loudly, and later, when I was old enough, it became my task to mix a raw egg with some milk and put it on the Vestry table before his sermon, to 'lubricate' his throat.

He decided to move to Lehrte, near Hannover, where he stayed for twenty-seven years until his retirement. My parents left the little Westphalian village of Buer with heavy hearts. Several times a year father was asked back to preach on special occasions.

The verdict of many who saw Lehrte was: the best thing about it is the station. Why? It is so boring but there is always a train to take you home. Or: the best thing to do in Lehrte is not to leave the station just to change trains.

It was not a pretty place, but I loved it. I loved its ugly water tower; the vulgar, ultra-modern clinker-built town hall; the church, built in 1870, a building devoid of any beauty, at least from the outside; the busy, exciting station and the many railway crossings which cut the little town into numerous sections and were a nuisance to drivers and pedestrians. Sometimes a queue of cars waited in front of the closed barrier, tooting impatiently. This made the guard in his tower-like house open the window: deliberately leaning out of it, he lit his pipe and, with the stateliness of an emperor, watched the growing crowd from above.

All sorts of trains passed through this little town; it was in fact a very important railway junction. There were endless goods trains, slow and fast passenger trains, a new electric train consisting of one coach only, and lastly the *Fliegende Hollaender*[1] on its way through from Brussels to Berlin. It was the fastest train in Europe. Once my aunt travelled on it. She had rung the night before from Brussels and I had promised that I would be at the station to wave. Proudly I told my friends, collected a gang of them and, in good time before the train was due, we stood at the station. Finally the signals announced its approach. Excitedly, I fumbled for my handkerchief, but before I had even got it out of my pocket, the brown and white larvae-like train had shot past, leaving a small group of children huddled against the fence, frightened by the pressure of its speed. All we could see were two red lights disappearing into the distance.

Lehrte was divided into two parts, the village and the town. We lived in the village. About thirty farms lay closely beside each other and flanked the village street on both sides; only a few lay tucked away in some off-shoot of the main street. The centre of it was the village green, called the Lindenberg, with six large old lime trees. A long time ago the village green had been in a different place, in front of the oldest farmhouse, which had since crumbled away. But the old oak, also the oldest in the village, still stood, gnarled and decayed, determined to survive its rivals, the younger limes.

---

[1] The Flying Dutchman

Not far from the village green stood the old 12th century church, a building of rough pink and grey sandstone with its lead spire perched on a squat whitewashed tower, pointing towards the sky like a witch's hat with a cockerel as a weathervane. The church stood slightly above the road, surrounded by a thorn hedge which hid the ancient tombstones and the rusted iron crosses of the churchyard.

Almost opposite was the Rectory into which we moved in 1932. The house lay back from the main street of the village, flanked by two old barns and guarded by tall acacias, a weeping willow in the middle of the lawn, and an enormous old oak tree. A long path of stone slabs led to the heavy front door with its brass handle and lock, fit for any stately home. A double and a single gate of wrought iron gave entry to the yard and house. The Rectory was a typical timber-framed cobb house of the 17th century. It looked like a friendly face, which even remained friendly in rainy weather, as the old bricks never seemed to change to the sad and dreary colour some houses take on when the rain wets their walls. Its many windows, thirty-two of them, made the house very light inside, and when the sun was shining, they twinkled in happy reflection.

It could be said that this Rectory was not exactly modern or even convenient for a housewife, but it did have running water and a bathroom and, of course, electricity. With the years, Mother insisted on various changes, but not nearly enough of them were effected before the war broke out, when everything came to a standstill. Most of the numerous plans for alterations never left the drawing board.

Large tiled stoves heated the rooms. Coal and logs had to be carried from the outhouses across the yard, and, as most of our living-rooms were on the first floor, many buckets of coal had to be taken upstairs. The lower and the upper hall were icy in the winter and no stove could even begin to heat them. We got into the habit of running across them in the winter months, to get to the warmth of the rooms and kitchen as quickly as possible. The lower hall had stone tiles and the upper one had wide, old wooden planks, which were highly polished and dusted every day. I once saw Mother going halfway down the stairs and when she was at eye level with the floor, she looked through the banisters to see if there was any dust left on the boards. There was. The maid was fetched immediately and the last speck of dust removed.

In the summer we had our meals upstairs. I always felt rather uncomfortable because a large picture, easily ten foot in length in a heavy black frame, showing in most horrifying detail the 'Destruction of Jerusalem', dominated the hall. I tried to avoid looking at it when passing it. But sitting at the table the nicest food was somehow made less tasty by suddenly coming eye to eye with the gory happenings in the picture. I tried sitting with my back to it, but the mere knowledge of the 'things' behind jumped on to my shoulders like an *alpdruck*[2].

I far preferred the winter months when we had our meals in the cosy little room downstairs, which was also our nursery.

Numerous doors with decorative brass handles and locks, each different, so that every door had its own particular sound when opened or shut, led from the upper hall into various rooms: six bedrooms, a bathroom, father's study, the large drawing room, with its four windows facing south and overlooking the garden, and mother's salon, called the 'Green room' because everything in it was green. The velvet sofa and its matching green armchairs, the bow-legged mahogany chairs around the mahogany table had green velvet seats; even the carpet was green. Here mother sat at her desk writing letters. She preferred to give her tea-parties in this room rather than in the large drawing-room next door.

In the summer, blinds were drawn half-way to protect the furniture from the sun, but the open windows let in enough air to allow the white muslin curtains to play flirtingly with the light breeze.

In the autumn, we hardly had to lean out of the window to pick a juicy bunch of grapes which grew all over the south wall of the house. In the winter all the windows were tightly shut and each one was paired with another set brought down from the attic. Thick velvet curtains, held in place by heavy brass rings, replaced the playful muslin curtains which now, gathered tightly with a wide band, hung sad and lifeless all through the winter months.

Towards the end of February, pots with crocuses, tulips and hyacinths, still in their infancy, were put between the windows and gradually, through the next two months, came into flower. On a particularly warm, sunny and spring-promising day, the windows were opened. Drops of melted snow hung from the gutters above, sparkling with rainbow colours in the sun and dripping steadily onto the snow below, just missing the windowsill. It was not until the end of April that the double windows were finally unhooked and taken back to the attic,

---

[2] Nightmare

the velvet curtains removed and folded, then packed into the camphor chest, and, at last, the white muslin curtains were released from their tight grip to play once again in the breeze.

Father's study was on the north side of the house, facing the courtyard. It was a dark room. The wallpaper had been originally of a light colour, but Father's constant smoking of pipes and cigars had made it brown. Brown also were his desk, chairs and table, as were the cushions and blankets on the sofa. Most of the books which stood shelf upon shelf along the walls were of brown leather with golden lettering; the shelves reached almost as high as the ceiling, but leaving enough room for large old Bibles lying on their sides. These were old family Bibles. One of the most precious possessions was an old Koran, a beautifully-bound small book.

At least twenty pipes of different shapes and sizes hung neatly arranged in a stand on the old smoking-table in the corner. On the shelf below stood cigar boxes, piled on top of each other, of 'Handles Gold' and 'Havanas'. The little drawer above, with its decorative brass knob, took care of the pipe cleaners and matches.

Two things in that room concerned me most. One I feared, the other I loved. The one I dreaded was a long ruler of red lacquer, slightly faded, its varnish cracking. It stood, leaning against the wall, on the smoking table, and the only time it was used was on my brother's and my own behinds. Father hated using it and only reached for it in extreme cases of naughtiness. It was used on my own behind far more than on my brother's, who bent over as told and took his punishment stoically, without uttering a sound. I fought back like a wild cat, biting and hitting out, trying to snatch the ruler out of my father's hand. This infuriated him so much that my punishment always ended up being far more severe than originally intended.

The thing that delighted me was a wooden money box on the desk, about a foot long. It showed a black boy kneeling down in prayer on a grassy hilltop. As soon as a piece of money fell through the slot in front of him, he nodded his curly head in thanks, and resumed praying.

One picture in the study fascinated me. It showed Daniel in the Lions' Den, in a ray of sunlight looking up towards the window, with the lions standing behind him, one licking his feet like a faithful dog.

The attic was huge and covered the whole of the house. Two ordinary-sized windows at each end and numerous small ones on the tiled roof gave ample light during the day. It was a lovely place to be in but, when the daylight began to fade, I was scared to go up by myself. Whenever I had to fetch something from the loft in the evenings, for my mother, I went to extremes to find somebody to come with me. Mostly I ended up by bribing my brother that I would not tell that he was reading in bed when lights should be out. Reluctantly he would come with me as far as the attic door, where he would sit down on the upper step of the short but very steep staircase.

The switch for the electric light was outside the attic, and what I was really afraid of was that somebody could switch it off while I was inside. A horrid cousin had once done just that and I had nearly died of fright. My brother would never do that; I could rely on him.

Everything that appeared harmless and friendly during the day took on a threatening shape when the light became dim. The bunches of beans in the pods hanging up to dry looked like heads of Red Indians, and the rows and rows of corn cobs for the chickens looked like daggers.

The atmosphere was completely different during the day. It was a cheerful and exciting place in which lingered a sweet and mysterious aroma, coming mainly from the drying herbs, which hung in small bunches from the beams - camomile and peppermint for colds and tummy-aches, garlic and onions, and, most of all, from the apples. The floor space was vast and, although numerous bits of furniture were stored there, it was not in the least cluttered. Wide, hard floor-boards sustained a great weight, and even our roller-skating, which produced quite an alarming noise and was only permitted when my parents were out.

Four attic rooms lay tucked under the large sloping roof. They were the apple room, the Christmas store room, the room for bedding and the smoke room.

Three of them would have made lovely bedrooms, but they became too hot in summer and too cold in winter. Looking down from the attic windows one saw the village from an unusual angle. One looked down upon the red tiled roofs of the cottages and their neat gardens of flower-beds and fruit trees. The dreaded farm dogs appeared small and insignificant, the ferocious gander was a small speck. Only the church spire stood as usual, dominating, grey and large, reaching out to the sky.

The apple room was the second largest of the four rooms. White muslin bags full of dried apple rings, prunes and hazelnuts hung from the ceiling. Apples and pears, carefully sorted into their varieties lay, not touching each other, on the shelves. Little tags nailed onto the shelves told their names. Each fruit had been carefully picked in the autumn by my mother. Most of the apple trees in the garden were of a dwarf variety, but the pear trees were tall, old and dangerous to climb. This did not deter mother from climbing into them, completely fearless, and determined to get every pear, however impossible and dangerous it seemed to the onlooker. Precariously, she balanced on the brittle branches, not giving in until the last pear was safely and carefully put into her basket.

Twice a week in the winter months, Mother went up to the apple room and selected the ripe fruit and took away what was rotten or wormy. She had chosen her fruit trees so carefully that we had a variety of ripe fruit right up until the spring. The nicest were the 'Christmas pear' and the 'Napoleon's butter pear', so large and juicy that one was too much for one person, but too little for two. It was a ritual to eat them, either after lunch or in the evening in father's study just before bedtime, off fruit plates hand painted with a golden rim. They were peeled with delicate fruit-knives with blue and white Meissen handles. They were delicious fruits and deserved precious things.

Next to the apple room was the small Christmas store room. Labelled boxes contained everything to do with Christmas: painted crib figures, candleholders and tree decorations. There was also a flat box full of long narrow silver strips, called 'Lametta' which were hung from the Christmas tree branches like frozen rain.

The smell of beeswax candles and the faint fragrance of pine needles never left that room and was powerful enough to transmit a Christmas mood, even on a hot summer day. At the other end of the loft was the biggest room. In it stood enormous wooden boxes. One of them had father's name written all over it and it was lined with pages and pages from exercise books in Greek, Latin and Hebrew. They seemed to me like drawings of crosses and dots and circles. This box had been father's book trunk and had followed him to every university he had been to. Now it contained heavy winter coats and furs, sprinkled with anti-moth crystals and camphor. Other boxes were filled with feather duvets; this was of course during the summer only. In the winter they were almost empty except for the light summer eiderdowns. I did not like this room very much. The smell of mothballs was unpleasant and the contents of the boxes uninteresting, except for one bit of furniture.

It was an invalid commode of mahogany whose lid bore a monogram. The fascinating thing about it was the huge chamber-pot inside, decorated with delicate bunches of roses and green garlands. Every time my brother and I went into this room we lifted up the lid and admired this beautifully painted but incredibly large vessel. Once I heard my brother, when he was closing the lid, murmur, "Quite impossible!" And he shook his head at the same time.

I was much more interested in the small room in the middle of the loft where most of the house's flue pipes met and went into one big chimney. Around it a small room had been built. This was the smoke room, into which led a tiny door made of gauze to keep out the flies. Here the smoked sausages were kept and the hams hung from large hooks. They were wrapped in muslin bags, yellowed from pepper and fat. It was the only room with a padlock; only mother had the key and it was mother only who decided which sausage to take down. I had never seen anybody else cut the ham except mother. I hardly ever missed this occasion and watched her, fascinated, as she took down the ham and put it onto the little table to take off the bag. Carefully she scraped off the powdered pepper with the big sharp knife and then cut into the pink ham bordered by strips of white fat. I liked it best when she started to cut a new ham. Once the bone appeared the ham became ugly, for she skilfully cut around the bone, so that eventually a nasty stump, like an amputated limb, stuck out, and this repulsed me. Each time mother sprinkled the newly cut bit with fresh pepper before she put it back into the muslin bag. But before it went into the bag she looked smilingly at me, cut a very thin slice and handed it to me on the knife. This was the moment I had waited for. The ham was so tender and delicious, it melted in my mouth.

One big treasure stored in the loft was the toboggan. My grandmother had bought it in Lausanne for us. Its front was gracefully curved like the horns of a ram, its slats were thick and round. It was not a piece of factory work, as my grandmother pointed out to us, but a piece of craftsmanship. My brother was not very keen on tobogganing, but I was. From the first snowflake until the last bit of snow had melted the toboggan and I were inseparable friends.

There was also the old sledge, a Victorian bygone, like a wheelchair, only on rails and painted in green and gold. It was pushed from the back. Once my brother and I took it out for an airing in the winter. I sat, wrapped in a blanket on the cast-iron seat and my brother pushed. It was hard work at first. The runners were rusty and left narrow brown marks in the snow, but after a while they glided easily over it and my brother began to try all sorts of tricks, like sharp turns, to upset me, but the sledge was well-balanced. We had great fun but it was spoiled by the village children, who almost killed themselves laughing and shouting rude remarks at the unusual sight. This stopped us from taking it out again, but we soon found many other purposes for it. We imagined it to be our tram, train, plane, even our pony cart.

One of the greatest secrets my brother and I ever shared was the 'preaching'. An old, disused lectern started it off. My brother began to preach in the loft. Later in his life he never had the slightest wish to become a parson, but at this stage in his young life it must have been there. One day he appeared in my father's long winter coat, a Bible pressed against his chest. Slowly he walked towards the lectern and began to preach. I was his sole congregation, sitting on a footstool below him with folded hands. Almost in the same voice as my father, he read a short text from the Bible and then began to tell stories, keeping up his parson's voice throughout his favourite stories, such as 'Winnetou', 'Quo Vadis', and, for my own special benefit (or the Sunday school children's benefit, as he announced), a fairy story. I was fascinated. A more ardent listener no parson could have wished for, but then, not all sermons were as interesting and captivating as my brother's stories. Alas, everything comes to an end. After a while his repertoire petered out and the stories repeated themselves a bit too often and I became bored. One day my footstool remained empty and there was no congregation. I think my brother must have been aware of his lack of inspiration because he made no attempt to claim me back. I often wonder for how long he went on preaching to himself in the attic.

As much as I loved the attic, I hated the cellar. There was no real cellar underneath the house, but a small dungeon-like vault with immensely thick walls. It had been built onto the house, halfway above ground. A pair of stone steps led from the kitchen into this dark, dank place. Two small windows with iron bars let in very little light. Along three of the cellar walls were shelves, on which were stored wine and bottles of fruit juice. I had a real horror of this place. Little did I know that later I should have to spend the greater part of three years in there.

My earliest childhood memory goes back to the age of two. I was lying in a cradle; somebody I did not know bent over me and gave me a wooden spoon. I started to play with it and banged it rather too hard on the edge of the cradle (it must have been a fairly rotten spoon), and it broke in half. Silver stars and a large orange moon with a grinning face looked down on me. My mother explained to me years later when I mentioned these memories to her that an amateur dramatic group of our village performed the play by the well-known German author Matthias Claudius, *The Moon has Risen* - for which I was borrowed. Of the play I remember an enormously tall man with a top-hat trying to take me out of the cradle into his arms. Naturally, I was terrified and began to scream. The play had to stop and mother rushed from the audience onto the stage to pacify me, without any result. I refused to get back into the cradle and soon was fast asleep on her lap and the play had to go on without me. Father referred to my little episode as the Intermezzo and burst into laughter every time he was reminded of it. I was never borrowed for any acting again, but a certain dismay of men in top hats remained.

The next thing I remember happened six months later. My brother had been very ill with a kidney complaint and needed my mother's sole attention. I was very much in the way with my liveliness, so it was decided that my father should take me to my maternal grandmother in Schleswig-Holstein, a long journey for a two and half year old who could not sit still for one minute.

The actual train journey I can't remember, but apparently, after a short period of looking out of the window I said in a loud and urgent voice that I had to spend a penny. Father was at an absolute loss. Never in his life had he been confronted with such a problem before, and despite all the advice mother had given him, she had forgotten to mention this vital detail. Luckily, a very nice woman in the compartment had watched this situation smilingly and offered to take me. I do remember sitting in a large waiting-room in Hamburg afterwards with a glass of milk in front of me and father urging me to drink it. I did not want to and no coaxing, pleading or bribing helped. I sat with my mouth tightly shut, refusing to take even a sip. Then my father had a brilliant idea. He remembered how much I loved clinking glasses, and so with every sip a beer glass and a milk glass met and the milk was drunk. It was a long process but it kept me occupied.

I can't remember anything of my stay with grandmother, except that I missed my mother dreadfully. It was obvious that I was homesick. Apparently I ate little and was, much against my nature, very quiet. At last mother came to fetch me: I think father dreaded another journey alone with me. I can remember the immense joy in my heart when I was told of her coming. When finally we fetched her from the station, I was wearing white knee socks, a thing for special occasions only, and I was skipping for joy beside grandmother. It had rained during the night and this had left little puddles on the path, over which I jumped, not always missing them, and my white socks became splattered with mud. Grandmother's scolding could not stop me, nothing could stop me, for my mother was coming. And then I saw her coming towards us. I can remember so well the thought which came into my head - it hurts me to think of it now. I suddenly thought, why should I run towards her? She had sent me away and I did not like it. A few feet away my mother stood with her arms outstretched and I stood stock still, pretending not to know her.

With tears in her eyes mother cried, "Don't you know your mummy any more?"

"Oh, yes I do!" my heart cried out, but I shook my head and took grandmother's hand and didn't talk to mother at all, only looked at her.

That night mother and I slept together in the big double bed. When I woke next morning I saw her looking lovingly at me. I could not restrain myself any longer, but flung my arms around her neck and sobbed all the homesickness of the last few weeks out of me. I wouldn't let her out of my sight or let go of her hand for the rest of our stay.

<hr/>

When my brother was well again, mother wanted to surprise my father for his birthday with a professional photograph of his children.

She took us to Hannover on a sultry August afternoon. Dark clouds hung from the sky and looked menacingly through the vast glass roof of the studio. Lightning illuminated the whole of it and frightened me. I buried my head in my mother's lap. Nothing could persuade me to pose for the picture. The photographer had to wait until the storm was over. My dress was of white organza with red embroidery, and I wore a little necklace of tiny moonstones. My brother wore a white sailor's suit.

For the first time, mother had put a white ribbon into my unruly blonde curls. I did not like this at all and constantly tried to get it out. In the end mother lost her patience with me, especially as the photographer began to get impatient too as the thunderstorm went on and on, and she slapped my hand. This produced tears and an even longer wait. Finally the portrait was taken and all of us smiled happily, and the white bow in my hair stuck out like a starched white pigeon. I remember the photographer asking mother if she would allow him to take a few more photographs of me for advertisements, because I had 'such lovely eyes'. Mother was horrified and refused with great certainty.

One winter morning - it must have been in 1933 - our house was suddenly full of people. It was at the time of the great unemployment. The church was trying to help. With a group of volunteers mother had sewn clothes until late into the nights, and now every room was stacked with coats and jackets and all sorts of other garments. Father had been to his former parish and collected food from the farmers. They had given so much that he had to hire a van to transport it back. He had also been given clothes, material and shoes from three draper's shops in our town. These were owned by Jews, called Simon, Maschekatz and Meinrath. Their generosity had been overwhelming, and there was no doubt that most of the gifts had come from these three.

More and more people crowded into the house; men and women with pale drawn faces, dressed inadequately for the winter cold. An unpleasant smell spread about the house. Unpleasant also was their behaviour; their manners were rough and they could become dangerous. They took the help offered as a matter of course. They became angry and rude if a garment given to them that was not exactly the right fit or to their liking. My brother and I had been told not to leave our nursery on that day, but of course, I did and tried to ascend the crowded staircase with my favourite doll under my arm.

At that very moment the riot started. I saw fists lashing out everywhere; blood squirted from noses and mouths. The shouting drowned my frightened crying, especially when my doll was snatched from me. I most certainly would have come to harm, had not two strong arms lifted me up and carried me to safety. They were the arms of a policeman. Suddenly all was quiet: the police soon restored order and they stayed in the house until the last person was fitted out, which was late at night. My parents were both so tired that I never got told off for leaving my nursery. Losing my doll was enough punishment in itself.

When I was five years old I started to go to the Kindergarten. My brother had been going to school for quite a while now and the mornings had become lonely and boring for me. I must have had a few playmates, though I can only remember two. The funny thing about these two was that they were uncle and nephew. Their father and grandfather respectively, was a crude and enormously large person, who wore a shiny leather apron. I never saw him without it. He was a pub owner and a coal merchant at the same time, and lived not far from our house. His loud, unpleasant voice could be heard for miles, and every child in the village was afraid of him, as were his own five children and his wife. His youngest son, Ernstchen, the same age as myself, had been an after-thought, and Alex, a year younger, was the illegitimate son of his eldest daughter. These two were my friends. Ernstchen's mother had a small sweet shop, but although he tried to convince me that lollipops and gob-stoppers were far cheaper in his mother's shop, the fear of meeting his father led me in my early childhood to the extravagance of spending more for my sweets at another shop.

Unfortunately, I sometimes had to take shoes to the old shoemaker who lived in the attic of Ernstchen's house. Steep, narrow wooden stairs led to his workshop. Ernstchen's father hated a lot of people in the village, but mostly my father. Soon after our move to Lehrte, my father turned one of our barns into a church hall. Up until then Ernstchen's father had been allowed to store hay for his horses there and he also made use of the lovely fresh eggs our hens had been laying. All this came to a stop with the conversion of the barn and he resented it. He completely ignored my father but got his own back on me.

Every time I had to go to the shoemaker I tried to sneak into Ernstchen's house without being seen, but most times I was unlucky - his father was lying in wait for me. I even tried taking off my shoes and going up the stairs without making any noise at all, but every time he had seen me going up and waited for me to come down again. He stood at the bottom of the stairs, legs apart, his fleshy arms tattooed with snakes and naked girls. He grinned when he saw me hesitating to come down with my shoes in my hands.

Sneeringly he shouted, "Are you afraid, you little holy one?"

Every time I thought my last moment had come, but he never touched me, and he moved just a little to let me pass. A shiver went through me when my arm came in contact with his dirty leather apron. Then he turned triumphantly round and shouted spitefully after me, *"Pastoren Scheisser!"*[3]

It was I myself who made this situation even worse. On a fine autumn morning I was collecting acorns in the yard with Ernstchen and Alex. We were going to sell them to Frau Kruse for her pig. I liked Ernstchen very much but not so much Alex, and with this his uncle agreed heartily. As I was putting acorns into my basket next to Ernstchen, his little round face came close to mine, and I suddenly had the desire to kiss him, which I did. I don't know what came over me next, but I bit him also. He at once let out a piercing yell and ran home with his hand over his cheek.

It wasn't long before his father, with a still frightened Ernstchen beside him, rang the doorbell and triumphantly showed my parents the tooth marks of their vampire daughter. I can't remember if he demanded compensation, but I was sent to my room for the rest of the day and was given 'prison food', as we called it - dry bread and a glass of milk.

Ernstchen did not come to play with me again for a long time, nor did his nephew. When he finally came back, he always kept a certain distance from me.

As I grew older, I grew less frightened of his father. I even dared to make some extra loud noises going up the stairs to provoke him. He gave up waiting for me at the bottom of the stairs, but never failed, when he saw me, to shout a rude remark after me.

I loved seeing the shoemaker and always spent a considerable time with him. He lived alone. Sometimes mother gave me some soup for him, which I carried in a little white milk can. Every time he said politely, "Please thank Frau Pastor for me," and he emptied the contents into a very dirty saucepan which he put onto the small round cast-iron stove next to a pot of hot liquid glue, in which stuck a blackened wooden spoon. I loved the smell of this glue, and always asked if I might stir the delicious, yellowish, almost transparent mixture. He let me, but only a couple of stirs and then he said quite firmly, "That's enough." The mess in the little room was incredible. Shoes and boots of all sizes lay in a big heap beside his chair, but the funny thing was that one never had to wait for more than a couple of days for the repair of one's shoes. The repaired

---

[3] Shit of a parson's daughter

ones stood ready for collection on a small table, some highly polished, some as dirty as they had been on their arrival.

In spite of being a very busy man, he always seemed to have time for a chat and he knew exactly what I was waiting for. He had a parrot which lived in a cage near the window above his work top. One could ask anything under the sun, and the bird always knew the correct answer. Each time I thought of something really difficult which he could not possibly know, but the bird was a miracle: he knew the answer, and replied correctly in a very human, slightly hoarse voice.

By and by I noticed a certain resemblance between his voice and that of the shoemaker, who always sat with his back towards me when the bird answered. One day I told him of my suspicion but he laughed and, with some nails between his teeth, said in the parrot's voice, "No, no, it isn't true." I knew it was.

The highlight was his zither which lay on the bed next door. It was a beautiful zither of ebony with mother-of-pearl decorations. Every time I went into his bedroom to fetch it, gooseflesh came all over me, for on the chest of drawers, in a large dome-shaped jar filled with methylated spirit, coiled a dead adder. Without once taking my eyes off this extraordinary bedroom decoration, I fumbled for the instrument and went backwards out of the room, and shut the door very firmly behind me, then handed Herr Domeier the zither.

He stood up, wiped his dirty hands on the even dirtier apron, which still showed, here and there, the original green colour. He pushed aside the boots on the small table and very carefully put the instrument on it. He twiddled with the numerous pegs, and then plucked all the strings with his thumb to see if it was in tune. I could not judge if he played well or not; but for me it was heavenly music. I looked, fascinated, at his fingers with the long dirty fingernails as they pressed down on the strings for an extra loud and impressive vibrato.

Anyway, to the Kindergarten I had to go and I didn't like it one little bit. I loved Tante Lisbeth, the Kindergarten teacher, but I didn't like any of the other children. I can't remember why, I just did not like them and refused to join in any of their games or to sit down at the same table with them. For a while they let me be, thinking I would get used to them, but I didn't, and after a few weeks I became so impossible that I was allowed to stay at home again.

Once in a while I stayed a weekend with Tante Lisbeth, mostly when mother had one of her migraines. Tante Lisbeth lived at the other end of the town and our maid took me, pushing her bicycle, on which she had fastened my small suitcase. She held on to the bike with one hand and to me with the other. I carried a little basket into which I had packed my nightie and my toothbrush and my doll. Tante Lisbeth had so many things in her flat which delighted a child's heart, but the nicest thing was her voice, and she kindled in me the joy of singing and of listening to music. Her brother, who lived with her, was very amused by my singing. There were one or two letters I could not yet pronounce properly, like the 'sch' which I pronounced as 's' only. He always asked me to sing '*Soene Luefte, soener sall, soener Fruehling ueberall.*'

Not only could Tante Lisbeth sing well; she told stories most beautifully, and all three of us sat after supper in the cosy kitchen, I in my nightie on her lap, sucking my two middle fingers, until my eyelids dropped and her brother carried me to my bed, both of them tucking me in tenderly.

One night it was not quite so peaceful. I had a great dislike of onions and there were plenty in the fried potatoes for supper. Tante Lisbeth insisted that I should eat them, but suddenly I took my plate and emptied the contents onto the floor. This earned me a severe smack. On top of it, I was sent to bed early without a story. Above my head hung a luminous cross which looked menacing in the dark and frightened me. I had told Tante Lisbeth I did not like it but she said it was there to comfort people. Every night I pulled the blankets over my eyes, so that I could not see it, but that night I kept on looking at it out of the corner of my eyes, and instead of feeling frightened, let alone comforted, I felt very, very miserable and homesick. I began to weep quietly. I was used to saying my prayers with my mother beside me, but this night two small hands folded by themselves and ardently I prayed, "Please, God, deliver me from these unjust people."

Next morning deliverance came. Everything had been forgotten and I was playing happily, when my brother suddenly arrived to take me home. Tante Lisbeth was very surprised. I should have stayed for another few days as arranged, but my brother, Gewi, insisted. I packed my little basket, and hand in hand, Gewi taking his duty to look after me very seriously, we walked home. Everybody was surprised to see me, but all the same, mother, more or less recovered, took me into her arms and said how nice it was to have me back. It turned out that my brother had acted entirely on his own because, as he confessed, he had missed me.

When I was five years old I still sucked my fingers, which, as a result, had started to grow crooked. When I developed measles and the doctor came, mother asked him at the same time to look at my fingers. I have always had a most unnatural horror of doctors and illness. Once, when mother had helped a woman who fainted in the street, I asked her afterwards, "With which hand did you touch her?" and avoided that hand for a long time.

The doctor gave mother two small wooden splints for her to fasten on to my fingers with a bandage. Furiously I looked at the doctor, took the splints from the bedside table, jumped out of bed, and before anybody could stop me, threw them out of the open window. But it had done the trick. The horror of the splints was enough to make me stop sucking my fingers.

My terror of illness was so vivid and exaggerated, that the sight of a drop of blood would drive me into hysterics. One evening when I could not get to sleep I heard voices and footsteps going backwards and forwards across the hall. I got up quietly and opened the door and saw our maid coming out of my father's study carrying a basin of blood.

I shot across the hall, shouting, "What has happened to my father?"

When I burst into his room I saw him sitting in his armchair, with a woman whom I did not know holding under his arm a basin into which dripped blood. I was almost beside myself on seeing this. Mother, startled and horrified by my sudden appearance, tried to explain that this nice woman was only putting leeches on father's arm and that he was perfectly all right. In fact he smiled quite happily at me. But what did I understand about all that? I started to scream and actually went for the woman, who after a few quiet words from mother, packed her bags and hurriedly left the house. Only then did I start to calm down. I was pale, I trembled all over and my heart was beating wildly. Mother wrapped me in a blanket and carried me back to bed, gave me a sugar lump dipped in milk, and sat down beside me until I fell asleep. I don't know whether father had any more of such horrid treatments, but most certainly not in our house.

—————◆————

My parents were a handsome couple. I was very proud of them. Both were tall and slim, with dark, almost black hair. Mother's was curly, but father's was straight, with a parting to one side and the other, fuller side resting in a slight swoop on his large forehead.

Not only was I proud of their handsome looks. I was proud for what they were, that they were our parents. In my childhood I took for granted everything they did, but when I grew older, perhaps from the age of ten, I began to realise how much of their lives they devoted to us children and to everybody who needed their help. I have seen them utterly exhausted in the evenings, especially during the war, not just with physical fatigue but mainly with worries, never about themselves, always about others. In spite of this, they never failed to show us and give us their love. They found time to go for walks with us, to play games with us and read to us.

The nicest thing was when mother, before our bedtime, sang with us from the big old song book, called Kinderland, which showed in colourful and descriptive pictures the content of nursery rhymes and folk songs. I can still see mother's fingers hovering, slightly shaking, over the keyboard of the harmonium when she tried to read the music and text at the same time. Gewi and I sat each side of her on the tall and slightly sloping oak bench, I resting my head on her shoulder. I loved singing the cheerful songs, but oh, when it came to the sad ones like 'Haenschen klein' or 'Morgenrot Leuchtest mir zum fruehen Tod', or 'Nun ade Du mein schoen Heimatland' where the picture showed a young man leaving home to earn his living, waving a last farewell to his mother, who stood crying at the small wicket gate, drying her eyes with the corner of her apron - then I could not sing any more. Tears choked my throat and I moved even closer to mother. But even mother's clear voice, or was it perhaps the mournful sound of the harmonium, seemed to fill me with utter sadness. I suffered badly from homesickness every time I went by myself on a holiday, and the older I got, the worse it became.

I adored mother; I thought everything about her was beautiful. Her oval face with the delicate complexion could go very brown in the summer. Her nose was thin and perhaps a little too long. Her lips were always a fraction parted by a front tooth which slightly overlapped the other. Her large blue eyes gave her face a sunny, kind expression; they were also sympathetic and laughing eyes. Very rarely did they appear otherwise, but when there was a very good reason they could suddenly look strict and penetrating. Then it was no good to tell a lie - when those eyes looked at you like that, you had to tell the truth. It did not happen often; we almost loved it. We actually sometimes asked mother to make her *'Polizeiaugen,'*[4] as we called them. But it wasn't the same when there was no reason for it. She over-exaggerated, and we all, including mother, burst out laughing.

Mother dressed well. She loved nice clothes though she was by no means extravagant. On the contrary, she was very thrifty. Father was utterly hopeless with money, so mother looked after the finances. We were not rich but comfortably off. Twice in their lifetime after each of the last two wars, my parents lost their savings through inflation. We did not often have luxuries, only on very special occasions. My parents had their annual three week holiday, which they spent mostly in Bavaria. Father's 'luxuries' were books and concerts in Hannover, and mother's were the occasional new dresses, and plants for her garden. Mother worked hard. With the help of one maid and once in a while with the help of a gardener, she looked after the house and large garden.

A lot of guests filled our house throughout the year; friends and relations and parishioners. Mother did all the cooking; she was an excellent cook. Flowers and pretty things made the house look cheerful and cosy. Parishioners sought not only father's advice but mother's as well. Her training as a nurse came in handy. I remember one girl coming to her in a very distressed state of mind. Mother found poison in the girl's handbag. She took her in and looked after her for several weeks. When the girl got better she went back to her own flat but committed suicide a few days afterwards. These things made mother very sad. She grew grey prematurely, and I often wondered if it was because of all the sadness she saw, especially during the war. Like father, she was loved and respected in the parish: people sought their comforting and help and they were always ready to give it.

Father called mother mostly by her Christian name, but in the diminutive Paulinchen as she was also called by our friends and relations. Gewi sometimes called her Paulinchen as well, but I liked to call her *Dotte* once in a while.

She once looked after a small boy suffering from TB. He could not pronounce her surname, which was Gotthardt before she got married,

---

[4] Policeman's eyes

so he called her *Dotte*. Mother had been very fond of the little boy, who died, and she still talked about him once in a while. Perhaps because of a little jealousy on my part, I sometimes called her *Dotte* and mother smiled every time I did so.

Physically I felt closer to mother than to my father. I loved it when she stroked my hair with my head in her lap or when she kissed my forehead or cheek, or when she hugged me and tucked me up in bed at night. That physical contact with mother made me secure and happy. When I was about 8 years old I wrote a poem about her which ended with:

Mein groesster Wunsch ist, denn ich bin klein,
ein Kangeruh Baby bei Mutti zu sein.[5]

I adored my mother but I worshipped my father. To him I went when I was frightened, when I wanted advice, when I had done something wrong. I sat on his lap with my arm around his neck but I did not cuddle up to him. Father treated me from an early age as a pal, a friend.

Many years later, on his death-bed, he stretched out his hand to me and said, "We have always been good comrades and understood each other. It has been one of my greatest joys."

Father was very sensitive. He knew when something bothered me. He would put his arm around my shoulders and ask, "What is it?" I could tell him everything. He gave advice, comfort, faith to me, the child, with the same seriousness and conviction as he did to all his parishioners. Comforted, relieved and cheerful, I left his study many a time, skipped across the hall and slid down the banisters back to the nursery downstairs.

Besides being handsome, father was also very clever. A scholar of theology and philosophy, he was also a scholar of ancient languages. He spoke Greek, Latin and Hebrew fluently, and talked four European languages. His greatest hobbies were reading and music, his greatest gift his sermons, which were powerful, faith-giving and uncomplicated, so that young and old could benefit. Father's sermons were printed in numerous booklets all over Germany. He took the greatest trouble to

---

[5] My biggest wish, for I am tiny,
   is to be a Kangaroo baby with Mummy.

prepare his sermons on Saturday nights until late into the morning. It was the only time when nobody was allowed to disturb him, not even mother. But on many a Sunday morning at 3 or 4 o'clock she would quietly open the study door and whisper, "It's time for you to go to bed."

From when I was about six years old, I used to accompany father on his way to Matins. To avoid the churchgoers we took a different route, and a slight detour took us along the little river, over the bridge, through an alleyway and across the patch of grass with the tall elms to the vestry door at the apse of the church. I walked beside or behind him, carefully carrying a mug, half filled with a raw egg beaten with milk, which father drank just before the sermon to lubricate his throat. We never talked on our way to church. I knew father was preoccupied with his sermon and I would not have wanted to disturb him. In the vestry, on cold winter days stood a small electric bar heater over which we warmed our hands. A churchwarden usually waited for him and, after discussing one or two things went back into the church. The organ quietly played an introduction and muffled coughs and clearings of throats came from the waiting congregation.

Father put on his black gown, gathered from the yoke in many folds. When I was still too small to reach up to him, I climbed onto a chair to tie the white starched bands around the collar, carefully tucking in the ends. Whenever I was not there to do this, father forgot about the ends and they remained sticking out from under the collar. Having done this, father wanted to be alone. We shook hands solemnly and I went home.

My brother had his Sunday duty as well. His job was to light the candles and to put out the collection plates. He then took up his post in the porch and, of his own accord and, if I remember correctly, against father's will, counted the arriving congregation, nodding a good morning to those he knew, continuing with his counting which he recorded in his private notebook. He always had, and still has, a passion for records.

After church I once again went to the vestry, and untied father's bands and put them carefully into the big, fat Bible which lay on the table. This time we walked hand in hand the usual way home, father raising his hat non-stop because everybody knew him. Sometimes he stopped and talked to somebody. When it took too long I grew impatient and tugged at his sleeve. We continued our walk in cheerful chatter. Sometimes we hummed one of father's university songs which he had taught me, sometimes we played a game when father put his large soft hand over my eyes, leading me along, going this way and that way, sometimes turning around in a full circle, and I had to guess where I was.

Father had a lot of female admirers. In no way did he try to charm them - he had a natural charm which women found irresistible. He enjoyed female company, especially intellectual female company, but he always preferred mother's though she was not an intellectual. Her common sense, sound opinions and fairness father valued more than anybody else's.

Ever since his student days father wore a small moustache until one day in Hannover, at the beginning of the war, a man mistook him for Adolf Hitler, who indeed had the same moustache, haircut and even the same mackintosh, a light brown one with a wide belt. Father was wearing one on that day. He was taller than Hitler, but the man undoubtedly thought it was his idol. He jumped off his bike, saluted him with an outstretched, rigid arm and shouted, "Heil, mein Führer!" He was most disappointed when father put on an expression of loathing and then looked into a shop window to discover that his reflection looked indeed a little like Hitler's. Without losing a moment he went to the nearest barber shop, had his moustache removed and his lock of hair over the forehead cut very short. He then bought himself a black mackintosh with a thin belt and burnt the other on his return.

⟹◆⟸

I very often heard mother complain about our maids; how troublesome they were and how she wished she could do without them. I could not see anything wrong with them at all. I liked them, but looking back I can understand that often they must have been more trouble than help.

Apart from our first three maids, mother took in young girls who came from Homes for unmarried mothers; some had been in prisons, some in mental homes.

One time this proved to be almost fatal. This particular maid was called Marie. I liked her because she was always smiling. As I was only five years old at the time, I could not distinguish between a cheerful smile and an insane grin. I thought it funny when one day, during a Bible reading her face became very red and she could not control her giggle, which started me off of course, and we were both sent out by my father. She went on giggling in the kitchen, until I got fed up and went into the garden. Gewi knew that she was slightly 'round the bend'. Mother had a soft spot for all unwanted girls, but this one proved to be a bit too much.

Once my parents went away for the weekend and left us in Marie's care. Mother had given Marie some money to buy cream cakes for our Sunday tea. On Sunday afternoon Marie put a large bowl of whipped cream on the tea table and nothing else. We had been looking forward to our cream cakes and did not know what to do with this large heap of whipped cream. We piled it onto slices of bread, but the three of us made only a small impression on the mountain in front of us. As it was summertime and we had no fridge, the cream would have gone off by the evening. Suddenly I had an idea. I fetched as many of my village pals as I could find; it was a great treat for them to have whipped cream and in no time all the cream was demolished on slices of brown bread with sugar.

But it was in the evening that Marie frightened us. I must have been asleep for a while when I suddenly felt something touching my throat, and when the pressure became greater I opened my eyes and looked into Marie's grinning red face, which came very close to mine, and her hands tightened around my neck. Gewi slept next to my room, and he must have heard some noise because he appeared just at that moment. He threw himself upon Marie, small as he was, being only ten years old, and Marie rushed out of the room and left us, totally shaken, sitting on the bed.

Then Gewi had the bright idea that we should leave the house as quickly as possible and quietly we crept out of the garden door and knocked on Oma Thiele's, our neighbour, window. We spent the night on her sofa.

My parents were horrified when they heard of the danger we had been in, especially when they saw the marks on my neck. Marie went back to a mental home and it was the last time mother took in mentally unstable girls.

But of course there were others: Helene, for instance, who came from a prison and swore that she would never steal again. Father called her *"Die fromme Helene"*[6] after a story by the writer and caricaturist Wilhelm Busch, whose work he liked very much. Indeed, Helene sat during our Bible reading at lunch time with a very pious expression on her face. She loved reading aloud from the Bible. Once a day, a leaf from a religious calendar was torn off and a short text from the Bible was read out by each of us in turn. Once, when my parents weren't present, Gewi insisted that Helene should read from Genesis, chapter 10. Helene was thrilled and with no idea what lay ahead of her, started to read, only to give up after the second verse; but Gewi was adamant that all 32 verses had to be read. Her enthusiasm for reading the Bible was very much less after this.

One day a friend of mother's, who was staying for a few days, missed a considerable amount of money from her handbag, which had been in her bedroom. It turned out that Helene had once again succumbed to her old habit, and confessed that she had taken quite a few other things as well, which we had not even missed up till then. That was the end of Helene's stay.

The other memorable maid was Hilda, from Cologne. She came to us with a large tummy, three months before she had her baby, which she later had adopted, much against mother's advice. Hilda and I got on very well until one day, after she had had her baby, I told her that she had lost a great deal of her beauty. It was a cruel thing to say and quite untrue; it was something I had picked up from my friends who said that mothers lose their beauty when they have had babies, and I, six or seven years old, believed it. After that announcement our good relationship was spoilt. Hilda did not stay long with us. She was vain and man mad. One night mother saw a man climb into Hilda's bedroom window, and that was that.

Our first two maids were super. Emma had come with my parents from their previous parish and she stayed for four years until she got married. When she left I cried my eyes out. On the day when Emma left and Else started, I sat outside, underneath the kitchen window, and sobbed for Emma. Else noticed me and came out and sat beside me. She put a small package into my lap.

"It's for you," she said. I unwrapped it with tears still dropping

---

[6] The pious Helene

onto the paper. A rat made of dough, with two currants as eyes, real whiskers and a tail appeared. "You can eat it," she said, but I shook my head and said that I would rather not. I hated rats but I did not like to tell her that. She came from Hamelin. Else and I became good friends and she stayed with us for six years. She got married to the local carpenter and called one of her two daughters Renate, after me.

Every summer, Dina came and helped in the garden. Dina had a room in an outhouse belonging to a farmer. Once when I was 'exploring' the village with some friends, we came upon a very narrow path between two barns. It was almost too narrow to squeeze through even for us children, and it was dank and dark and unpleasant. A window with iron bars in front of it caught my eye. "Dina lives in there," I was told. I looked through the bars. Dina was not there. The room looked more like a cell with its bare white-washed walls, a neatly-made bed with a crucifix above it, a chest of drawers, a small table and a chair, all the furniture Dina possessed. Dina was a very ugly person with a heart of gold. Her greasy grey hair hung in strands over her face. Her nose was large and crooked; she squinted and the only tooth she had left was one enormous front one which stuck out onto her lower lip. She was tall, even with a hunched back. She must have been about 55 years old. She wore long skirts with an equally long apron on top, and man's boots with thick socks. She was deaf and partly dumb, for there was something wrong with her throat. From the bottom of her neck to the top of her chin hung loose flesh, like a turkey's neck, and when the sun shone sideways on to it, all that flesh became transparent. Poor Dina could only make some peculiar guttural noises and nobody could understand them, but she managed to make herself understood by sign language. Dina worked hard in the garden and was utterly reliable. She was an ardent Catholic, and when she had tea with us she crossed herself before she slurped from her tea mug and dipped the bread into it. She was feared by some village children and made fun of by others. Gewi and I did neither; we were very fond of her. When she first smiled at us we thought she was crying but it was just the way the muscles of her face worked.

One day Dina stayed on after work to look after my brother and me whilst my parents went out for the evening.

It was a warm summer's evening and just beginning to get dark, but it was still too warm to go to sleep, so Gewi and I were reading. We suddenly heard somebody singing and we tiptoed out of our bedrooms towards the sound. The door to the drawing room was wide open. To our amazement, we saw Dina sitting on the low window ledge, her head leaning against the wall. She looked dreamily out of the open window at the full harvest moon, singing in a low, soft voice, a song about Mary and Jesus. Dina, who could not talk and made the grunting sounds of an animal, was singing! We could not believe our ears; not only was her voice beautiful but it was clear as well, and we could understand every word she sang. I wanted to go to her, but Gewi took my arm and shook his head. She could not hear us, of course, but we withdrew a little so that she could not see us either, and we stood devoutly listening to her singing. Then we went back to bed, leaving a lonely, dreaming Dina gazing at the moon and the stars.

⇒•◇•⇐

Twice a month mother went to Hannover to shop. When we needed new clothes, or perhaps as a treat, we went with her on the 13.29 train from Platform 5. Taking us firmly by the hand, she confidently crossed the Ernst-August Platz and the even busier Georgstrasse where trams and cars in an almost continuous stream missed each other by a hair's breadth. On a peninsula, jutting out into the traffic, stood Hannover's most-frequented *Konditorei*[7] called *Kroepke*, or as father called it *Der Ziegenstall*[8]. Heavily made-up ladies sat at small tables near the windows. *Kroepke* was a dome-shaped building, entirely made of glass, so everybody knew what went on outside and inside. Here sat ladies dressed in furs and large hats drinking mocha and eating lashings of cream cakes, smoking cigarettes from long holders and gossiping. I never had the chance to go inside. It was destroyed in the first air-raid on Hannover.

Mother always shopped in the same shops. *Karstadt und Saeltzer* for our clothes, *Werner und Werner* for father's shirts; *von der Linde* for linen and material; the *Reformhaus* for any special food; and, last of all, the *Markthalle,* an enormous building with a glass roof where every kind of food was sold: citrus fruit, precariously stacked in pyramids, vegetables scrubbed and artistically arranged, a hundred kinds of various

---

[7] Café
[8] Goat stable

breads and cakes, fish and meat. Going past the meat stall, I turned my head aside. Rows of deer, hare and wild boar stared with glassy, sad eyes at the passers-by. Every year in the autumn wagon loads of hare and deer were driven through the village after a day's shooting, a most depressing sight.

Mother steered towards the stand which said *Arberg's Delicatessen*. Sausages of I don't know how many varieties hung above the counter. Mother bought *Fleischsalad*[9] and thin smoked *Frankfurters,* my favourites. We could smell the fish stand from a long way away. A fishmonger with a cart and dapple-grey horse came twice a week to our house to deliver fresh fish. But the fish stand here offered more: lobster and crabs; crayfish; smoked eels; smoked salmon; buckling; roll-mops and *Kieler Sprotten;*[10] shrimps and prawns; wafer thin slices of smoked haddock twisted into a long curl, and rows and rows of salads in milky glass dishes. Mother bought shrimps for our supper, a small shiny black smoked eel for father and *Kieler Sprotten* which lay tiny and tightly packed, golden and smoked, in a wooden box which had in black lettering *Kieler Sprotten* written all over it.

Our next stop was the *Sprengel* sweet shop. *Sprengel* was the best chocolate in the whole of Germany, and it was made here in Hannover. Mother bought a small bag of liqueur beans, and for Gewi and me chocolate drops covered in 'Hundreds and Thousands'.

We would put our noses against the glass partition of the counter and inhale the aroma of the extremely good and bitter chocolate. We were given one drop each by the shop assistant, a good habit all German shopkeepers have. A sweet here, a slice of cheese or sausage there, even a tiny curled-up shrimp, children were always given something. Mother put the chocolate drops into her bag.

"For later," she said. Our treat before we caught the train home was tea in the *Kakao Stube*, a smart and well-known *Konditorei* in Hannover, of Art Nouveau style, crammed full of little round tables and customers, in a hazy atmosphere with a small orchestra playing sentimental music.

Gewi and I always chose the same - hot chocolate, the cafe's speciality, with mountains of whipped cream on top and a slice of cake

---

[9] Meat Salads
[10] Smoked Spratts

made of layers of meringue, sponge cake, whipped cream and ice cream, topped with thin curly bits of chocolate. We ate every scrap of it and made it last as long as possible. We ate the cream on top of the hot drink with a spoon with a little of the liquid. In the end we stirred it into the cocoa and drank it the proper way, not leaving a drop in the cup.

On the way home in the train mother opened the bag with the chocolate drops and in spite of our large tea we ate them as well.

If mother had bought a dress or other garment for herself she presented herself in it to father after supper. Father approved every time. He stood up from his chair behind the desk, put his arm around mother's shoulders and said lovingly, "My beautiful little Paulinchen."

Gewi and I looked at each other, giggling. We were very happy, lucky children.

———◆———

Two lovely old farms touched our grounds on both sides, but the many trees in the garden hid their buildings. Each boundary fence had a little gate which let us communicate with each other in an intimate and friendly way without having to use the formal front door entrances from the road.

On the right lived 'Oma'[11] Thiele with her husband in a couple of rooms of the large farmhouse. Her son and family occupied the rest. Oma Thiele's drawing-room window was low to the ground. We hardly ever bothered about the formal entrance but climbed through the window; the first time I stood in front of her window she lifted me over the low sill. She immediately went to the cupboard in the corner and took out a smoked sausage and cut off a thin slice for me. This sealed our friendship right away. Oma Thiele's sausage tasted far better than ours, I thought. Many times when I was playing in the garden, I stopped suddenly to knock at her window and ask for a slice of sausage. Sometimes, when I had been knocking too often, she gave me an extra thin slice, but she never refused it, not even in the war.

In the winter months she spent most of her time at her spinning wheel. I used to watch her through the window. Of course she had seen me, but pretended not to, and when I finally knocked, she always appeared

---

[11] Granny

to be completely taken by surprise, which made me laugh. When she was spinning, she took off her right shoe, and her small foot in the thick black stocking pushed the treadle up and down in an even rhythm. She sat slightly bent over the wheel, and wore golden half-rimmed spectacles. On her lap lay a lump of uncombed and unwashed fleece from which she plucked a thin thread to feed into the little aperture and an even thinner thread wound itself onto the spool. When two spools were full she stuck them into two long needles of an upright stand and plied them together into hanks. These hung from her mahogany secretaire, waiting to be washed, before they were made into thick winter socks for her husband and herself.

The nicest thing about Oma Thiele was her chestnut brown hair. Not a strand of grey in it, always shiny, and there was lots of it. She wore it in a tight plait coiled on top of her head, and two combs kept any stray bits of her hair in a tight grip around her temples.

A large seashell lay on the chest of drawers, white from the outside, a delicate pink leading into its mysterious inside. I was compelled to lift it to my ear every time I saw it because Oma Thiele said that one could hear the roar of the sea. Indeed I heard it, first faintly, then more and more until I thought the waves would take me with them out to sea and I quickly, but very carefully, put it back onto the chest.

Her room always appeared to be sunny and warm. A stove of green tiles reached as far as the ceiling. Its lower half had two iron doors with brass knobs for coal and wood and ashes. The top part had three different compartments, each with a decorative double door of cast iron. In the lowest and hottest stood a kettle with ever-simmering water. The second was for baking potatoes or apples and the third, which was only just warm, had an oval shaped shiny black warming stone which periodically went on to Opa Thiele's (Grandpa Thiele) lap to warm his hands in the winter.

Oma Thiele's kitchen was tiny, and there was no running water, but two enamel buckets stood full of spring water on a low bench, with a large ladle hanging from one of them. All her cooking was done on a *Grude*. This was an old-fashioned, but most efficient cooker used in almost all the farmhouses. It was about six feet tall, with an oven for baking and roasting and another compartment on top for keeping food warm. A tank on the side with a tap gave constant hot water. A tray on rails full of hot ashes was pulled out twice a day, and very carefully the ashes were pushed to the sides with a shovel on a long handle, until the red ash appeared and a new lot of small anthracite was put on top. Once again it was embedded with the ashes previously pushed aside. This kept it going for about ten hours and gave enough heat to cook on. It required careful handling, otherwise the fine ash would cover everything with dust. I liked to watch Oma Thiele replenishing her *Grude* with new coke. In the winter, when for a few moments the glowing ash lay exposed, I warmed my hands over it. To my great joy my grandmother presented mother with her *Grude* when she moved house. Mother was very opposed to this old object, but my arguments that it was ideal for warming hands on, and even more Oma Thiele's advice, made her change her mind, and it was installed. For the first week Oma Thiele came twice a day to show mother how to 'feed' it, and soon mother got used to it and never regretted having it. Especially during the war it proved to be most economical, and it always kept the kitchen warm because it never went out.

Whenever we had turnips, bread soup or one of mother's peculiar North German dishes, I went to eat with the Thieles. As soon as my face appeared at the window at lunch time Oma Thiele knew why I had come and she got a plate and spoon for me. I sat down at the table on which stood a large white terrine. They always had soup and it was always bouillon. Little stars and letters of the alphabet were the only visible contents, but it was delicious. Opa Thiele had a long white beard. He sat on the black oil cloth covered sofa, a napkin tucked into his collar, and he slurped his soup very noisily, leaving stars and letters hanging from his beard. He had had a stroke and could not help it because he could only put his spoon sideways into his mouth. On that side the spoon had worn away and one could always tell which was his spoon.

On a warm day his wife would lead him to the stone seat in front of the house where he sat hour after hour, his hands folded over his walking stick which he had dug into the earth in front of him, his chin and beard resting on his hands, his eyes fixed on the approach of every passer-by, following them until they were out of sight. Sometimes Gewi and I sat with him, but we hardly ever talked. He didn't talk much to his wife either. He was what one could call a laconic person.

One summer day I saw Oma Thiele working in her vegetable garden, in her large old-fashioned sunbonnet. I liked giving her little surprise presents when she was out and which she would find on her return, such as a drawing I had done or a bunch of flowers. This time it was a snail made out of plasticine which I put on her table. I suddenly saw a long plait of chestnut brown hair hanging from her secretaire where in the winter hung her spun wool. I had never seen anything like that before and didn't know what to make of it. Quickly I fetched my brother and quite out of breath pointed to the plait.

"Well," he said, "that is Oma Thiele's artificial hair," and softly he stroked the shiny plait. I myself could not touch it. I had thought her beautiful hair so much part of herself, and when I saw her wearing it the next time, I could not keep my eyes off it and was puzzled how she managed to glue it on to her head every day, but I never asked her about it.

The neighbour on the other side was also a farmer, called Busch. Frau Busch was almost completely deaf. On my arrival I always managed to startle her. It didn't matter how loudly I knocked at the door or banged it shut. I remember her standing at an old-fashioned stone sink tackling a mountain of plates and saucepans, the sweat dripping off her forehead into the washing-up water. In the summer, swarms of flies settled everywhere in the kitchen; the sticky flypapers hanging from the ceiling were full of them. Frau Busch seemed quite an old woman but I never saw anybody helping her, except in the war when she had a Polish girl. Years of hard work and sorrow had aged her prematurely.

The Busch's had three children. One daughter was married a long way away, and the two sons were helping on the farm. Heinrich, the younger one, was weak in the head since he had had meningitis at the age of sixteen. He seemed quiet and harmless, which indeed he was, except when it 'took him' which happened about twice a year. Then he got into such a state that he smashed everything in sight and went for people, except for my mother who was fetched every time he had one of his attacks.

I remember once he had climbed to the top of the house and sat astride on the ridge, dismantling tiles and throwing them down. We tried not to let mother go, but she was fearless. She had a ladder fetched and climbed to the top of it and talked to Heinrich. We could not understand what she said, but after a while the distraught young man came down and let himself be led into the house by mother.

Every time he ended up in the lunatic asylum for treatment. When he was released, after about four weeks, he returned home pale and very quiet, avoiding any human contact, hiding in the barn. For quite a while he never walked, but always ran like a hunted animal. I could hear him talking to the calves in the barn in a gentle voice, and he looked after them beautifully. After a while he became more himself and started to communicate with his family again. Heinrich and I were very good friends.

Two large cherry trees stood in their garden, and when it was time for them to be picked, Heinrich fetched me. He climbed into the tree and threw down into my apron underneath, the most delicious ripe black cherries. Once he took a couple of cherries, whose stem was still joined together and put them behind my ears. They dangled and bounced like two heavy rubies when I moved my head. He was also most anxious that I should spit out all the cherry stones, but sometimes I had so many cherries in my mouth at once that I did swallow some. I did not tell him.

Heinrich's hobby was reading; he was always carrying a book in his pocket. He told me many a story. Some I understood, some I did not. I can't remember seeing very much of Heinrich in the winter, but in the summer we used to sit on a bench in front of a well from which they drew their drinking water. It was covered with a wooden lid with a hole in the centre, large enough to let a bucket through. The bucket was fastened onto a long rusted chain, coiled umpteen times around a beam with a handle which, when turned anti-clockwise, let down the bucket under the clanking of the chain until it hit the water with a dull thud. It was not quite so easy to get it up again, and when I sometimes turned the handle, Heinrich put his hand over mine to help me wind it. The chain would creak and wind itself slowly back onto the beam until the bucket appeared, full of cool, crystal-clear water. Several times I asked Heinrich to lift me up and let me look into the well, for I was eager but afraid at the same time to see the mysterious inside of it, but Heinrich always refused. It even made him angry. His brother, Ernst, once took off the lid and lifted me up, because I was not quite tall enough to look over its rim. He held me tightly when I leaned over to look into it. At first I could not see anything at all of the water, only stones, slightly green, with bits of ferns and grass coming out of their cracks. When my eyes got used to the darkness of the well, I spotted the water far, far below. I became frightened and closed my arms tightly around Heinrich's brother's neck and asked urgently to be put down. But sometimes, when nobody was looking, I took a little stone and dropped it through the opening, quickly put my ear against the well and waited for the splash. It was hardly audible, because the stone was only small and it sounded far away and hollow. Whenever I read Grimm's fairy story of *The Princess and the Frog* it was this well that I imagined.

———▶◆◀———

The day came when I had to go to school. I was six and a half years old. My brother had just finished his four years at the *Volkschule* which every German child had to fulfil before changing to another school. He now started at the Gymnasium for Boys in Lehrte where Latin was the main subject. French and English were also taught as foreign languages. Pupils of this school wore a cap indicating which class they were in. It started with a dark blue one for the first form, the *sexta* which my brother was now proudly wearing. The eighth and last form was called prima and once the *Abitur* was successfully passed, University followed. I looked with the greatest respect upon anybody wearing a school cap. It was the only sign that showed the difference between schools.

My first school year was spent in the old church opposite our house. Ever since the new church had been built, in 1860, the old one had been halved and one part was used for school beginners who lived in the village. These first year pupils were known as the 'A.B.C. Archers', of which I now became one.

I was fitted out with a brand new leather satchel which was worn like a rucksack on the back. All it contained on the first day was a small blackboard, a wooden box for the thin stick of chalk and an oval case for a small damp sponge. It was a very special case of thin wood, heavily lacquered with black paint. The lid showed a landscape with a windmill, a couple holding hands and a lamb grazing beside them. It was given to mother on her first school day, then to my brother and now I became the proud owner of this little box. I still have it, standing on my desk; I keep elastic bands in it.

It was the custom that on the first school day mothers took their offspring to school. About fifteen little children walked demurely alongside their mothers, holding on to their hands, in their Sunday best, with new satchels on their backs. Some of the children were so small and the satchel so large that the sight from behind was a comic one. We all waited in front of the solid oak door of the church which was still closed. The sight was not a happy one; it looked more like a funeral than a happy occasion. Mothers were constantly wiping their eyes and making remarks like, "This is my last one," or, "This is my first one." I couldn't make head or tail of it; I was as happy as a lark, and so was mother beside me.

I was dressed in my favourite dirndl and wore white knee socks. For the first time I wore my hair in plaits. I held my head very upright lest they might come undone. I kept on glancing at mother, in case she might be overcome with tears like the rest of them, but was reassured by her happy smile.

There was one thing I was not happy about, though. Every child held a large object under its arm, called a *Zuckertuete*: it was a cone of cardboard filled to the brim with sweets. It was the custom that on this 'sad' and important first school day every child should be comforted with one of these - except, of course, me.

"Dreadful things," mother had said, when I mentioned *Zuckertuete* a few days before. "Quite unnecessary!" I had been looking forward to one of them and had spent some time looking into shop windows where these sugary comforters were displayed in gold and silver paper, like enormous ice-cream cones, topped with a white rufflet and silk ribbon of a garish colour. Some even had an inscription written on them such as, 'For our little darling'. It was one of this kind I had in mind and I was most disappointed when I did not get one at all. At the same time, I think I must have been the happiest child on this first school day.

A partition divided our small cosy classroom from the rest of the church, of which we had a horror as we were told that it was full of skeletons and other frightful things. A peep inside through the windows was impossible because they were too high off the ground and the door to it was always locked. Our teacher told us, on the first day, that whoever did not behave would be locked in there - and I was very nearly the first one to experience this.

We were taught on the first school day how to write the small 'i' and our homework was to write ten rows of these on our blackboards. Full of enthusiasm, I threw myself into the task after lunch. Crooked and drunken-looking 'i's' appeared, laboriously written, with penetrating squeaks from pressing the chalk too hard. After the third row I had had enough. The sun was shining and beckoning and I wanted to play on the swing. My blackboard was shoved back into the satchel with the idea of finishing off in the evening. But I forgot all about it until bedtime when sleepily I took out the blackboard and saw, to my surprise, ten neat rows of i's. My brother had written them. Should I wipe them out and write my own? I decided against it. Next day when the homework was inspected, the teacher looked at me sternly. "Who has written this?" he asked.

"My brother," I answered in a small voice. And it was then that he told me if it ever happened again I would be locked into the next room. I made sure I never gave cause for this threat again.

My special friend of the first school year was Ilse Rust. We looked very much alike. Both of us were skinny with lots of curls, only Ilse's eyes were blue and mine brown.

"You even laugh in the same annoying way," our teacher used to say, as we were always giggling.

One thing Ilse took very seriously was her family name: Rust. There were numerous 'Rusts' in the village, all well-to-do farmers. Every one had an additional name like: Great-Rust; Dr Rust; Zacharia Rust. Ilse's father worked for the railway, and they lived in a small house near a large meadow, so Ilse invented her own double-barrelled name and even insisted at school on being known as 'Meadow-Rust'.

Beside Ilse's house stood one of the largest old farmhouses, surrounded by lime trees. The childless widow Klunder lived there with her old maid Else. She was so rich, Ilse told me, that she went shopping in Hannover by taxi, which was after all, 28 kilometres away. Ilse also confided in me that one day she would inherit Frau Klunder's fortune, because she was so fond of Ilse. She had given her permission to go into her large garden any time she felt like it and eat the strawberries and greengages - so Ilse said.

One afternoon we did just that, and as we were sitting in the tall grass stuffing ourselves with the delicious fruit, and I was once again being told by Ilse of the great wealth awaiting her one day, a threatening shadow fell upon us, and behind us loomed Frau Klunder dressed in the deepest black, all six feet of her.

She grabbed us by our shoulders and pulled us up in front of her. "You wicked little thieves," she shouted, and pushed us away disgustedly. Completely surprised, I looked at her and then for Ilse, who was nowhere to be seen.

I was very much ashamed and stammered, "I thought it was allowed to come here."

"Why should it be allowed?" she thundered. "Ilse is a very wicked girl and now she is leading you astray too."

I wasn't quite sure any more if Ilse was going to inherit her fortune after all. I was terribly afraid that Frau Klunder would go straight to my parents, but this did not happen until a little later when, once again, she caught us at our misdoing.

The winter was the time to empty the slurry pits on all the farms. Every day horses pulled long containers plastered with muck, along the village street. Through the opening at the top overflowed the smelly dark juice which trickled onto the snowy white road leaving a nasty brown track behind.

Now Ilse had the bright idea of opening the tap at the end of the barrel, which lets out the slurry. She thought it would be such a laugh if the farmer arrived at his field and found the slurry had all gone. She dared me to do it - and I did. Little did I know with what tremendous force the liquid came out. I was at once covered from head to foot and stood dripping in the road, surrounded by an evil-smelling lake of slurry. To my horror I saw Frau Klunder witnessing it all. Now she was steering in the direction of my parents' house. I followed her shivering with cold and trepidation. Ilse was again nowhere to be seen.

Needless to say, my parents were horrified when they heard what I had been up to, and when the proof of it stood small and very unwholesome in front of them, I was severely scolded and punished.

I am sure Frau Klunder meant well in telling my parents that Ilse was leading me astray, but they did not stop me from playing with Ilse or the rest of the village children. My parents pointed out to me what was good and what was bad. Young though I was, they told me that they had faith in me and were sure that I would not do the many wicked things in which the village children indulged. As a matter of fact, it was the village children themselves who would not let me take part in their naughtiness. When they decided to go and steal peas or carrots from the fields surrounding the village I was not actually allowed to pick the forbidden fruit, but was posted as sentry to give a whistle when somebody was approaching. Or should they all decide to pile into the little outhouse - the loo - I was pushed aside and told to wait outside. When I asked what they were doing in there they would not tell me.

It may have been because they lived in awe of my father. In 1934 the position of a parson was still revered. Although religion as a whole did not mean much to these youngsters - their parents were certainly not of the church-going type - at the same time they were brought up to show respect to the clergy, which was also combined with a certain amount of fear. Nobody could have been kinder to children than my father, but as soon as they saw him they scattered. So I gained a certain protection from them. They put up with my going about with them but I never became a 'sworn-in' member of their gang.

The people I was afraid of, and almost started to hate at an early age, were the farmers' rich widows, dressed in black, opulent and corpulent, trotting to church every Sunday, and then gossiping maliciously about their neighbours for the rest of the week. They appeared to me like gangsters in black uniforms who spent their time behind lace curtains spying, especially on me. Frau Klunder was their ring-leader!

My school pals came from the poorest families. Many lived in houses, long condemned, belonging to farmers. Their mothers came from Poland or Silesia after the first World War to work on German farms. They were known as the 'Beet Girls', as they were cheap labour to help with the sugar-beet harvest. Most of them married farm workers and settled down. Their German was poor, their husbands, mostly, were communists. I remember the men, and their children copying them, greeting each other with tight fists, shouting: *Heil Moskau.*

The wives had a raw deal. They were bound to the farmers in return for living rent free in their miserable houses, and each had to look after a large plot of sugar-beet land. The work started in spring with singling out the small plants, keeping them free of weeds during the summer, and in the autumn pulling the beet out, cutting off the leaves and throwing them into the carts beside them. From the age of six the children had to help, and the younger ones stood shivering in their inadequate clothing beside their mothers. The winter started early, the ground became hard with frost, and often the beets were pulled out in snow and ice. No wonder the classroom in the winter was filled with constant coughing from the children's infected chests.

Their fathers led a lazy life. Often laid-off by the farmers for their slack attitude towards work, they lay on their sofas in the kitchen, foul tempered, yawning and belching. Just as their children were afraid of my father, I was afraid of theirs. They looked at me mistrustfully, but at the same time I liked going to their houses: their wives could not have been kinder. In spite of being poor, they ate well. All their money was spent on food and nobody in the family was undernourished except the mothers, who always looked ill and thin.

Every morning I went to fetch Helga to walk to school together. She had a twin brother, Willi, and her mother was a particularly kind and hard working person. Every time I was given a lovely warm crisp roll with lots of butter and jam. (At home we only had rolls on Sundays.) The husband looked at me begrudgingly, but the mother urged me to have another roll. I never saw any plates on the table. All slices of bread and rolls were prepared by the mother on the not too clean surface of the kitchen table and delivered into the ever outstretched hands of the children and husband. The main meal was cooked in one large stew-pot on the stove. At mealtime the pot was put in the centre of the table, tin spoons put beside it and everyone leant over and started to slurp the stew into their mouths as fast as they could. I avoided going at mealtimes, for I could not have got myself to join them.

Apart from the awful smell which dwelled in these kitchens, they were very cosy in the winter. It was always warm on dark winter mornings. The smell of the paraffin lamp on the table mingled with cabbage and fat meat, already prepared for lunch, boiling away on the stove, and the lamp's dim light hid the grime on the walls. The small windows were never opened in the winter and thick condensation formed behind the dirty lace curtains and trickled down the inside of the panes. A white enamel bowl with greyish water, a few small soap bubbles and some hairs floating on top, was the evidence of the family's morning wash. This same bowl was used afterwards for washing-up, washing the clothes and for making cakes. The mugs were of enamel too, with chipped black patches showing through.

Once or twice I had a glimpse of their bedroom. The whole family slept in the same room. It smelled very damp, with peeling wallpaper, straw mattresses and dirty red and white checked bed linen. There was a large chamber pot under the bed. Their pride and joy was the parlour, mostly facing north and therefore sunless. A sofa, a few rickety chairs, a table with a black oilcloth upon which stood a cheap crystal bowl, a sideboard with Woolworth china, and vases with garish coloured paper flowers. On the window-sill stood well looked after geraniums and a myrtle tree, and always a jam jar of cut flowers, filled with daffodils or asters according to the season, their stems cut too short with only the heads sticking out like drowning children.

There was never enough money for clothing or fuel. Nobody helped them except the church. Later in 1936, when Hitler had come to power, they were offered work, new houses and a better life. They took it and all the other advantages that came with it. Suddenly they turned from being communists to socialists and large and small fists unclenched into a thunderous 'Heil Hitler'.

These were my friends until I was ten years old. I took them into our house but they didn't feel at home, in spite of my parents' kindness. They talked in whispers and unlike their usual behaviour, were quiet and bashful. Once they entered the garden they became their natural selves again. We climbed trees, set the swing into such violent motion that the frame began to rock and we ate all the plentiful fruit, forbidden or not. We were told to eat only the apples and pears and plums which were lying under the trees, but we had a cunning way of throwing ourselves against the tree trunk or branches so that the fruit fell off and showered the ground underneath. Sometimes we teased Heinrich from next door, who was watching us silently from behind the fence.

When we became too loud and boisterous we were told to go to the meadow at the end of the garden, where there were tall trees and a hazelnut grove. Two large mounds, where once weeds and rubbish had been dumped, but were now overgrown with grass, were excellent for our little handcarts to roll off or for us to race down with scooters and bicycles. These were things my friends did not possess and were a very good reason for my popularity.

On a hot summer's day, father sat in his arbour after lunch, reading. This was a small lawn surrounded by tall yew trees with an opening cut into it which looked very appropriately like a church door. He sat in a large cane armchair, surrounded by books, smoking a cigar.

Mother also had her private little corner in the garden: a sunny retreat surrounded by mock orange and lilac. It was quite large and every year on mother's birthday, the 21st July, when the weather was good, we had tea there with guests arriving all through the afternoon. It was nicest there in the summer evenings, when my parents sat with friends in the secluded arbour drinking. I could hear the clinking of their glasses, their laughter, and the faint, drowsy twitter of birds when I was lying in bed. Through the open window drifted the scent of the orange blossom.

Sometimes I heard the clanking of the chain when Heinrich or his brother drew a bucket of cool water up from the well. I used to get up and stand at the window, looking down into the garden. I could not see anybody, for the trees and bushes surrounding the arbour were too high. The garden looked so forlorn, the only traces of the day's activity were the watering-can left on the path and the hose pipe with its tap still slightly dripping, coiled like a sleeping snake on the lawn. The sky was still pink from the setting sun. In the distance, behind the garden gate over the little river, rose a thin blanket of mist.

Sometimes I did not go back to bed but dared to creep up to the arbour in my nightie and tell the grownups that I could not go to sleep. Mother lifted me onto her lap, wrapped her shawl around my knees and I cuddled against her warm shoulder. I hardly ever remember being carried back to bed, but I do remember the feeling of complete happiness, the heavy scent of blossoms and the drowsiness which slowly came upon me, making the voices and laughter of the people around me go further and further away.

I had my own little summerhouse of wood, painted green with white windows. It even had white lace curtains and a white picket fence gate. In front of it stood a large magnolia tree whose stem had split in half, but each half was a thick trunk, large enough to climb onto. My brother was the owner of the one on the right and I of the one on the left.

The summerhouse was furnished with a small wooden nursery table, four matching chairs and a bench, all painted green. Every year in the spring, when my maternal grandmother stayed with us for four weeks, she gave them a fresh coat of paint. A miniature stove of cast-iron, about a foot square, was my pride and joy. It had belonged to my grandmother in her childhood, and it had a real brass rail in front which from time to time I polished. But the great thing was that you could really cook on it. A methylated burner heated up the small enamel saucepans. Raw fruit was boiled to a pulp and sweetened with plenty of sugar and presented to our guests, who mostly consisted of our long-suffering maid and mother, who sat on the uncomfortable small seats, praising our cooking.

My brother and I had our own little garden where we could plant and sow whatever we fancied. My brother's was always the same; every Spring he planted his wallflowers and forget-me-nots and sowed radishes and parsley. It was well looked after and always weed free.

Mine was different every year. Once I transformed it into a rockery and wished for a gnome. Mother was horrified, but I pleaded with her to let me have one, and next time she went to Hannover she brought one back for me. It was only a small one, but I was terribly happy. It had the usual red nose and a hood and wrinkled trousers. I had to promise mother that he would not stand in a prominent position, so he found his home behind a rock. I planted flowers around him and held conversations with him. He became a very good friend. I even gave him a Christmas present, a little frog of stone which from then on sat at his feet.

Beside my small garden was the swing, which was also used by mother and our maid for beating the carpets on once a week. A large sand pit, surrounded by a wooden seat, a see-saw and, my favourite, a merry-go-round, made out of a huge wagon wheel which squeaked incessantly, kept us happy for hours. The garden was a paradise for me and my friends. Careless hours we spent in play, not always peacefully but always happily.

The nicest part of the garden for me was the meadow in summer, when the long grass swayed in the breeze together with daisies and wild cowbells, buttercups and dandelions. The grasshoppers chirped all day long until late into the night. I was always longing to walk through the long grass, touching the stalks and petals and finally lying down in it, completely hidden, smelling the aroma of the various herbs and looking up into the blue sky.

Alas, it was forbidden, as the grass was cut twice a year by a man from the village as hay for his goats. After it was cut it became coarse and uninteresting, and it was no fun lying on the shorn meadow. After a couple of weeks it was green again and flowers and grasshoppers returned. When the man came to cut the grass, he brought along his son, who was a little older than I was. I did not like him at all. He always stuffed his pockets with our plums and pears and he was very rude. Once he took a cotton sanitary towel from the washing line and held it, like a dead fish, in his fingers waving it in front of me.

"Do you know what this is?" he asked.

"Of course I do," I said, "that is a flannel."

"That's just what it isn't!" he shouted.

"It is..." But before he could explain it to me, his father had grabbed him by the collar and told him to get away, and boxed him behind the ear.

My brother Gewi, perhaps because he was four years older than I, very seldom played with us. He was by nature much quieter than I was; he was a dreamer. He sat for hours reading books. His favourite occupation was going to the end of the garden to the wrought-iron gate from where he gazed towards the horizon. There he stood every evening, with his hands in his pockets, looking at the sky and the clouds and drawing his own conclusion about the weather for the next day. He was mostly right. When we were expecting guests, I was the one who fetched them from the station, whilst he sat, next to Opa Thiele on his stone bench, waiting for us to come down the road. As soon as he had spotted us, he got up and went indoors. He was very shy and hated any sort of demonstration, and never showed his feelings openly.

He was very sensitive. Once he knocked over a little boy when riding his bicycle. The boy unfortunately was laid-up with a damaged knee for a couple of weeks, but there was not a day on which Gewi did not go to inquire about him, and he used all his saved-up pocket money to buy him presents.

Sometimes he had funny ideas. On one very hot day in the middle of summer, he noticed a pair of ear mufflers lying in the corner of a shop window, obviously overlooked and forgotten after the clean out of the winter displays. They were of black buckskin on the outside and of red velvet on the inside. He had just enough money to buy them. He then walked about on a hot day proudly wearing this contraption on his head. He was about eight years old then.

I was apt to tease him when he did these peculiar things. This made him angry and he would pull my pigtails, until I apologised.

One Sunday morning we were alone in the house as everybody had gone to church, I had unfortunately been teasing him again, and he put a toy clockwork bird onto my head. It got entangled with the masses of curls. Eventually it stopped turning. Its pointed beak, however, went on pecking into my scalp and I shrieked with pain. My brother put his hand over the bird to stop it and so we sat, with the bird in my hair and Gewi beside me with his hand on my head, until my parents came back from church. Mother had to cut a great chunk out of my hair to free the bird.

One day, in the autumn of 1934, father was raging through the house. The black, white and red old German flag had to go; instead every household was compelled to display the red and white Nazi flag.

"This Hitler flag and a rectory don't go together," father shouted. "I won't have this rag hanging from our house."

Mother tried to pacify him. "We will buy a very ordinary small one," she said. And a very ordinary, small one was bought, and when this miserable rag hung for the first time from the centre window of the house, the string with which the long handle was fastened to the window-ledge became loose and the flag slipped to half-mast.

"Leave it like that," father said. "That's just right."

On the eve of this particular autumn day I saw a torch light procession for the first time. An endless column marched through the street, men in brown shirts and black breeches, displaying on their sleeve the Nazi emblem, in long shiny, highly polished black boots which kept in step with the song they sang: *S. A. marschiert, Die Fahne Hoch.* Their left arms swung backwards and forwards like stiff pendulums and in their right hand they carried a torch. I ran out of the house into the street and was fascinated by this sight. Never before had I seen anything like it. The light of the torches illuminated the faces of the men, who looked sternly ahead and sang. This was almost as nice as the Easter bonfires, I thought, and I couldn't understand why my parents had not told me about this wonderful procession. Suddenly my brother appeared beside me. He grabbed me by the arm and pulled me away.

"Come home," he said, and when I tried to resist, he whispered into my ear, "These are the Nazis and we are not joining them."

"Why not?" I wanted to know. "And who are the Nazis anyway?"

By and by the circumstances were explained to me, that a man whose name was Adolf Hitler was ruling Germany and that the Nazis were his followers, but that a lot of people were not, and we were amongst them. I really didn't understand very much of it, but I soon learned that I was never to tell anybody what was discussed in our house.

<hr>

One morning everybody in the street stood and gazed up into the sky. The 'Graf Zeppelin' was supposed to fly over the town and they were waiting. I too stood and looked eagerly upwards, putting my head so far back that I nearly fell over.

It was a breezy autumn day; large white clouds hung like puffy featherbeds from the sky. We expected the airship to make a tremendous noise and were taken by surprise when suddenly a large oblong object emerged silently out of a cloud and floated like a shiny silvery fish. We saw the undercarriage clearly and some said they saw the people inside. It was a breathtaking moment, gone in almost a flash before the tail end disappeared into another white cloud. It was the first and last time we saw the airship. A few weeks later it went up in flames.

After a happy first school year we were moved up to the big school, an ugly building opposite the new church. We had been guarded by our teacher like a shepherd guards his small flock of first-year lambs. Suddenly we were released into a large field with four hundred sheep. We felt forlorn and orphaned, but not for long, because our new teacher was equally nice, a small man with a round red face, smelling very strongly of drink.

To my joy I discovered some of my older playmates in the new classroom, though I could not make out why they should be in the same form as I, when they were two and three years older. It was explained that they were hopelessly stupid and would soon have to attend a different school, which our teacher referred to rather ironically as 'the Academy of the Elite'.[12] I had always looked upon them with such respect, but now they presented quite a different picture as they sat sheepishly and uncomfortably at their desks, which they had outgrown.

There was 'Lanky Emil' whose arms and legs were far too long for his age and could not be accommodated by the infant desk any more, so he sat sideways. Next to him sat two sisters, called by the surname of Grosskopf;[13] both of them were the despair of the teacher.

"Such big heads and nothing in them," he used to shout. There was only one year between their ages, but they were as different as day and night - one enormous, the other tiny, both completely gormless. They reminded me of two monkeys, one an Orang Utan, the other a Marmoset.

Very quickly I made new friends. There was Annemarie, who was frightened of almost everything. There was Anneliese, whose father

---

[12] A school for educationally subnormal children
[13] Big head

was a teacher at the same school. She had long blonde pigtails and deep blue eyes which filled with tears at the slightest upset. And there was Gabi, dark-eyed and dark-haired. I liked her best but, unfortunately, I could never become her best friend because Anneliese had got there before me.

Going to tea with the Boedeckers (Gabi's family) for the first time was a great treat for me. They lived in a large, beautiful old farmhouse. A huge glass double door divided the entrance hall from the inner hall. When I rang the door bell two older girls, one blonde, the other dark, opened the door. Gabi had told me proudly of her two sisters - how very clever they were and that they went to a school in Hannover every day. I soon envied her for having two such nice sisters. They obviously adored their much younger sister and showed great kindness towards her new schoolmate. From the first moment I felt happy and very much at home at the Boedeckers.

In the same house there also lived their spinster aunt whom everybody just called *Tanta*.

Tanta looked after the cattle and, when Gabi showed me around the farm and we came to the cow stall I asked Tanta if I might scrape the 'Pennies' from the cows' rumps. These were small round bits of dried dung and Heinrich had taught me how to remove them, so that the cows were made more comfortable. Laughingly she handed me the scraper and they all stood around me watching, bemused at their small guest enthusiastically cleaning the cows.

Gabi dragged me away to see the horses just being fed by her father. Out of a large oval shaped shallow basket he poured the chopped oat-straw into the manger, and the horses, hungry after their day's work, put their heads into the cribs, shaking their manes with pleasure and pulling at their chains to get their heads closer to the food. All we could hear was a rhythmic munching and the clinking of their chains.

It was a warm, sunny Spring evening when Gabi showed me her own small garden for the first time. It was full of pansies and wallflowers, and the butterflies moved gently on the dark red and brown blossoms as we sat on her rickety self-made garden bench, a small plank of wood balanced on some bricks.

Gabi was a serious girl, Anneliese was sentimental, Annemarie timid and I was always cheerful. We made a good quartet for many years.

For three years we stayed together in this school, adoring our teacher except on the days when he smelled even stronger of drink and his red face took on a purple colour. We soon learned when he was not in the mood for any sort of a joke and that we had better sit quietly and do our work, so Ilse and I refrained from giggling. The slightest noise upset him and whoever was responsible had to suffer. Of course we were punished when we deserved it, and quite a few times I had the cane, which fell upon my outstretched hand with a whistling blow. With my head bent so as not to show my tears I went back to my seat and immediately put my hand on the cool metal lid of the built-in ink pot. I never showed my hand to my parents, for fear of being punished once more, but our maid was most sympathetic, and my punishments earned me pieces of chocolate and biscuits.

One day Herr S. said, "Who would like to learn to play the mouth organ?" About six small hands shot up - mine was amongst them. On the next day we carried a Honer mouth organ of one octave in our satchels, copied notes of music from the blackboard with special attention to the in and out blowing. It was not difficult and soon six little Larry Adlers were happily blowing away.

At the same time my grandmother gave me a violin. Because I was still rather small it was a half-size one and music lessons were arranged for me with Fraulein Pook. My first lesson disappointed me for I had thought I should be able to play a tune the same day. That did not happen until weeks later, and when finally I was able to play a fairly recognisable one, nobody wanted to listen.

Fraulein Pook had a great rival, who was naturally her enemy, in the town. It was Herr Posen, who also gave violin lessons. He was a very handsome young man, very popular with the ladies, so quite a few mothers preferred to send their children to him. Fraulein Pook referred to him as a five-o'clock tea fiddler, and father dismissed him with one word: shocking.

It took me half an hour to walk to Fraulein Pook's house at the other end of the town. Proudly I carried my violin case for the first time, together with my music satchel, into which I had put the Mozart Sonatas which father played from time to time. I had never met Fraulein Pook before and when Emma, her maid, opened the door to let me in, I thought she was my new music teacher. I was horrified to see that she looked almost like a man, with a very visible moustache and long hairs on her chin, but when she told me in a deep stammering voice that Fraulein Pook was in the music-room, I was most relieved.

But not for long, because Fraulein Pook also looked like a man, except that she did not have any excess hairs on her face. Her hair was certainly cut like a man's, her voice was as deep as Emma's and she was smoking a large cigar. Her fingertips were brown from nicotine, and her breath smelled of tobacco. I had to sit close to her on the sofa. She drew an apple on a piece of paper, halved it, quartered it, divided it into eight then sixteen pieces and in this way explained the timing to me.

She took my violin out of its case, held it in front of her and sighing deeply, said, *"Ach, Gott,"* and told me the names of the strings, what a fret-board was and introduced me to the frog on the bow. I was allowed to hold the violin under my chin, together with the blue velvet chin cushion and she led my bow by pushing my elbow across the 'E' string. A most excruciating noise was the result and a cloud of dust from my bow, which I had rubbed with resin for half an hour before I set out. Her four canaries started to object and had to be covered up. I could never understand why she had to have canaries in her music-room anyway, as they spent most of their lives being covered-up with a blanket. Even if one played well, they objected and made more noise than violin and piano together.

It took a long time before I enjoyed playing the violin and I wanted to give it up lots of times at the beginning. My mother practised patiently with me, until I started to practise on my own regularly every day and began to enjoy it. When I finally played my first small pieces by the great masters, modified for beginners into the first position, I grandly wrote to my grandmother, 'I am now playing Mozart, Beethoven and Bach.'

The highlight of the school year was the day's outing. I remember one to the Harzmountains, which stands out as a specially happy one, because both my parents came. It did not often happen that both of them were free at the same time. Apart from visits to my grandparents in Hannover, I can only remember one holiday in Berlin with both parents.

A group of 25 children, most of them accompanied by their mothers, stood excitedly on the platform on a July morning. Each carried a small rucksack and was fitted out with tough walking shoes which by the end of the day caused everyone painful blisters. The weather was promising and the sun was still low and rosy as the train sped along, past woods and meadows where cows were lying on the dewy glistening grass, chewing the cud.

Shrieks of joy and amazement broke out at the first sight of the mountains. Our own countryside was as flat as a pancake for miles and miles. Not the smallest hill broke the monotony of it, though there were woods. I kept on glancing with pride at my parents who looked so different today. Father appeared years younger in his travelling suit of salt and pepper tweed with matching cap, such a nice change from his usual dark suits and hat. And mother, who mostly wore smart dresses, was today dressed in a dirndl. All this made me very happy.

When, after two hours, the train finally stopped at our destination, Bad Harzburg, a small town surrounded by wooded mountains with patches of green fields here and there, our excitement had reached its peak. A four hour walk to Goslar lay ahead of us. Our teacher went on in front, swinging his walking stick as he strode along. Taking out the mouth organ from his jacket pocket, he began to play the *Happy Wanderer.* Everybody followed, singing and trusting his sense of direction. We looked like the children following the Pied Piper of Hamelin. We started along the small but fast running river called the Ocker, but soon our steep narrow path led us far above it and we looked down onto the white foaming water as it rushed over the rocks into the valley.

Parents shouted to their children to be careful, hanging on to them for most of the walk. Thank goodness I was not one of them. Ilse and I were in our element, darting from one rock to the other, always discovering new things, running back from time to time to our parents to make sure that they also were enjoying themselves.

Our own enjoyment was rather dampened when we saw 'Lanky Emil', his face deathly white and his eyes half closed, walking slowly beside mother who had put a helping arm around his waist. He had already been sick on the train. He suffered from migraines. It had been suggested on arrival that he should stay with his mother at the station and catch up with us by train when he felt better. This was very much opposed by his mother, a robust person, who said quite firmly that she had saved up and paid for this trip and was jolly well going to enjoy it. And this she did, leaving her son completely in mother's care.

After a two-hour walk we stopped to rest and to have our lunch in a *Biergarten.* Poor Emil flopped onto the grass; there he lay outstretched, not able to live or die. A small group of grown-ups and children stood around him looking sympathetically at this heap of misery. Mother knelt beside him, wiping his forehead with her handkerchief soaked with Eau de Cologne, whilst the rest of us sat under cheerful sun umbrellas eating our sandwiches and drinking lemonade through straws.

The day became hotter and hotter, our walking after lunch slower and slower. The singing had stopped altogether and Herr S. had put his mouth organ back into his pocket. His face had become redder after lunch and was beginning to take on the alarming purple colour, but he stayed in a good mood. Father caught up with me, took my hand and told me to walk slowly for a while beside him. He brushed the curls from my damp forehead and demonstrated how to breathe in deeply the delicious mountain air and the sweet scent of pine trees. It was good for the lungs. I did not stay beside him for long, as I was still charged with plenty of energy. Herr S. shook his head when Ilse and I overtook him and said to father, "These two are doing the whole walk twice over."

We arrived at the old Imperial town, Goslar, in the afternoon and were dragged to see the castle, in which we took not the slightest interest. We were beginning to get very tired. We got our second wind on the way home in the train when we talked incessantly of our adventures. Even Emil had sufficiently recovered to join in, though his memory of it all must have been rather hazy and unpleasant. By and by we became quieter and one by one dropped off to sleep.

When we arrived at our station our eyes were small and blinking. In a daze we got out of the train and walked stiffly down the platform, because of blisters and aching leg muscles, a different little group from the boisterous one in the morning; quiet and tired but carrying in our young hearts a memory of a very happy day which stayed with us for a long time.

⇒◆⇐

In the Winter of 1938 for the first time I heard an all-male choir perform in the church. The choir members, all dressed in black, looked like cut-outs silhouetted against the lit-up altar as they grouped themselves in front of it. The rest of the church was dark. They wore a peculiar get-up: wide-sleeved blouses held in by leather belts over loosely-fitted trousers, which were tucked into high black boots. Their hair, beards and moustaches were equally black. They were Cossacks.

Never before had I heard such wonderful voices. Their deep richness not only filled the church but penetrated into one's inner self and it sent shivers down my spine.

After the concert they were invited to supper at the Rectory. Silently they followed mother and me through the dark evening, dressed in long black coats and fur hats. During the meal they became more talkative and their dark eyes began to sparkle. The choirmaster stood up, raised his wine glass towards my parents and with a deep bow expressed his gratitude for their hospitality. Their faces became relaxed and cheerful and the hall filled with the vibration of their laughter, which was as deep and rich as their voices. Their German was not very good but good enough to tell us stories about their homesteads in Southern Russia, about their families and ponies. One of them performed a dance in a peculiar squatting position; with his arms stretched out in front of him he danced to the rhythmic clapping of his comrades. When they said goodbye they kissed the sleeves of our coats. Some of them had tears in their eyes.

I can't remember ever being bored. Admittedly I had my brother and friends to play with, but if they weren't around I was quite happy on my own. In the winter I played with my dolls; this was before I was able to read. Once I could read, at the age of seven I think, my dolls became very neglected. I adored reading. My grandmother had given us lots of books which once belonged to her children. Fortunately, my brother loved reading too, and we both sat for hours completely engrossed in our books. The only maddening thing sometimes was that Gewi insisted on reading aloud: when this happened I put my fingers in my ears and tried not to listen.

The lovely old books we read could not be found anymore. Most of the children's books in the shops at that time were Nazi-orientated. My first spelling book at school started with, 'Heil Hitler, Toni, how is your cat?' I need not mention my father's remark on this. It became a standing joke that every time he asked me what I had learned at school that day, he said, "Oh I know, Heil Hitler, Toni!"

'Christening' was one of our favourite games. It started with the actual birth when I had to recline on the sofa with a blanket over me and Gewi was the doctor delivering the child.

When I was twelve years old mother enlightened me about the facts of life. Until then I drew my own conclusions, altered at times by horrendous information from various pals. I am sure my brother, being that much older than I, must have known more about it, but he certainly did not let on.

Until I was about eight years old I believed in the stork bringing the babies. There was a stork's nest on our neighbour's chimney, and every May Mr. and Mrs. Stork returned to the same nest. Sometimes they raised a family, sometimes they didn't, but the storks standing in their nest on one leg became a familiar sight. It was supposed to be good luck to see a stork in flight and it was then that one had to express a wish like: *Stork, Stork Guter, bring mir einen Bruder,* or *Stork, Stork bester, bring mir eine Schwester.*[14] I was longing for mother to have another baby, and I shouted and pleaded my utmost whenever I saw a stork in flight. Once, when mother and I went for a walk and came upon a lonely gypsy caravan beside the road, we heard a baby crying from within. I was quite sure its mother had abandoned it and begged mother to go and fetch it so that we could take it home, but mother assured me that its own mother would come back soon.

Gabi's father had told her that the foals lie under the cobbles in the stable and that the horse paws them from underneath the stones. Once we saw a horse doing just that. Gabi and I sat quietly with pounding hearts on the feed bin, watching it. The noise of the horse's hoof was alarming and sparks started to appear.

"It's coming soon now," whispered Gabi, but the horse gave up and continued feeding out of the crib. I asked mother where babies came from and was told that each mother, before the baby was born, carried it under her heart

Once, when coming home from school, my friends and I passed a cottage from which suddenly came a most dreadful yell.

"It's Frau Albin having her baby," one of my friends said knowingly. Now I knew two things; that I had to put the doll next to my heart and let out a fearful scream when Gewi pulled it away from under the blanket. The christening followed in a grand style, and Gewi was once more in his element acting as a parson.

There was always something to look forward to throughout the year; festivities like Christmas, Easter, Whitsun and birthdays. Christmas was the nicest. It started with the beginning of Advent when a large

---

[14] Bring me either a brother or a sister

wreath of fir branches was hung from four wide red silk ribbons suspended from the ceiling in the hall. Four fat red candles were stuck onto it. A smaller replica appeared on the dining room table. For each of the four Advent Sundays a candle was lit at tea and supper time. Two Christmas calendars, one for my brother, one for me, hung against the nursery window. The scene they showed was mostly a little town with snowy roofs, where each window had a number corresponding with the date up to the 23rd December. Finally, on the 24th the double stable door was opened and the Nativity appeared.

Each Advent Sunday night we were allowed to put our slippers onto the window-ledge for *'weihnachtsmann'*[15] to fill during the night. Even when we did not believe in Father Christmas any more we kept up this practice until the war put an end to the supply of presents. I tried to keep awake to see Father Christmas come, but fell asleep every time and dreamed up during the night, felt for the slipper on the window-ledge, pulled out a instead of the slipper overflowing with delicious things. Sometimes I got chocolate Father Christmas and indulged in a midnight feast. Of course I was disappointed in the morning when I saw a dismantled Father Christmas and crumpled-up silver paper beside the almost empty slipper.

The 6th December was a dreaded day for me. It was St Nicolaus Day, and St Nicolaus appeared in person. He came towards the evening, dressed in a red coat trimmed with white fur, a long white beard and a red hood. He carried a sack on his back and in his hand a switch of birch twigs; this of course was only for the naughty children. I always had a bad conscience and hid behind the sofa as soon as I heard his voice. He always found me and dragged me out from behind it, told me not to be frightened but to be more obedient and more diligent at school. It was marvellous how exactly he knew about all our shortcomings, especially about father who sat in the armchair, very much amused by it all, smoking a cigar and putting a couple of them into the large coat pocket of Father Christmas. Gewi and I had to say a poem which went like this:

> *Lieber Guter Weihnachtsmann*
> *Sieh mich nicht so boese an*
> *Stecke deine Rute ein*

---

[15] Father Christmas

Ich will auch immer recht artig sein.[16]

After that he began to unpack his sack. Everybody got a present and it was always just what we wanted. How did he know? When we had thanked him and promised to be good children he went, but not before giving father a friendly tap on his shoulders with the birch twigs and telling him to go to bed earlier. Father did most of his writing at night and never went to bed before 2 or 3 o'clock.

Later, of course, we knew that Father Christmas came from a large department store called Karstadt, in Hannover, and that mother had hired him, telling him exactly what to say and what to bring. When the war started he stopped coming. He most likely had to enlist and ended up somewhere in Norway or Russia.

Early in December mother started baking ginger biscuits and a special kind of dark treacle biscuit with lots of spice in it. Gewi and I helped her cutting stars and half-moons out of the dough and decorating them with a hazelnut or almond. Just before Christmas the kitchen looked like a factory producing endless Christmas Stollen (fruit loaf), all of which found their way into the homes of the needy. Our own biscuits were stored in large tins and every day at tea time a plate of them appeared on the table.

Mother was in charge of the Nativity Play performed by the Sunday School children. Each year the play varied. My fervent wish was to be Mary, but it never happened.

"Your hair is too curly and fair," mother said, and that was that. I hated my hair. So many of my friends had long dark hair, just right for Mary. I always played an angel, and Gewi was always a shepherd. He did not mind; he didn't like acting anyway and always had to be coaxed into it.

Once he got the giggles. I don't know what started him off, it was so unlike him because he was always so serious. I was very easily infected by giggles and although Gewi controlled himself quickly, I could not, and was sent out by mother in the middle of the play. Of course this

---

[16] Dear Father Christmas,
   Please be kind to me,
   put away your stick
   and I promise to be good from now on.

ruined my chances completely of ever being Mary.

My brother was very good with his fret-saw. I was hopeless with the needle. I tried to crochet but it was not much better either, and the saucepan holders which were meant to be square turned out to be a peculiar conical shape. But mother made use of every little present we ever gave her. My favourite presents to give were boxes of match wood which I painted; fortunately they were very fragile and broke easily, so it didn't matter that I produced them year after year. I was very bad at keeping my presents a secret. Once I told father what his present was. As soon as I left his study I sat down and cried, full of regret at having told him. Father heard me crying, came out and said that he had already forgotten what it was. I believed him and was happy again.

A great treat before Christmas was the children's opera to which my grandmother invited us every year. It took place in the Opera House in Hannover. 'Haensel and Gretl' was my favourite opera and 'Frau Holle' came next. The Opera House was very beautiful: its chandeliers sparkled and the red plush seats in our box with its gold brocade felt soft and grand. I wore my best dress for these occasions, and grandmother lent me her delicate pair of binoculars made of mother-of-pearl.

After the opera we always had a quick walk around the Christmas Fair before we caught the train back. There were huge Christmas trees with white electric candles, brightly lit stands covered by canvas roofs on which the snow lay heavily and sparkled in the light, glittering jewellery, chocolate hearts hanging from silk ribbons, every kind of toy, and the lingering smell of roasted chestnuts and fried sausages served on a paper plate with a crispy roll and lashings of mustard. Father Christmas in his full regalia cracked jokes or kissed a frightened child. Above all stood the impressive Marktkirche, known for its green copper spire which was now floodlit. Its deep melodious bell behind the golden clock rang out every quarter of an hour.

A few days before Christmas, a large Christmas tree was brought up the stairs into the drawing room and from then on the door of that room was locked. Only mother was allowed in there. Happy were the days when I still believed that mother was working behind the door with Father Christmas or, as mother said, with the Christ Child Himself. She had a marvellous way of making me believe in things. I sat in front of the door with my ear against it, listening to the mysterious noises going on inside. Sometimes mother would ring a tiny silver bell which made me believe that the Christ Child had just flown in through the window. When I requested, in a timid voice, for Him to talk to me, mother answered in a thin sweet voice which for years I did not recognise as her. Once she left a very delicate golden hair on the threshold which for a long time I treasured as that of the Christ Child.

My behaviour most certainly improved before each Christmas. The atmosphere in the house was so exciting and beautiful and I lived in awe of what went on behind the closed drawing room doors.

The morning of the 24th was wonderful to wake up to - it was the most special day of the year. Gewi and I wrapped up the presents we had made. Mother was busy in the kitchen preparing the goose with apple and raisin stuffing for the following day, and the finely shredded red cabbage to go with it was put onto the stove: the longer it simmered the better it was.

Tonight's meal was, as usual, carp - 'Carp Bleu' as it was called - with creamy horseradish sauce and parsley potatoes. Our maid was scrubbing the tiles in the hall shouting angrily at us as we dashed backwards and forwards, hopping over the wet floor and her bucket, to get more wrapping paper from the chest in the hall. Father was typing in the study, preparing the many sermons he had to deliver during the next three days.

The day improved as it went on. At about three o'clock the work was done and a hush settled over the house. Two more hours to wait before Mass started. These quiet hours in the afternoon on the 24th were always very special to me. There was nothing much to do except wait, but it was just this that I liked, and Gewi felt the same. We were both completely different in temperament, but for certain things we had the same feeling. Confidently we sat in our nursery, our noses pressed against the double window. Looking out into the wintry garden, we watched the birds snatching the last bits of crumb or nut from the bird table before retiring for the night. The clear sky got redder with the setting sun, until a pale first star appeared. Suddenly the sun set and the pinkness of the sky changed to a cold pale blue which very quickly became dark. The curtains were drawn and the tea brought in; all four candles on the advent wreath were lit, one had nearly burnt itself out but the fourth still had a long way to go.

I shall never forget the afternoon of one Christmas Eve. What was so special about it was that I had mother all to myself. My brother had gone out with my father and our maid was in bed with a cold. Mother was upset because she had broken a small bulb for the campfire of my brother's toy fortress which he was to get that evening. Apparently this bulb was very important. I knew the shop where I could get it, but as I was only five years old and the shop was a long way away, mother was very reluctant to let me go. I assured her I would be alright.

With the small bulb inside my mitten, I set off. There was hardly anybody about. Everyone, it seemed, had done their shopping and were now busy putting the finishing touches to the preparations indoors. The shop windows were lit up, but the shops themselves were almost empty. A dummy figure of Father Christmas appeared in almost every shop window; his head was continuously nodding and his eyes rolled from left to right, his grin from one ear to the other. They were not very becoming images, in fact they were rather frightening. I got the bulb from the electrical shop. Here and there I could see through the windows a lit-up Christmas tree. The light of the street lamps threw long shadows onto the pavement and the thin snowflakes danced and glistened in their light.

When I turned into our drive I saw mother's face looking out of the window from father's study and before I had reached the front door she had opened it and took me into her arms. She had obviously been very worried about me. I think this was perhaps the first time I realised how much mother cared for me, and it made me so happy that I shall never forget that moment. Mother took me to father's study where she had prepared tea just for herself and me, and my happiness was complete. I sat on her lap and she stroked my curls, and softly hummed a Christmas carol.

Christmas Vespers was at 5 o'clock and we all went to church, which was packed every year, mainly with children. It was said that mothers sent their offspring to Vespers because it gave them a chance to do the last preparations in peace at home. The only time mother sat in the 'rector's pew' was at Christmas. It was right next to the altar. She hated to sit 'in front' and usually had her seat next to the entrance. Tonight she sat here for our benefit so that we could get a full view of the two tall Christmas trees at either side of the altar. On their wide dark green branches stood white wax candles, all alight; they lasted exactly the length of the service. I found it difficult to listen to what father was saying. Thank God that for once he kept his address short. The last carol was sung with great fervour by old and young. Excitement and anticipation of the things to come that night were reaching their climax. But it was a long time yet before we had our presents and supper. Mother had prepared several small Christmas trees, beautifully decorated with candles and small silver balls, as well as presents of food and warm clothes for the sick and suffering in our neighbourhood.

One of these families was Mr. and Mrs. Rettich. I shall never forget the first time we took them a Christmas tree. They lived in one of the oldest houses in the village, shared with many others. Their two rooms, a kitchen and a bedroom were at the top of the house. A large wooden double door, through which a horse and wagon could easily fit (that was exactly what the door was for originally) had a smaller door on one side through which we went into a dark interior which had an uneven earth floor. A smell of goats and pigs, which were kept in little compartments on either side of the hall, filled the airless place. We climbed the rickety stairs and mother knocked at the door. A thin-faced old man opened the door, holding a small oil lamp in his trembling hand. His wife lay on a shabby sofa in the kitchen. The stove gave out ample heat; through the cracks in its surface, flames threw a red glow. Our shadows danced and quivered on the ceiling. The smell in the kitchen was unbearable. Frau Rettich had been paralysed for years and never left the sofa. The smell was of dirty clothes and urine, although the kitchen itself was very clean. I wanted to leave the room for I was beginning to feel sick, but Gewi caught me by my wrist and held it tightly until we left. He was so much wiser and nicer for his few more years than I was. When the candles on the tree were lit and their light fell onto our faces, I saw tears rolling down the old couple's cheeks. They had never expected the Christmas tree, let alone presents, and would have spent this evening as all other evenings, alone and cheerless in their minute kitchen by the dim light of their oil lamp.

The sick woman held mother's hands and squeezed them and muttered something incomprehensible, for her speech had gone long ago. A lump came into my throat and, glancing at Gewi, I saw that he too was fighting back his tears.

And now mother said, "Let's sing 'Silent Night'." How could she expect us to sing and especially this, the most moving carol, but we did, and the old man joined in with his thin, quavering voice.

It was after having been to see people like this old couple that we had our own Christmas. By now we could hardly wait.

At last the little silver bell from within the drawing room told us to come in. The room looked the same every year, and each year we greeted the tree and the crib with the same joy. The scent of the tree and the sweet smell of the honey candles filled the room. The tree reached the ceiling, under its lower branches was the crib, a thatched open stable about four feet long with Mary and Joseph kneeling in front of the manger, in which lay the Christ Child with his halo. Donkeys and cows crowded around, all the figures being made of plaster and beautifully painted. Fresh green clumps of moss and rocks, which I recognised as being from the garden, made up the fields around, on which sheep and lambs were grazing. Shepherds stood in awe looking up at the delicate wax angels which were suspended from the lower branches. The largest, the angel Gabriel, hung very low. They were all of different sizes and the one furthest away was the smallest, a tiny delicate angel not more than an inch in size. Every year a new piece was added to the crib. This year we spotted a well in the middle of the field; it had a small silver bucket on a lever which let the bucket disappear into the well. Behind the crib stood a cross of pale pink roses made of tissue paper. An electric bulb from behind illuminated it.

Mother started to play 'Silent Night' on the harmonium and father accompanied her on his violin. He could play and sing at the same time, something which I found very difficult when I joined them with my violin. I could not possibly sing as well.

All the time we were singing, we could not help glancing towards the row of tables which were arranged on one side of the room. They were covered with long white starched tablecloths on which lay our presents. Finally, after what had seemed like ages, mother led everybody to their own table. A large plate of sweets, marzipan and chocolates stood in the middle of it and round it lay the presents, so many of them, that we did not know which one to open first. We shrieked with joy, on receiving the gift we had wished for, ran to our parents, embraced them wildly, and rushed back to open the next present.

Our maid was pleased with her table. In her clean white apron, she stood in front of it with a wide grin on her face as she opened her presents. Mother never failed to make us feel that our home-made gifts were, once again, just what she needed and wanted.

The meal followed, taken in the Christmas room. All the time the candles burnt on the tree. We watched as they burnt out, one by one, and when the last one flickered feebly in its holder, it was time for us to go to bed.

Getting up the next morning was easy. Still in our nighties we crept into the drawing room, where a fire was already lit. The smell of the burnt-out candles from the night before still lingered about the room. We reassured ourselves that our beautiful presents had not been just a dream. When we were old enough - from the age of six, I think - we went to church with mother, but before that we stayed at home in the charge of our maid who was also in charge of roasting the goose.

Once, when I was still very young, I stood in front of the crib and looked at the Christ Child. For some reason it was made of marzipan. I had a passion for marzipan and I remember taking it out of the manger and nibbling a little at its feet and then its legs. It looked ugly without them, so I ate a little more and finally I ate it all. I did not tell anybody but felt terribly guilty. When at tea time the candles on the tree were lit, I went to the crib (no-one had noticed the empty manger) and I thought that Mary looked very sad as she gazed at the place where once her child had been. I burst into tears and confessed to mother what I had done. She did not scold me, but very quietly said, "How sad!" For that evening the manger remained empty and my brother looked at me most reproachfully. The next day a little wax angel replaced the Christ Child, and Mary's face, I thought, looked a little happier.

A week later it was new Year's Eve, which I never liked. Going to church at 5 o'clock reminded me of Christmas Eve the week before. Now it was all over, this was an anti-climax. Instead of the cheerful Christmas Carols, mournful hymns were sung. Father's voice thundered from the pulpit, "We do not know what sorrow is waiting for us in the coming year, therefore..." It all struck me as being very sad, and when I was small I put my head into mother's lap and went to sleep. I remember the smell of her leather glove as she put her hand on my head.

New Year's Eve is the time for fireworks, hot punches and doughnuts. Until I was ten years old I was not allowed to stay up, but I did not mind, and even when I was old enough I never really enjoyed it.

There was no particular time to take down the Christmas tree or decorations. We kept the tree and crib until the needles started to drop.

When that time came, everything was taken off carefully, wrapped in tissue paper and put back into the labelled boxes which were taken to the room in the attic.

The tree was thrown out of the window. Without a sound it landed on the snow below and was put in front of the woodshed to be chopped up in due course for firewood. For a short time a patch of pine needles showed where it had landed but it was soon covered with fresh snow. The once beautiful Christmas tree sometimes stood for weeks leaning against the shed, and bereft of its needles it awaited the end. The only sign of its former glory was a thin strand of silver paper which fluttered in the cold wind on one of the bare branches.

Birthdays were almost as exciting as Christmas. I always thought that father's birthday was even nicer than my own.

Every year he was serenaded by a group of young girls and women between the ages of eighteen and thirty, a Bible Group he had founded when coming to Lehrte, who met once a week. As soon as we heard the shuffling of shoes and whispering and stifled giggles, my brother and I rushed to the stairs. From the top step, dressed in our pyjamas, we watched as the early well-wishers grouped themselves at the bottom of the stairs. Suddenly the whispering stopped, one or two cleared their throats. Then silence followed until one of them raised her hand. Immediately lovely voices in soprano and alto sang father's two favourite hymns. One was 'Praise the Lord, the Almighty', and the other 'Auf Adler's Flüegeln getragen' was about being carried on the wings of an eagle to heavenly heights. They were the same hymns every year. Father stood behind us in his dressing gown. His birthday was the only time I ever saw him in his dressing gown, except occasionally just after the war when he was very ill. When they finished singing he went down and shook hands with them and they presented him with a bunch of flowers and a book.

None of them could stay as they all had to dash off to their jobs but the next time the 'group' met, they were given cakes and coffee. On fine summer evenings they persuaded father to have the meetings outside on the lawn and these evenings ended up with country dancing. I watched from my bedroom window. They saw me and waved their hands and called me to come down. In my bare feet and my nightie, I danced with them under the weeping willow to the sound of the accordion. Father and mother joined in too, but not my brother - he stood with his hands in his pockets all by himself. A row of village children sat on the stone wall under the oak, watching us.

Parishioners came throughout the day to congratulate father. In the evening he sank into his chair, saying, "What a tiring day a birthday is!" Something I could not understand.

One of father's birthdays turned out to be a sad one. My grandfather, who was in his 80th year, often came to preach to give father a day off. He had come to this birthday celebration to do just that. Matins was from 10 to 11.30 and Sunday School started at 11.45. I had arrived early and was surprised when suddenly the big double doors opened and the congregation appeared, sad-faced, some crying. A kind woman took me aside and whispered that grandfather had fainted in the pulpit. I rushed into the church and saw him lying in front of the altar on the deep red carpet, his head resting on the cushion which was used by brides to kneel on. He looked very pale and had his eyes closed. An ambulance took him to our house. Grandfather was a healthy man and after two hours he recovered. Grandmother stayed beside him all day as he lay on the sofa, and held his hand. He was told by the doctor not to preach any more but he continued to do so until be was 86.

He was of great help to father at the beginning of the war. We sat with trembling hearts lest he should faint again, but he never did. It was a touching sight when father and son, one tall and dark-haired, the other bent from age, his hair snowy-white, stood side by side at the altar giving communion. Father held the chalice with the wine, grandfather gave the bread.

Whose ever birthday it was, a garland of flowers surrounded the birthday King's or Queen's place at table. The presents were laid out on a small side table. In the middle stood a candleholder indicating the age. It delicately refrained from revealing the age after eighteen.

<hr />

I didn't like the summers nearly as much as the winters, though I can only remember summer days as being hot and sunny. I always longed for the winter, the snow and all the joys it brought with it.

When the first snowflakes came floating down from the dark bluish-grey sky, I sat with my nose pressed against the windowpane watching them as they came faster and faster and bigger and bigger, settling on the frosty earth and covering the frozen puddles. Everyone was prepared for the snow and knew that it would not melt but would remain with us for the next four months. My sledge was waiting next to the front door, oiled and polished with a new rope to pull it. For the next few months we would be inseparable friends.

After the first heavy snowfall everything seemed transformed. The light in the house grew a shade brighter even when the sun was not shining. Outside, everything was quiet. Now the snow muffled the sound of the noisy cart-wheels, the large uneven cobblestones lay deep under a white blanket and the clatter of horses' hooves was silenced. Instead there was a jingle of harness, and the snorting of the horses produced a small white translucent cloud in the clear frosty air.

People dressed in fur boots and fur hats shuffled carefully along the footpaths. Soon the activity of shovelling pathways from front doors to the road set in. I, too, got hold of my small shovel from the sand pit and joined in. Our path to the road was a long one and several others had to be made to the woodshed, wash kitchen and chicken house. Hands began to get cold but by beating them across the shoulders they soon warmed up again. A large snowplough had pushed the snow to each side of the road, leaving high banks near the pavements. It was up to the pedestrians to make a breakthrough here and there.

Soon the beauty of the first snow was spoiled when ashes and sand were scattered and the snow became slushy and brown. Disappointed by the sight of it, I opened the door to the garden. Here the untouched snow lay feet deep in front of me. Its surface sparkled in the sun like a veil of diamonds. Trees and shrubs, shortened by several feet, emerged out of the white mass, their branches bent under the weight of the snow. Over everything spread a great stillness. Sometimes a very small branch succumbed to its sudden weight, broke with a brief sharp crack and fell silently with its burden on the ground, leaving a slight mark on the white surface, which, apart from a few traces of delicate feathery hopping marks of a bird, was still untouched.

Behind the garden lay my winter paradise, a disused clay pit cum rubbish dump with 50 to 100 metre long slopes falling steeply to the lake below which lay dark, deep and menacing. It was an ugly place in the summer but now it looked different in its coat of glittering white. These slopes were our only chance of tobogganing; mother very reluctantly let me use them and I had to promise only to stick to the smaller slopes, which I am afraid I did not. There was one slope of 100 metres, called the 'death track' leading straight onto the lake. The sledge zoomed across the ice until it was stopped by the slopes on the other side. Some daredevils had erected a narrow passage of drums at the bottom of the slope through which the sledge was steered at a tremendous speed. Of course these drums were empty, but inaccurate steering resulted in the most awful crashes with nose-bleeds and bruises.

It took a good twenty minutes to re-climb the steep slope, which had become icy from our constant use. Often, nearly at the top, one of us slipped, let go of the rope and the sledge shot down into the pit. We had to try again. Our coats and gloves were covered in snow and, as soon as the sun started to set, the snow froze, they became stiff and our faces went blue with cold. It was time to go home.

By the time I reached our front door, my hands were hardly able to clean the snow off boots and coat. The gloves became completely useless, small icicles hung from them, and my numbed fingers fumbled to unbutton my coat. My 'snow suit' must have been dripping wet every time, but the next morning I found it hanging dry and warm on the hook in the hall and the woollen gloves were once more soft and comforting.

Mother was waiting with the tea in the drawing-room. Every time she said on my return, "I am glad you are back safe and sound," and she rubbed my cold red hands until they were warm again. After I had drunk the hot cocoa my cheeks began to glow with the warmth of the room and the contentment inside me.

A sizzling noise from the stove promised baked apples filled with raisins and topped with sugar. Through the outer double window, which was covered with 'ice flowers', came the last rosy glimmer of the setting sun. Mother got up and drew the curtains and pulled the lamp low over the table. In a very definite voice she announced, "Time for homework."

The cuckoo clock ticked noisily as we sat at the table, my brother and I bent over our books, mother over her mending and our maid shelling dried bean pods or helping with the mending. These were the winter days and evenings I loved and longed for.

Neither my brother's nor my bedroom had a stove and they were icy-cold. It was so cold in winter that the walls glistened with thousands of tiny particles of ice, which I could scrape off the walls with my finger-nails. The bathroom was equally cold except on two days a week when we had baths. The water cylinder was a two foot wide copper container about five foot high, a small cast iron stove underneath heated the water to such an extent that the cylinder started to bulge dangerously. When the hot water was drawn it spurted out of the tap in alarming gurgling spasms so that the bathroom filled with dense steam and the electric ceiling light appeared like a full moon on a misty night. It was highly dangerous; what's more, the electric light switch was in the bathroom itself. It was a handsome little switch of brass, which gave us all shocks, more than once, but we survived.

On non-bath nights we had a good wash in my parents' bedroom where an old-fashioned tiled stove gave out ample heat. In front of the fire stood a large, low, rubber tub into which a large basin with warm water was put. We stood in the rubber tub to wash ourselves and could splash as much as we liked. Our nighties were put on top of the stove and were lovely and warm to slip into. I remember one evening when my parents were out, and my maternal grandmother, who was staying, supervised our washing. She had, like my mother, some peculiar ideas about health. One of them was to plunge one's feet into icy cold water after one had just washed them in warm water. I refused to do this and she gave me a smack on my bottom, whereupon I called her the dreaded word, *"Arschloch!"*[17] That was too much for my grandmother. She took out the hot water bottle which warmed my bed and I spent a freezing night without it.

The winter mornings were cruel. No stove was lit yet and the mornings were dark. School started at 8 o'clock. My dressing was done up to a certain stage under the eiderdown, then I made a dash into the bathroom to clean teeth and have a quick wash. We ate in the warm kitchen. Hot cups of rye coffee with bread and butter and honey revived us before we set off for school in a temperature not more than 15 degrees below freezing, with the pale stars still twinkling in the morning sky.

One day, in January 1938, I came home from school feeling very ill with a sore throat and aching limbs. Mother's remedy for colds was a drastic one, but mostly very effective. After a hot bath I was wrapped into an ice-cold wet sheet with only my arms sticking out; warm blankets were put on top with a hot water bottle. A glass of piping hot elderflower syrup ensured that I was bathed in sweat, and according to a famous

---

[17] Arsehole

doctor called Kneip, this was the best cure for colds.

But it did not work this time. My temperature rose and I felt more and more ill. The next day red blotches appeared all over my body. The doctor diagnosed Scarlet Fever. There were two dreaded children's diseases: one was Diptheria, the other scarlet fever. In both cases the death rate in those days was high. Both were strictly hospital cases as they were very contagious, but mother pleaded with the doctor to let me stay at home. Knowing her ability as a nurse he allowed it.

Four weeks of complete isolation followed. I remember little of the first two weeks, except that when I woke up one day after a deep sleep, I found myself in my parents' bedroom. Father had been banned and was in the spare bedroom, and mother, in a white overall, was sitting beside me holding my hand. She had tears in her eyes. Apparently they were tears of joy as I had just overcome the crisis and was on the mend.

It took a long time before I was allowed out of bed. My brother and father appeared at the bedroom door waving to me from a distance. Outside the bedroom hung two white overalls, one for the doctor, one for mother; also a basin of water stood on a stool with some disinfectant, the smell of which loomed over the whole house. Mother had taken the utmost care that nobody else caught my illness. I lapped up all mothers' lavish attention. She carried me to the open window so that I could breathe the fresh March air. Sadly I looked at the vanishing snow, through which already peeped crocuses and pearl hyacinths. I had missed out on a lot of tobogganing. I felt weak and very tired. I had caught glandular fever as well, had become very thin and the mere thought of food nauseated me. Cod liver oil and malt was forced down me, which made it worse.

The summer came and I was still poorly. Mother decided that sulphur baths would do me good, so off we went - mother, Gewi and I - in the summer holidays to stay with my grandmother in Bad Segeberg.[18]

Every morning mother took me to the pump rooms where I was immersed in a horrid-smelling bath. For the first week I felt like dying. It was a long walk to the pump rooms from grandmother's house. I felt so weak after the baths that mother almost had to carry me back. Indeed, one day I fainted. Mother gave up taking me and from that day I felt better and became stronger.

---

[18] Schleswig Holstein

One of the nicest things was the scent of the lime avenue in which my grandmother lived. Every morning, Dollie, her maid, swept the pavement in front of the house which was covered with white lime blossoms; the scent drifted through the open windows and the house was filled with it. At night the street lamp in front of the house threw mysterious shadows onto our bedroom ceiling, and my brother and I watched from the window when the man came to light the gas lamp.

Through my illness I had missed a lot of school and I had to catch up on a great deal. My Godmother in Westphalia, who had spent some time teaching in England - she was an Oxford graduate - invited me to spend a few months with her. I adored Aunt Emmie and her adopted daughter, Hanna, who was much older than I, and I was most enthusiastic. They lived in a pretty little house in Buer, where my parents lived before we moved to Lehrte. I had been there several times before and I knew it well.

I was meant to go to the local school for two months and Aunt Emmie was to give me lessons in the afternoons as well. The schoolmaster was a fanatical Nazi who proudly wore the Party emblem on his lapel. He was very friendly when Aunt Emmie introduced me to him on the first morning. The trouble started after she left. He made me stand in front of the class with my right arm outstretched in the Hitler salute.

Three times he made me say, 'Heil Hitler', and when my voice wasn't loud enough, I had to shout it another three times. It had not been made compulsory at that time to use the Hitler Gruss, and it was the first time that I had been obliged to use it. When I finally got it to his liking and wanted to take my seat next to a girl I knew, he shouted that I could not sit there, and pointed to a desk at the far end of the room at which I had to sit by myself. For the rest of the morning he completely ignored me. I did not mention this to my aunt, but when the next day he pulled my pigtails in a very painful way, I burst into tears. My only comfort was that now I had a desk mate, a curly-headed gypsy boy, who had been treated in exactly the same way by the young Nazi when he appeared that morning. Finally I began to understand why we were given this unjust treatment. Again he came and pulled my pigtail so hard that my face hit the desk and he shouted, "We will teach you a lesson or two. Gypsies, Jews and parsons are all alike, they are the vermin of Germany."

Ignanz, the handsome gypsy boy, shrugged his shoulders; he could not care less. Had he not shared in my misery at school, I should have complained to my aunt about the teacher. Ignanz and I became good friends; he was my first love and what could have been more romantic? Alas, it did not last long.

Every day after school I went with my new friend to his gypsy wagon which stood at the edge of the village near the stream. His mother was not a bit surprised when she saw me and she showed me his tiny baby sister who lay on bulging pillows asleep in a cupboard - which served as a bed. I kept very quiet about my friend to Aunt Emmie. I knew she would not approve. For nearly a week after school I went back to his home with him. Once I saw his sister being breast-fed; she had enormous black eyes and her hair was as curly as her brother's. On her tiny wrist she wore a silver bracelet. Ignanz had a habit of scratching his hair. I soon did the same and when Aunt Emmie noticed it and looked into my hair, to her horror she discovered lice. She was almost beside herself when I told her about my daily visits to the wagon and she forbade any further visits.

I did not tell her that I was sitting next to Ignanz at school. I wanted to pay one more visit to the gypsies to say goodbye. In my ignorance I told his mother that I had caught lice off them and that my aunt had forbidden me to come any more. Somehow the kind gypsy woman took umbrage at this and she took the frying pan with potatoes from the stove and threw them at me. This was the sad ending of my first romance. Two days afterwards, Ignanz did not come to school for the gypsy wagon had moved on.

School without Ignanz was unbearable and then I told my aunt about the treatment I was receiving. The very same day she took me away from school, but here she met with opposition from the teacher who was not prepared to let his little victim go as easily as that. Aunt Emmie produced a doctor's certificate that I was still not well enough to attend school, and he had to let me go.

In the Autumn of the same year I noticed that my parents often looked worried and sad and talked in whispers to their friends.

I overheard words like 'Jews' and 'Concentration Camp' mentioned. I did not ponder on it; the last word was completely new to me and I did not know its meaning. But I knew of the Jews who played quite an important part in our small town - did not four of the largest shops belong to them? Most of the population bought their shoes in Herr Simon's shop, including us, and dresses and materials were found in Herr Maschekatze's at a very favourable price.

Herr Maschekatz was a particularly generous and friendly man; he never failed to escort mother out of the shop, bowing deeply and opening the door for her. He did not overlook me either, calling me, 'my Little One' and gave me remnants of material to make into dolls' dresses. His son Daniel went to school with my brother and his younger son, Herschel, an enormously fat boy, was in my form. He was always being teased, not because he was a Jew, but for his size and clumsiness. We did not know any difference between the Jews and ourselves; the only difference was that, like the Catholics, they went to their own church. Quite a few Jewish families had left the town since 1935; gone to America, it was said.

Father was often seen in long conversations with the male Jews; they looked a bit alike in their sombre suits and black hats. Oma Thiele, our neighbour, sold most of her vegetables to them, and in summer, her fresh strawberries.

On the evening of 9th November 1938, the telephone rang whilst we were having supper. Father answered it. When he came back, his face was sad and he looked pale.

In a quiet voice he said, "They are burning the synagogues in Hannover." Whenever he used the word 'they' it meant the Nazis. We went outside and looked to the west towards Hannover, where the sky was blood red from the fires.

Father said, "There will be revenge."

I took his hand, which I did whenever I was frightened and he was near. His hand was so big and comforting.

"Why do they burn them, father?"

Before he could answer my questions, a group of S. A. men in uniform marched past us shouting in unison, "Exterminate the Jews get rid of the vermin!" I had heard that before and gripped father's hand tighter.

They were marching in the direction of the town and going to do just that. All night they beat up the Jews, plundered their shops and houses, made bonfires of their books and enriched themselves with their valuables. Sleep did not come quickly to me that night; had not the teacher mentioned gypsies and parsons as well as the Jews? Was it to be us next?

The town looked a sad sight the next morning with broken glass everywhere and the smell of the dying bonfires. The broken shop windows were crudely repaired with planks of wood on which was written, 'Who buys from Jews is a traitor'. Daniel and Herschel never came to school again. I only saw them once again when they walked with their eyes downcast beside their mother, completely ignoring me. All visits to theatres, cinemas or any other public performance were forbidden to the Jews. They found themselves not only unwanted but homeless, jobless, penniless, and compelled to wear a large yellow star on their clothes, so that everybody recognised them, despised them and even spat at them.

When I met Herr Maschekatz some time later, I hardly recognised him, for the handsome middle-aged man had turned into an old man, walking bent with a stick. As always, I curtsied to him and bade him good day. He stopped, looked around him and, as nobody was to be seen, put his hand on my head and said, "Little one, it is better you ignore me from now on!"

When I told my father he looked at me sadly and said, "He is right, you had better not greet him any more, but you can pray for him." This I did, and for Daniel and Herschel too. At that time I thought of so many people I had to pray for, it became something like a compulsion. Eventually my list got so long that I often fell asleep before I could mention them all.

———◆———

The only holiday we ever had with our parents, except the North Sea holiday when we were very small, was when we celebrated the golden wedding of my grandparents in Berlin in the summer of 1939.

The golden wedding took place at the summer residence of my uncle in Berlin-Sacrow, a district for the rich with beautiful houses and large gardens running down to the river Havel.

Uncle Claus was the eldest of my grandparents' eight children (six of them were still alive). Like his brothers, he was tall and handsome. I liked him very much indeed, but unfortunately I only saw him twice.

He was married to Aunt Clarutschka, who had a German mother and a Russian father. She was very fond of children and young people. They never had any children of their own, so Aunt Clarutschka invited children of her numerous friends to come and stay with her. Gewi was a frequent guest and spent at least one holiday a year with her. He felt very much at home in these beautiful surroundings. I was quite unaccustomed to the wealth and luxury of my uncle's place. For the first half of the week my parents and I stayed at the large and comfortable flat in Berlin-Charlottenburg in the Nymphenburgerstrasse.

A butler looked after us, Annie, the cook, provided scrumptious meals and Louis, the chauffeur, drove us wherever we wanted to go in the open 'Opel Admiral'. Father's brother and wife led a completely different life from that of a country parson. Uncle Claus had studied under Max Reinhardt to become an actor, but changed his mind and went into Science and Politics. He became Manager of the Chemical Industry in Germany. Uncle Claus was very different from his brothers and sisters; he hardly ever smiled and seemed to be miles and miles away with his thoughts. He loved sport, the only Ungewitter who ever did, apart from myself. Every day before breakfast he trained with a professional trainer in swimming and rowing.

On my first evening in Berlin I was taken by Louis to fetch my uncle from his office. I waited for him in a large hall with a fountain. I sank into one of the voluptuous, soft leather chairs and I was so tired by my journey and all the new impressions that I curled up and went to sleep. When I met him for the first time he asked me what my name was. I thought it was a silly question because surely he ought to have known what his niece was called. I told him my name was Renate.

He said, "Are you sure? How do you know that this is your name?"

I told him everybody called me so, and then added as an afterthought, "And, anyway, I also know myself." He thought that was very funny and laughed. I think that was the only time I ever heard him laugh.

I fell head over heels in love with Uncle Claus. Unfortunately he was a very busy man and did not spend much time with us, but when he was present I watched his every movement. I thought him most terribly handsome.

On the morning of the golden wedding, the family fore-gathered in the conservatory for a short service taken by my father. I even watched

Uncle Claus through my folded hands during prayers. He did not believe, like us, and whilst everybody else had their heads bent in prayer, he looked out of the window and seemed far away with his thoughts.

I was overjoyed when, on my last evening with them, he told me to sit on his knee. He asked me how old I was and if I had learned to speak English yet. I told him that I was changing school that autumn and would then begin to learn other languages. He told me to make a special effort with the English language, and once I could speak it well, he would buy me a beautiful new dress. These were almost the last words he spoke to me and it was the last time I saw him.

The golden wedding was on a lovely summer's day but the clouds of war hung low. The grown-ups sat in the garden until late in the evening. From their anxious faces we could see that all was not well. Uncle Claus had more inside information than any of his family and his absent gaze and his seriousness, I am sure now, were there for a good reason.

Aunt Clarutschka was the complete opposite. She was small, vivacious and always laughing and she talked with a foreign accent.

One afternoon I went with my parents to Dahlem to visit the wife of Pastor Martin Niemoeller, the former submarine Commandant, who since 1931 had been the leader of the 'Bekennende Kirche' opposing Hitler. In 1937 he was 'put away' by the Nazis. After his imprisonment I included him in my nightly prayers, and countless Germans prayed for him throughout the war, until his release in 1945. After the first week my parents went to Bavaria, and Gewi and I stayed with Aunt Clarutschka in Sacrow. With us stayed another boy, the same age as us. His name was Heinz Goering, a nephew of Herrmann Goering. Heinz was full of fun. One morning he came to breakfast in an embroidered Russian dress which he had found in a cupboard, and nobody recognised him until he started talking.

Under Louis's guidance we rowed across the River Havel to Posdam to the impressive Schloss which belonged to Frederic the Great called Sanssouci. Terrace upon terrace, each with its orangery, stretched up to the castle, a beautiful building in baroque style. Louis took me to see the *Bradenburger Tor, Unter den Linden*, the *Zeushaus* and the Zoo, and we watched the changing of the *Wache*[19] in front of the *Neue Kanzlei* on a Sunday morning.

---

[19] Guard

The highlight of the whole holiday for me was when he took me to see Leni Riefenstahl's film of the Olympic Games of 1936 in Berlin. Gewi and Heinz had been taken by my aunt when the Games actually took place. I had, up until now, only seen pictures of it in magazines. I had a very good reason for going. Besides Jessie Owens I looked for another person, called Trudi Meier who had won a gold medal in gymnastics and who came from Hannover. Not only did she live there, but I had become one of her pupils. After the Games she started to give gymnastic lessons in Hannover as well as in our small town. Every Thursday afternoon thirty girls stood in pale blue tunics in a straight line in front of her. The age group was from six to sixteen. Trudi Meier, in a white track suit which bore the emblem of the Olympic Games of five coloured rings, greeted us with "Heil Hitler" and taught us to use the parallel bars and the horse, to climb the rope and to do movement to music. Trudi Meier had dark bobbed hair; the older girls copied her hairstyle in admiration, and once again I cursed my own curly blond hair.

When she appeared in the film, standing on the rostrum receiving the gold medal and shaking Hitler's hand, I felt proud to be one of her pupils.

In the evenings Aunt Clarutschka told us stories of her childhood. We sat at her feet on the terrace and listened to her adventures of when she toured Russia with her father, who had been a well-known architect, and had designed the main railway station in Moscow. The river was below us. Once in a while a pleasure steamer with rows of windows lit up, Chinese lanterns swinging in the breeze to the music, glided past. Then the only noise was the lapping of small waves from the swell of the passing steamer against the rowing-boat anchored at the bottom of the garden.

There were always guests at her house, mainly actors and politicians. Uncle Claus was not a Nazi. His high position in Berlin compelled him to get on well with many fanatics of the Party but he did not care to entertain them. His sad face and silent behaviour revealed to those who knew him well the conflict he was in.

Although my father and my grandfather implored him for information he shook his head and would not talk about it. He had probably been sworn to secrecy and knew what was at stake if any information should pass his lips. Families had started to disappear and innocent children were drawn into the punishment of their parents who had disobeyed the orders of the 'Führer'.

Uncle Claus was determined not to bring any unnecessary suffering upon his family and remained silent like so many others.

I remember meeting Robert Ley and Herr von Ribbentrop at my uncle's house. Herr von Ribbentrop suddenly pulled a bright red yo-yo out of his pocket and began to play with it, and then gave it to me.

This was our last holiday in Berlin. A month later, on the 1st September 1939, the Second World War started.

———⇒·◆·⇐———

The 1st of September 1939 was a beautiful sunny day with a definite tinge of autumn in the air. During breakfast we heard a voice from the road shouting through a loudspeaker, "*Achtung! Achtung!*" We rushed outside; a van covered with the Nazi flag was parked just in front of our entrance gates. Again the voice shouted, "*Achtung! Achtung! In the early hours of this morning the Führer's troops have invaded Poland. Germany is at war!*"

The national anthem and the Horst Wessel song followed, blaring out of the loudspeaker at full volume. The van moved on, leaving groups of people behind standing dazed and silent in front of their houses. The silence was very noticeable after the din of the songs and the impact of the grave announcement. Shocked, everybody stood for a while and then went on with what they had been doing. Just when we were about to do the same, our neighbour's nephew who came every summer from the Ruhrland, came running up to us, dressed in the Hitler Youth uniform. His arm shot up in the Hitler salute, his heels clicked and he shouted at the top of his voice, "Great Germany has declared war. Long live the Führer!"

Father's face suddenly became very red. He took one step towards the boy and said in a very angry voice, "Shut up, you stupid boy, you don't know what you are talking about!" Father was so angry that I feared he would hit him. This would have been a grave offence because anybody in the Führer's uniform was not allowed to be punished. Instead, father turned round in disgust and walked into the house.

Mother followed father into his study. My brother Gewi stood as usual with his hands in his pockets, thinking. I was thinking too. School

Renate, six years old.

Renate and mother,
Gewi and friend
at North Sea, 1929.

Renate and Gewi, 1931.

Portrait of Renate, Gewi and their mother.

Renate's mother.

Renate's father.

The old village Church, Lehrte.

Village children in Lehrte, Renate in front with pigtails.

Uncle Claus.

*Gewi,
just before he joined the army.*

Domsuhl, Aunt Pauline's Farm in Mecklenburg.

Tom leaving his office in Lehrte.

Renate, 1945.

had not yet started. What was going to happen now? I was nearly eleven years old and I had no idea what was going on between the countries; of course I had read of wars but it had never occurred to me that war could happen now, right now. What was it all about?

I knew about the Jews and I felt sorry for them; I knew of Pastor Niemoeller and I prayed for him; I also knew that the Nazis were dangerous and that father said Hitler would destroy Germany one day. Was this going to happen now? I was very muddled. I suddenly remembered that I was invited to a birthday party that afternoon, but now there was a war on, was I still able to go? Would it be wrong to go to parties in critical times like this? It worried me and I decided to ask father's advice.

Father smiled, put his hand on my head and said, "I am sorry for all you young people. Of course you must go to the party." Then he drew me towards him, and said, "Promise me, never to lose your cheerful smile, whatever happens."

I went to my friend Irmela's party that afternoon. To start with we sat and talked in whispers about the war. We decided how we would help; we could knit socks and mittens for the soldiers and perhaps we could even help to nurse them.

"That will not be necessary at all," said one girl, whose father was a Nazi. "The war will be over long before we are old enough to nurse the soldiers." Little did I know that six years later I would actually be helping to nurse not just German, but French, Italian, Serbian, Polish and Russian wounded. During the course of the afternoon we completely forgot about the war, and were happy and carefree.

But when I walked home by myself, I found as I always did, that the red evening sky, as beautiful as it was, tightened my heart just that little bit. That evening it reminded me of blood and I remembered father telling us a short time before, that when he was staying in the Harz mountains with mother, they had seen some red clouds in the sky in the shape of a large sword. I suddenly felt very frightened and started to run towards home. Once inside I forgot again all my worries of the war.

During the course of the first week ration cards were dished out: blue ones for meat, red for groceries, pink for bread and flour, and yellow for butter and fats. Children under sixteen years received double butter ration.

The ration cards were delivered to the house by people (they all wore a Nazi button on their jackets) who, at the same time, took down detailed particulars of every member of the household.

On 3rd September, England and France declared war on Germany. Soon after that a man came and taught us about air raid precautions. He told us where to put buckets of water and sacks of sand, and he also inspected our cellar and shook his head and told us it was not good enough. We were told to use our neighbour's cellar, which came up to standard. Mother pointed out the thickness of the walls and ceiling, but he did not agree with the cellar windows being above ground. In the end he compromised, and a five-foot wall was built in front of each window, leaving enough space for us to squeeze through if necessary.

Nothing else happened that was different from any other autumn except that young men were called up. Ernst, Heinrich's brother from next door, came one day in uniform to say goodbye, and many others came to do the same. Father's new colleague, who had been sharing the parish for the last year, was one of the first to be called up. He was the father of six children.

The blackout needed quite a bit of organising with so many windows in our house. We started off with blinds made from blackout paper. On the first evening of a mock air-raid an outraged warden rushed into the house.

"For God's sake, turn the bloody lights off, your house is a direct target and a danger to everybody else!"

In some ways, mother wasn't very practical, and father had no idea whatsoever about practicalities. Apparently gaps either side of the blind let the light through, so now we used endless drawing-pins, until the sides became so perforated that the paper tore. From then on thick blankets were used; they hung from hooks at the top of the window and were held in place on the window-ledge by heavy books. Although no more light escaped, they weren't altogether satisfactory as they were cumbersome and an eyesore during the day. In the first few months we sometimes forgot all about the blackout, and would go into a room and switch on the light. Immediately angry voices shouted from the road and we felt like traitors. Luckily it was not until March 1942 that serious air-raids started. Then we all became so frightened that naturally everybody was extremely careful and not the slightest glimmer of light escaped anywhere.

The issue and trying on of gas masks was a frightening thing in the first couple of years. More frightening still, was the actual sound of the sirens. Hand sirens were distributed to various parts of the town and village. They were funny looking things on tripods. The village one was handed out to my friend Ernstchen's father. Although the sound was alarming, the sight of the massive figure winding the handle of the siren in front of his house with his grumpy expression, was an amusing one. He never took very long over it. In fact, people complained that they had not even heard the sound, when he took the machine which was still humming, the last notes becoming lower and lower, under his arm, and put it back into the corner of the bar and continued drinking his pint of beer. One day Ernstchen pinched the siren and gave us a demonstration. Unfortunately, the sound was louder than he expected. His father came and gave his son a good hiding in front of all of us, and then disappeared into the house, with a howling sound from Ernstchen and the fading humming of the siren trailing behind him.

⟹◆⟸

Changing to a new school was, for the time being, much more important to me than the war. When the holidays came to an end in the middle of September, Anneliese, Gabi and I said goodbye in floods of tears to our teacher for the last three years, and prepared to go to the local boys' school. Originally we were supposed to go to Hannover, to a girls' school, but our parents thought it safer, now there was a war on, not to travel daily to a large city. The boys' school had recently changed its name, under Hitler's orders, from '*Realgymnasium*' to '*Oberschule*'. Many things had changed by Hitler's orders. No more morning prayers were said; instead the national anthem was sung and some lines from 'Mein Kampf' or some impressive lines by the Führer were recited. Scripture lessons were made voluntary, and to make it difficult to attend them, they were tagged on the time-table after 1 o'clock, when it was time to go home.

The Oberschule was a good half-hour walk from our house. It was a large, ugly building dating from 1820, but at the same time it was impressive with a large well equipped gymnasium built onto it in recent years. A large courtyard with old elm trees surrounded it. The headmaster was just about to retire when the war started, and like so many others, he stayed on. His name was Dr. Pol. He was well over six feet tall with long white hair, and he walked like a stork - very deliberately picking up his legs higher than necessary and holding back his shoulders, he walked slowly and upright. He was very keen on posture and stopped students who slouched and made them do exercises. Immediately anybody saw him they straightened up and walked stiffly and unnaturally past him. He and his wife, who was also a teacher (she taught me English for six years), rode on their ancient bicycles to school every morning. They rode with their backs completely straight, looking intently ahead of them, ignoring all the 'Heil Hitlers' that students on their way to school shouted at them. They were both anti-Nazi and Dr. Pol confessed to father one day that the reason for cycling to school was because it saved them from acknowledging the Hitler salute as they needed both hands on the handlebars.

Our Biology teacher was an old man who was also due to retire at the beginning of the war, but stayed on. He was like a Teddy Bear to look at, round and small with fuzzy grey hair and he grunted a lot. He was known as Opa H. He never let on that he was anti-Nazi, but his ironic grin during the hoisting of the flag in the courtyard each morning, and the slack Hitler Gruss he gave, barely lifting his right hand, suggested what he thought of it all.

It was clear to us that Opa H was fed up with teaching; and he let us do what we liked, provided we were quiet. Whilst he read, or more exactly murmured, from the Biology textbook about the theory of heredity by Mendel or about the functioning of the kidneys in the human body, we did our homework. Sometimes a skeleton was brought in to show anybody coming into the classroom that some serious research was going on, but it stood grinning and completely ignored in front of the desk for the whole of the lesson.

Our History and German teacher was the exact opposite vivacious and strict. She was also an anti-Nazi but very diplomatic in her attitude. When she entered the classroom we stood up. Briefly raising the right arm and saying, 'Heil Hitler,' in a soft voice as she had taught us to, we took our seats again. Her name was Dr. Schaumann or 'Uschi' as we called her.

Physics and Chemistry were taught by Studienrat R. whose nickname was 'Paule'. He was a very nervous man and flew into a rage at the slightest provocation, so we were more than careful not to provoke him. He had been known to take a chair and throw it amongst the pupils.

His wife was known in town as 'Rosa Luxemburg'. He did not share her communist beliefs but he was not a Nazi either. On entering the classroom he took on a clown-like posture; his arm was gradually lifted in the salute and without saying a word he glared at us, sometimes coming very close to our faces. If anybody started to giggle he received an '*Erdnuss*' which was performed with the knuckle of the right index finger at the back of the head, a painful experience. We learned to out-stare him; this performance lasted for about three minutes, after which he suddenly dropped his arm, and everybody, without having uttered a single word, took their seats.

Apparently he boasted after the war that the 'Heil Hitler' had never passed his lips, and he got away with it.

The only two Nazi teachers we had at the beginning of the war were our Art teacher, Herr L., who was small and spiteful and who was known as '*Giftzwerg*',[20] and Herr Offenhausen, known as 'Offi' who taught Literature, Music and Mathematics. Offi was the biggest Nazi in town and did more harm to my father throughout the war than anybody else.

Yet I only remember him as a warm-hearted, kind man with a great sense of beauty and humour. In fact, he was my favourite teacher, whereas Giftzwerg was the most loathsome man I could think of. I must confess I did not have much talent for drawing but he never even tried to teach me, and looked at my attempts with the utmost contempt, teasing me mercilessly about being a parson's daughter. I ended up by doing the shopping for him. One day he made me go for miles to get some asparagus.

The sandy soil in our area was ideal for growing asparagus and farmers had large plantations outside the town. The asparagus was delicious, long white tender stalks, every bit of it melted in one's mouth.

During the war, farmers were committed to surrender most of their crop to the nearby canning factory, so unless one had a 'tame' farmer or 'connections', it was impossible to get any. A kind farmer supplied us during the season with two to three pounds for our Sunday lunch. Mother used to peel the stalks very thinly; a soup was made from the peel and the stalks were strictly rationed out, so that everybody got a fair share.

It was almost impossible to get any asparagus in towns. Giftzwerg,

---

[20] Poisonous dwarf

who lived in Hannover, was on to a good thing when he sent me to get some. The plantations were a good two miles from the town and each had its own small hut where the asparagus was sorted before it was taken to the factory. I knew where the farmer who supplied us with the vegetable had his hut, and as I didn't dare return to school without it, I asked him for our own weekly supply. There was no asparagus for our Sunday lunch that week. I confessed at home what had happened, but it was really up to myself to stand up to the teacher and tell him that I would not get any a second time.

Luckily, the season was a short one. He tried it again, but unsuccessfully, though I had to suffer for it in other ways. He made me clean the basins in the art room into which everybody tipped their unused paint and cleaned their brushes. I had to sharpen his pencils and empty wastepaper baskets - anything but do drawing or other exciting things which everybody else was doing and which I should have liked to have done, too. One day he did not come back to school. His house in Hannover had received a direct hit from a bomb and he and his family were killed.

As the school was not geared for girls we received the minimum amount of teaching in Needlework and Sport. The young sports teacher had been called up like all the other young teachers. Instead Frau S. taught us, but after the age of fourteen there was no more sport. The only games we played were rounders and football. Frau S. was a very tough person of about 55, with grey hair in a bun and the beginnings of a very definite white moustache. With the football under her arm, a whistle in her mouth and dressed in a track suit, she led boys and girls onto the football pitch. On rainy days she gave us demonstrations of how to climb the rope or pole. She looked so comic but, it was a brave undertaking at her age and she was obviously untrained for the job.

She was not very good at teaching needlework and I learned next to nothing. We had made a pact between us few girls that one of us would forget her needlework in turns, and as she was a person who could not bear to see anybody sitting idly by, she allowed that person to read aloud to us. We made sure that all our favourite books were read, and after the first ten minutes, our knitting or crochet work came to rest in our laps and even Frau S. got absorbed in the stories. Our most favourite one was *The Wonderful Adventures of Nils Holgerson with the Wild Geese.*

In every classroom hung a large picture of the Führer. In fact it had become compulsory for every household to have at least one picture of him. Father had been very clever. He had chosen a 'diluted version' as he called it, of the Führer. It was a photograph in which he and the former Chancellor, Hindenburg, were shaking hands and it hung in the darkest corner of the hall.

That autumn I saw a dead person for the first time. Opa Thiele, next door, had died. When Oma Thiele asked me if I would like to see him laid out, and say a final farewell to him, I did not have the heart to say no. Secretly I was afraid to see a dead person and, with a heart full of fear, I followed her up the stairs into the bedroom where he was lying.

I am glad that my first contact with a dead person was Opa Thiele. It took from me a great part of the fear I had of the dead. We entered a room in which the curtains were drawn, but a gap in them let in a shaft of the afternoon sun which ended in a pool of light on the wide brown floorboards. Opa Thiele lay on a massive oak bed with an expression on his face I had not seen on him before. He looked so much younger, so peaceful and so clean. His white hair and long beard were beautifully combed, and his hands were folded across his chest. He wore a long white starched night-gown, and on his feet thick black stockings which stuck out from underneath his gown like two pointed rocks.

"His feet were so cold," said his wife, sadly, "I put some socks on them." And she lovingly rubbed the stiff, cold feet of the old man. Two candles burned at either side of the bed and below his hands lay a bunch of dahlias. It was very quiet except for the buzzing of a fly which settled on Opa Thiele's face. Carefully I wiped it away. I said my farewell, and when we went out of the room we shut the door quietly behind us, so as not to disturb the peace we had left behind.

⇒◆⇐

I was only ten years old when I had to join the Hitler youth. Of course my parents were against it, but there was nothing they could do. It was not compulsory for grown-ups to join the Party, though most of them did. Sometimes their profession forced them to, but it was compulsory for every German youth between the ages of 10 and 18 to join this youth Organisation.

When it started on a voluntary basis in 1936 it had 100,000 members. During the war it rose to 8 million.

For quite some while I had secretly looked forward to joining. The uniform, the marching and the singing appealed to me. I went to the first meeting turned out to Hitler's liking, in a uniform consisting of a short blue skirt, white short-sleeved blouse with a black triangular neck-scarf which was held in place by a brown leather knot, white knee-socks and a light brown suede jacket, like a wind-cheater. My pigtails were neatly plaited and I brimmed over with enthusiasm.

Every Wednesday and Saturday at 3 p.m., the Hitler youth met on the tarmac square in the town park, girls on the right, boys on the left. The boys' uniform looked very severe with black wind-cheaters. In the summer they wore brown shirts, thin leather straps over their shoulders. A wide black leather belt kept up their short trousers. A boat-shaped black hat was pushed under the shoulder-strap. Round the neck, they wore the same black tie as the girls with the leather knot.

Twice a week throughout the year we gathered grouping around the flagpole, raised our right arms and sang the national anthem and the Horst Wessel song, a lengthy ordeal. Fortunate were the ones in the second and third row, for they could rest their arms on the shoulders of the ones in front. Quotations from 'Mein Kampf' were read to us as a black triangular flag with the white Hitler youth emblem imprinted, was raised to the top of the pole, where it remained until 5 p.m. when the same procedure happened again.

It very soon became rather boring for me and a few others. There was a small group, but only a small group, who thought it all a great hoot. We were the ones brought up by anti-Nazi parents, and were fortunate enough to learn from a young age that, behind the facade of this Organisation with all the various opportunities it offered, stood Hitler's technique of indoctrinating Germany's rising generation, at its most vulnerable age, with his ideals and philosophy.

The Hitler youth was indeed able to give us the things that appealed to us, which our school, with its ancient teachers and lack of materials, could not offer us any more. Here the young were led by the young. Sport, travel, crafts, music - a chance to do it all.

It was easy to get sucked into it all without noticing. Hitler had the gift of cunningly starting a campaign just at the right moment. He took the unemployed off the streets at the right time. The youths adored him and flocked to him because he provided them with things which would otherwise have been denied them.

Once a year, just before the summer holidays, a two day sports event took place in the vast new stadium in the town. Dressed in the shortest of black shorts and white vests, boys and girls competed in a miniature Olympic Game. The winning of 100 points justified a *Siegernadel,* a small silver pin, which the winner received on the evening of the second day, when he went onto the stage where the top nobs sat and shook hands with the *'Gauleiter',*[21] who pinned the award onto the vest. I think sport was the only thing I was good at: I received a pin every year, long-jump being my triumph - even my father did not mind my wearing it.

I made a new friend when I changed schools. Inge's father had been sent to Polen to reorganise the postal system in Posen. Inge played the piano very well, and we both qualified for the Hitler Youth Orchestra. It had its pros and cons. Pros because we were let off other things like marching exercises, cons because we had to perform at lots of functions; some were on Sunday mornings at the same time as church. Father forbade me to go. To start with, it didn't seem to matter, but as the war went on and the hatred towards the church became greater, I was commanded to appear. When I didn't one Sunday, a group playing drums and fanfares marched to the front door of the church during a service. Their blare drowned father's voice and he was forced to discontinue the service until they moved on. It was repeated several times until I reappeared on Sunday mornings whenever the orchestra was playing.

I wished I had never joined it. I felt so sorry for father and, worst of all, I felt I was betraying him. Father never said one accusing word to me. He knew that whatever they were trying to teach us - to which we had to listen - would not enter into my heart. Inge and I were often reprimanded, when we did not take things seriously. Inge had a great sense of humour and was very good at mimicking others, especially those in uniform.

In 1941, Lehrte received its first *Ritterkreuztraeger.*[22] Hitler youth and S. A. men formed a lane from the station to the house of this young hero. Every household hung out the flag, and a life-size portrait of the Führer was hoisted onto the platform next to where the orchestra was

---

[21] Political Head of the province
[22] A new war medal meaning: Bearer of the Knight's Cross

sitting. When we took our seats, I unfortunately tripped over one of the ropes which secured the picture. It started to sway precariously and, for a moment, it looked as if it was crashing down on top of us just when the train was pulling into the station. Fortunately it was saved, but almost everybody thought I had done this on purpose.

I can still see the horrified face of the young *Ritterkreuztraeger* when he stepped out of the train. Instead of being greeted, as I am sure he expected, by his parents and fiancée, he stepped straight into the hands of the 'Gauleiter' and his fellow leaders.

By the time he had listened to speeches, the orchestra playing and the ever-repeated national anthem and Horst Wessel song, he looked tired and cheesed-off. All the way home he had to acknowledge the 'Heils' and 'Sieg Heils' shouted at him. Oh yes, Hitler knew what would please heroes, but it did not go down well with all of them.

Because I had changed school and made a lot of new friends, playing with the village children had become less frequent. Sadly it was they who withdrew, calling me posh and stuck-up, but I did not feel like that at all, as homework, music lessons and Hitler Youth took up a lot of time.

My tobogganing with them came also to a sudden and sad end. It was towards the end of February, when the temperature had suddenly risen for a few successive days, that I was trudging through the deep snow across the field to the tip. I suddenly saw a group of men coming towards me, rather slowly, carrying something between them, which at that distance I could not make out. They were followed by children pulling their sledges behind them. When they came nearer, I saw that they carried a stretcher covered by a blanket with two shapes visible underneath. Puzzled, I looked at my friends. One of them said, "The Neumann brothers have been drowned!"

The ice had broken when their sledge hit the ice on the lake. One brother, aged nine, fell in. The other, one year older, tried to rescue him, but drowned as well. No grown-up was present. The other children, frightened and helpless, did not know what to do. By the time they had fetched help, both boys were dead. This had happened three hours before and all the time the other children stood and watched the men as they tried to get hold of the bodies from under the ice. Silently we followed the men on the way to the village to the home of the boy's parents.

I had never heard anybody scream with such pain as the mother did when she opened the door and saw the stretcher. Then she looked under the blanket and saw both her boys, her only children, dead. She threw herself upon them and remained motionless. Stunned from witnessing such grief, and the fact that we would never see our cheerful playmates again, we turned away and went home.

I could not eat my supper that night. I went to bed and cried in the dark bedroom. It was not for the boys I was crying; I believed that they were angels now, but it was for the mother and father. The pain-stricken cry, and the sight of the mother lying across her dead children did not leave me all night. When hours after I had gone to bed, my bedroom door opened and I heard mother and father come in, I pretended to be asleep. They stood for a long time silently at my bed. I had a feeling that they were praying. When father put his soft warm hand on my forehead, I felt comforted, but still very sad.

A couple of days later a group of children watched two white coffins disappear into the winter's earth.

From then on the pit was out of bounds to all children, winter and summer.

⟫◦◦⟪

In every classroom hung a map of Europe, and Asia and above it was a large portrait of the Führer in uniform. 'Offi', who had become our form master, had risen to be the town's highest Nazi official. On most days he wore the brown party uniform and shiny high black boots. He had fought in the first World War and a row of medals adorned his brown shirt. Offi produced minute swastikas on pins and on every school day morning from the start of the war, we marched with our soldiers and triumphantly stuck pins onto the map. Within twenty days, flags advanced towards Warsaw, and on 27th September the Polish capital capitulated. The war with Poland had come to an end.

"Nothing to fear from Russia," Offi shouted. "They are our allies and supply us with grain, cotton, oil and platinum."

And Great Germany, he boasted, gave arms and steel in exchange; there was absolutely nothing to fear.

In his smart, brand-new uniform, the 55-year-old, yet already white-haired man, looked suddenly young, as with shining eyes, full of conviction and enthusiasm, he told us, again and again, how wonderful the Führer was, how trustworthy and great. He would soon give us more *Lebensraum*,[23] and a rosy future.

During the winter of 1939 - 1940, German and French soldiers stood motionless on either side of the Maginot Line. Norway received Sweden's oil and Hitler's eye was fixed on Narvik. His next move was towards neutral Scandinavia. Britain had the same idea, but the Germans got there before them, in April 1940.

For the first time the German losses were heavy. We had lost six submarines and several other warships. Offi was not worried. "For Führer and Vaterland," he shouted, and stuck a swastika flag with a black pin head over Narvik and Oslo. His chest swelled with pride as, with his thumb tucked underneath the highly-polished brown leather belt, he marched up and down between our desks in his noisy leather boots.

The nickname for any high Nazi official was *Pfau*:[24] quite appropriate; small brains behind brilliant plumage, all miniature Hitlers with big mouths. But Offi was different. He had a good brain. He could be cruel and hard when in uniform but kind and soft when in civilian clothes, as we were to find out later. Now he shouted, "Let us sing the England Song," and we stood up from our desks and sang, 'Let us drink the cool wine and fly towards England.' Offi stood in front of us singing the loudest in his good bass voice, with a tight fist and his right arm stretched out towards England. Our singing drifted through the open classroom windows into the first warm summer's breeze which gently lifted the last blossoms from the budding fruit and blew them over the garden fences onto the pavements.

Every Monday morning we carried bags of scrap iron, silver paper, rags, bones, waste paper and other materials to school. Carefully they were weighed and entered into a book. Points were given for each item and those who had most points got a cheer. It slowly petered out. After two years there was nothing more to bring. At the beginning of 1941 things became scarce. Clothes and shoes were obtainable on coupons only; coffee, tea and cocoa were things of the past, and of other foods there was just not enough.

---

[23] Living Space
[24] Peacock

Those who had soldiers as friends or relations in the occupied countries were lucky. Woollen garments were sent home from Norway; coffee, chocolate and tea from Holland and Belgium, silk stockings and leather goods from France. The black market had started. Anything was obtainable provided one had something to exchange.

It was in the summer of 1941 that I met one of the nicest and kindliest persons I have ever known. Her name was 'Tante Krueger'.

On a sultry July morning father had sent me to fetch his diary which he had left in the vestry of the churchyard chapel. The new churchyard was a long way from the town, and even further from the village. I had been given a bicycle for my tenth birthday. I loved it, looked after it well, and later even took it into the air-raid shelter with me.

The churchyard was at least 6 kilometres from our house. It was like a huge garden with high, well-established hedges of yews and rhododendron bushes. In the spring, nightingales sweetened it with their songs. People came out in the early morning, and, sitting on the numerous benches, listened to the melodic chorus. It was not possible to see more than ten graves at a time because each row was surrounded by a tall hedge, and at each end of the row was a well which was continually fed with clear water from a fish's mouth, so the sound of water was always present.

At the end of a large well-kept lawn stood the ugly red-bricked octagonal modern chapel, into which I dreaded going, especially by myself. Long stained glass windows made it dark inside. To my relief no coffin stood, as it usually did - without the lid in front of the altar. I found my father's diary on the table in the vestry and was relieved when I was out in the warm, welcoming fresh air again. When I pushed my bike towards the exit, I noticed a middle-aged woman sitting by herself on a bench, completely dressed in black, a sign of the deepest mourning. She wiped her face continuously with a handkerchief.

I stopped. Curtseying, I said, "Good morning," and asked if she was all right.

"I am feeling a little giddy," she said. "Would you like to sit beside me for a while?"

I rested my bike against a tree and sat beside her.

"Aren't you Renate Ungewitter?" she asked.

"Yes, I am," I said, "and what is your name?"

She told me her name was Frau Krueger and that her husband had died suddenly from a heart attack a month ago.

"He came home from work, my Hein," she told me. "He was just going to ring the doorbell when he collapsed." She found him when she opened the door.

"I come every day, morning and evening, to water his grave, but mainly to be near him. And today is my birthday," she added quietly.

"Haven't you any children?" I asked her.

"I haven't anybody," she said.

I sat with her for a little while, and when she was feeling better, I said goodbye and cycled home.

I told father about meeting Frau Krueger and that it was her birthday. Father, of course, knew about her and where she lived, and in the afternoon I cycled to her house which was quite a distance from ours. In the basket on the carrier lay a bunch of roses, freshly picked by mother, and a letter from father.

Frau Krueger lived on the fourth and highest floor of a large apartment house belonging to the railway. Her husband had been an engine driver. I thought her house most depressing as I climbed the eight flights of stairs. There were two flats on each floor, and on every other landing I passed two small brown doors opposite each other. These were the lavatories and some of them were rather smelly.

At last I reached the top flat. Here the ceiling sloped and a stepladder stood under the trap-door to the loft. A shiny brass plate said H. KRUEGER. I rang the bell. The huge house was completely silent and I felt a little frightened when there was no reply. A small slate with a crayon on a string hung beside the door. Should I write Happy Birthday on it and put the flowers on her doormat? I rang the bell once more and a shadow appeared behind the frosty glass door.

"Happy Birthday," I said when Frau Krueger opened it, and I gave her the flowers.

She was very pleased and surprised and asked me to come in. Her flat was tiny, cosy and very clean. The drawing room had two small dormer windows, but the kitchen had a large window and was full of sunshine. We sat on the sofa, drinking delicious Ersatz cocoa[25] and ate home-made biscuits. Frau Krueger showed me photographs of her

---

[25] Cocoa substitute

husband; in fact they were standing everywhere, on her side tables and chest of drawers, and some were hanging on the walls, in all sizes. A black velvet bow was tied to each one of them. She talked about him all the time. They had obviously been very happy together. She suddenly asked me if I liked picnics. Picnics were something we hardly ever had, but I did like them. So we arranged a picnic for the following week.

We walked towards the wood, carrying between us the picnic basket, onto which two small canvas stools were tied. I had not noticed how small and round she was; she wasn't much taller than I was at eleven. She wore thick spectacles and her face was chubby, and though she was not attractive she was very kind and nice. We found a shady place at the edge of the wood and, sitting on our small wobbly canvas stools, we had our picnic. She must have saved her rations for the entire week, as the most delicious things came out of the basket. She herself had the appetite of a sparrow. My healthy appetite pleased her and she urged me again and again to take one more sandwich or a piece of cake. She told me that once a week, when the weather was good, she and her husband had come to this place for a picnic and how much they had always enjoyed it. We arranged another picnic for the coming week, and we kept it up all through the summer. Our friendship was sealed over numerous cups of cocoa.

Sometimes I went with her to the churchyard. Behind a large black marble tombstone she kept her watering can and a small hand rake. On the right side of the stone was written 'Heinz Krueger, born 12. 2. 1885 died 7. 6. 1941.' On the left it said, 'Luise Krueger, born 8. 7. 1889.' and then a blank.

"That's where I am going to rest," said Tante Krueger pointing to the left side and quietly added, "I will join you soon, dear Hein."

In fact she lived for another twenty years. I always felt very embarrassed when she held her little private conversations with her husband. I turned away and raked the path in front of the grave in a very special pattern to please her. I tried hard to cheer her up with nonsense stories or jokes or other silly things. At the start of our friendship she insisted on walking home with me. Before we left her flat, I sometimes wrote something funny on the slate outside her flat door, which she was not to look at until she came back. I hoped it would make her laugh then, when she returned to her lonely, empty rooms.

Tante Krueger refused to come into our house: she said she was shy, so we said goodbye at the gates of the yard. My parents would have loved her to come in, but even when invited she would not come.

One day I told her that mother was in bed with flu. Our maid had flu at the same time and father was looking after us and doing the cooking. He had no idea how to cook and everything was terrible. Without hesitation she came into the house, saw how badly help was needed, tended to the patients, put on an apron and started to cook. From that day she became a friend of the entire family, and she was in fact our dearest friend.

It was lovely to see her change once again into a happy, cheerful person. One of her greatest assets was her sense of humour. Maybe it was because she had no children, but she was most certainly over-anxious. She often said that one of my daredevil acts would give her a heart attack. When she came with me to the local swimming pool, she could not bear to see me jump from the 5 metre board and turned her head away, but I waited until she turned around again and then jumped. Mother said she spoiled me, but I liked it.

Sometimes, when I practised my violin, she would be in the same room attending to the mending basket. I really believed that she genuinely liked listening to my playing. She was very sentimental but not very musical. I stopped practising the things I ought to have done, and played things she liked, such as the *Largo* and *Ave Verum*. I played them badly; nobody else wanted to listen but Tante Krueger said, with tears in her eyes, so that she had to take off her specs and wipe her face with the sock she was darning, "It's quite wonderful." But I thought it was Tante Krueger who was quite wonderful!

———⋙◆⋘———

Offi's reassurance that we had nothing to fear from Russia did not come true. On June 22 1941 — Hitler had typically chosen the same date on which Napoleon had marched his troops into Russia — German troops were given the command to attack the Soviet Union.

It looked, to start with, as if a second *Blitzkrieg* was to follow. Offi's little swastikas rapidly moved eastwards and by the autumn stood threateningly in front of Moscow. We ran out of flags and quickly had to make more.

German troops appeared everywhere: Le Havre, Scapa Flow, Spitzbergen, Narvik, Tobruk, Crete and now Moscow. Offi was beside himself with pride, but father shook his head and said, "It can't go on like this."

A lot of people believed that victory would follow victory, that the war would not last long. Hitler shouted himself hoarse convincing them that it was true. Masses flocked to see him whenever he appeared in public. 'Hypnotic' was the word I heard mentioned in connection with his speeches. We were compelled to listen to them. Police patrolled the streets to make sure everybody sat next to the radio when Hitler talked to his people. All lessons stopped. We sat in our uniforms on these great occasions, on the hard school benches and listened to the voice which was so persuasive. We listened to the applause, wave upon wave of it, and finally we got up after two hours, stiff and bored, and sang the National Anthem with many thousands of others who had come to see him in the Berlin Stadium, finishing with a triple *Sieg Heil.*

Polish prisoners of war had arrived in our town. They were ordered to work mainly on farms. In the evening a German guard with his rifle over one shoulder collected them and took them back to the camp, a large building not far from our house, its windows secured with barbed wire. It was a sight quite new to us when, on a dark evening, this group of about sixty prisoners in their long heavy coats, walked slowly and silently back to their camp, with the guard and his rifle behind them. All we could see was a long dark line and the glow of their cigarettes.

Farmers soon came to the conclusion that they were lazy and always hungry. After a few months Polish girls arrived and were billeted on farms. A year later a number of Polish infants were born. In many cases the farmer's wife took charge of the infant during the day, when its mother was busy, but in the evening the Polish mother took over, feeding the baby with all sorts of unsuitable food, convinced that the German Frau starved her child. Very often it was sick the next day. All this presented quite a few problems.

Not long after the Polish prisoners, French and Belgian PoWs arrived. The Polish prisoners were now billeted with the farmers (and even more babies were born) and the newcomers were put into the large building with the barbed wire. They too were put to work on farms. Like the Poles they wore a khaki uniform and their language was the only difference. They were very cheerful and friendly but apart from their employers, we were forbidden to communicate with them. The farmers preferred them to the Poles, since they worked hard and did not have babies. They made fun of the guard when he came to collect them in the evening, but he took no offence; a packet of cigarettes from the prisoners soon put him in a good mood. Chatting and joking, in no special formation such as the Poles used to adopt, they walked to the camp. There was never an occasion when the guard had to use his rifle, and they were given enough food and treated well. I never saw anything to the contrary, but perhaps some were luckier than others with their employer.

I saw Herr Busch, our neighbour, packing a basket full of goodies and warm clothes and giving it to his French PoW. (the French were always shivering with cold), who embraced him and warmly shook his hand. After a while, they became part of the farming community. We began to chat to them and nobody minded.

All through 1941 the black pins moved rapidly forward on all frontiers. *Sondermeldung*[26] upon *Sondermeldung*, introduced by fanfares, came through the radio.

Since the autumn we had made a new friend. Hauptmann Alex, in charge of the large ammunition factory outside the town, was our frequent guest. Up until then he had fought at the Eastern Front; his reports were gloomy and his forecast of the future not encouraging. Only when he was alone with my parents did he dare to air his views. All was not well within the German Army in Russia. Hitler had fallen out with some of his generals. Hauptmann Alex had inside information. A deep crisis had arisen in the East and some generals had 'retired', which meant they had been given the push. Towards the end of 1941, Hitler himself took charge of the army.

With the beginning of winter the Hitler Youth got busy. Boys and girls, in pairs, wearing uniform, collected gloves, woolly hats, ear muffs, anything to keep our soldiers warm in the unusually cold winter of 1941 - 42 on the Eastern Front. We went from house to house after school until every household was exhausted of any surplus warm garment. Every pair of skis was confiscated, and we spent most of our spare time knitting. But not only the Hitler Youth knitted. Every household sat knitting, and

---

[26] Special announcement

small cartons were issued with *FELDPOST*,[27] written on them in large letters. They were filled with biscuits and something warm to wear, with a weight limit of 500 grammes. Hitler Youth collected the boxes several times a week, and took the heavy canvas bags to the collecting centre.

The *Winterhilfswerk*[28] came into action. Shivering in the bitter winter wind, we stood in the streets in our inadequately thin but smart uniforms. Wearing white knee socks, our knees red and blue from the cold beneath the short skirts or trousers, and with cheerful faces as commanded, because Hitler's youth had to be tough, we sold beautifully made carved figures, small enough to hang from the button of a coat. We sold, always in pairs, blue candles in aid of the Russian offensive, and blue candles and colourful figures adorned every German Christmas tree that year. Only Christmas was not called Christmas any more but: 'The night of the Sun Light', as the Führer had ordered.

In the New Year it looked as if once again Hitler's plan was going to work. A new offensive on the German side had started at the end of June. The aim was the oil sources on the lower Volga river.

On the map in our classroom the pins crossed the Don into the Caucasus, and at the end of August a triumphant swastika was stuck on the highest peak, the Elborus.

<hr />

There was a small room in our house which was hardly ever used. Its only window faced east and looked into the farmyard belonging to Herr Busch. It was tucked away between father's study and mother's green room. Once there had been a door into it from father's room, but a few years before, a bookshelf had been built to take father's ever-increasing store of books and put where the door had been, so there was no trace of it left. Now the only entrance to it was from the green room.

One day, when I came back from school, I noticed that the tall mahogany bookshelf with the glass doors and crisscross wooded slats had been moved in front of the door; nobody would have guessed that there was a door behind it. I thought mother must have been in one of

---

[27] Field post
[28] Winter help Organisation

her furniture-shifting moods and did not think any more about it. A few days later I heard a noise coming from the room, but mother said, "It must be the mice again."

On another occasion, I heard a muffled cough and knew that somebody must be in there. And then mother explained it all to me.

In 1941 there were still several thousand Jews in Berlin. Without the help of the Church they would not have been able to survive. With the ever increasing air raids on Berlin, more and more people became homeless. A lot of Jews, who up till then had kept themselves hidden in the houses of friends, became homeless and had nowhere to go.

Throughout Germany an underground Organisation, run by the Church, helped them to find further shelter. Up until now I did not know that my parents belonged to this Organisation, the members of which risked the death sentence, not only for themselves but their entire family, every time they opened their door to a refuge-seeking Jew. Many Jews were discovered - by the Gestapo - and together with those who had taken them in, were transported to concentration camps. But in spite of that, a great number of German people risked their lives and were willing to help.

Nobody knew about the hiding place in our house. Since the beginning of 1941 a household which had fewer than four children no longer qualified for a domestic help. It was fortunate that we were now without a maid. Tante Krueger was the only one who knew, besides my brother and me, and she would have given her life before she would tell anybody.

For eighteen months the little room hid these poor, unfortunate Jews. The longest each couple or single person stayed was a week; sometimes it was for one night only. The Gestapo were looking for them everywhere. Frightened of being caught, haunted by the knowledge of the danger they brought upon those who took them in, they moved on to the next place at the slightest sign of suspicion. Every time they moved on to the next hideout, a new address was given to them, never more than one address at a time. Continuously they were on the move. I know of one couple who in 18 months went to 66 different houses, but they survived, as did thousands of others. They had no ration cards and no coupons for clothes. Whoever took them in shared their own meagre rations with them and gave them warm clothes and most importantly, gave them sympathy and hope.

My parents were well aware of the danger they had taken on, not only for themselves but for us children as well. They also knew how much they depended on my brother and I never to murmur a word to anybody, not even to our dearest friends. Sometimes this was very difficult. The worst occasion was when we were told by our Hitler Youth leader to come to his office and were asked question upon question: how many rooms were in our house? How many people lived in it? Which they knew perfectly well. Who came to visit us? The same questions over and over again. We did not let on. They allowed us to go after two hours, only to repeat the same thing the next week.

After the first interrogation I cried all the way home. Gewi took my hand and talked to me reassuringly. He was now nearly 17 years old and would soon leave school. He told me that I must not show that I was frightened; they might think there was a reason for it. I must answer their questions as casually as possible without telling the truth about the room and its inhabitants. I had to promise him not to mention the interrogations to my parents as it would have added to their many worries.

The Nazis in our town were very suspicious of my parents, but so far had no evidence that they were helping Jews.

Offi, my teacher, and now the local *Gauleiter,* was most anxious to find something out. Nothing would have pleased him more than to take my father away from his parish, but Offi never tried to get any information out of me or my brother. Indeed, Offi and I felt a great mutual friendship towards each other. There was nobody who recited Moericke or Lenau, my favourite poets at that time, as beautifully as he did, and he liked my German essays. It was he who opened our eyes to the beauty of nature; when on a summer's day the temperature being too hot for indoor lessons, he took us into the fields and woods and we sat in the meadows singing old German folk songs. On those days he wore civilian clothes. Could this man, who was so sensitive and kind, really hate and be unjust? Or did he, like so many others in uniform, just do his duty?

On one school morning he took the hand of my class-mate, Ernst-August, and gently led him to the door of our classroom.

"Go home, Ernst-August," he said, "your mother wants you." His father had fallen under a train that morning and had been killed. Ernst-August was an only child, and Offi knew that his presence would comfort his mother.

Ernst-August's grandparents, on his father's side, were half Jews, which made him a *Mischling*.[29] From this day on, Offi was especially kind and caring for the boy, even though he had Jewish blood in him.

We tried hard not to draw any attention to the only east facing window on the first floor which meant that no electric light or even a candle could be used in it. Whenever the room was occupied, which happened once a month or so, the bookcase was eased away from the door just a little, so that the occupants could squeeze through and use the bathroom. It could only be done in the evening when visitors were not very likely. Either my brother or I kept watch from the windows facing the yard. Provided everything was all right, they sat with us for a while sharing our supper, after which mother packed a basket with provisions which they took with them back to the little room. Their faces looked thin and pale from worry and lack of fresh air. How did they get about from one place to the other unnoticed? They were given money and false identity cards, and they mingled with the crowds as naturally as their anxiety allowed them to. At that time there were a lot of homeless people in Germany, and it was not difficult to be disguised as one of them.

The first time the Gestapo arrived at our house they could not find anything. With a pounding heart I followed them from room to room. The relief when they left was more than I can describe. But they came again: this time it was not all right. However Herr Busch, our neighbour, had given us warning in good time. By chance, he had seen an S. A. man scrutinising the east side of our house over the garden wall. He, of course, had no idea what was involved, but he knew it could mean no good, so his warning saved our lives. The Jews left the house immediately; people constantly came and left, so that was no problem.

By the time the Gestapo arrived all was clear. There had been just enough time to move the bookcase away from the door to its usual place. Though there was no trace left of the Jews, the Gestapo were sure we had been collaborating with the underground movement. They took Father away with them to be interrogated in Bielefeld. It all happened so quickly that there had been no time to say goodbye to him.

We waited anxiously for his return. He was released after three days as they could not find enough evidence. When he came back he

---

[29] Jewish Aryan - second degree

was unshaven and very tired.

After they had discovered the little room we could not shelter the Jews any more. For the rest of the war the Gestapo kept an eye on us. Though there were no more Jews in our house, they could perhaps still find out that we had sheltered them. Every time they came we feared that they had found out.

⪼◈⪻

There was fighting everywhere now. Japanese planes had attacked American ships in Pearl Harbour in December of 1941. Japan and the United States were at war, and Hitler declared war on the United States a few days after the attack. Since the beginning of the war, families had received letters with the dreaded official Government stamp on the envelope. They read, 'We are sorry to inform you that your husband (son) has been killed in action.'

Black armbands on coat sleeves became a familiar sight, but the population of Lehrte also increased. The first people made homeless through bombing started to arrive in our town.

In the Spring of 1942, German towns like Luebeck, Cologne, Bremen, Wilhelmshaven and Hannover had their first major air raids. A massive automatic siren, higher than the two chimneys, now stood on our house, it being the tallest in the village. When it gave the alarm the whole house shook, and, for a minute, every other noise was drowned.

After the first air raid on Hannover the sky was as red as it had been when the synagogues were on fire six years earlier. I remembered how frightened I had been then, frightened about something I did not understand. I was frightened now. Had the revenge Father had forecast come so soon?

No bombs had as yet fallen on Lehrte, except for two which landed a few kilometres outside the town. Hordes of sightseers had walked or cycled out the next day to look at the craters in the middle of a corn field, and did more damage to the crop than the two holes.

Air raid alarms were a regular thing now. Almost every night the sirens howled. After those nights, school started two hours late and three hours of teaching was the most we could expect now. There was no homework for us on Wednesdays and Saturdays or on those days when the Hitler Youth needed us.

A homeless mother from Cologne moved into our house with her two children. With the first sounds of the sirens they rushed towards the cellar, where all three sat trembling and huddling together until the all clear was given. We had got used to the humming and droning of the enemy aircraft overhead on their way to Berlin, releasing their deadly weapons upon the unfortunate larger cities.

We had also got used to the deafening noise of the anti-aircraft guns which were stationed near the village. The fragments of their shells hit the roofs and I collected some of them the next morning to take to school. We sat in our warm kitchen during air raid alarms, feeling reasonably safe, as we were sure that bombs would not be wasted on a small and unimportant town such as ours.

But we were wrong.

One sunny July day, shortly before lunch time, we saw hundreds and hundreds of enemy aircraft flying overhead in perfect V formations towards the east leaving white fluffy tails against the clear blue sky, they sparkled in the brilliant sunshine like silver birds on migration.

"Poor people in Berlin," we said. This was going to be one of the first daylight air raids. They flew so high, we could hardly hear them. The anti-aircraft guns were silent, being unable to reach them because of their height. But suddenly they started to fire. White puff balls appeared in the sky and we noticed a much lower flying formation coming towards us from the east.

"Into the cellar at once!" Father shouted. We had just reached the cellar door when the air was filled with hissing and whistling sounds. The cellar lights went out and immediately after that the cellar began to sway. We fell onto the floor as a tremendous sound of rolling thunder came over us. The children screamed. Their mother was lying on top of them, like a hen protecting her chicks. I was clinging on to both my parents, too terrified to utter a sound. Several more times the hissing, followed by the thunder, repeated itself and every time the cellar heaved and plaster fell off the ceiling. Then all became deathly quiet.

Anxiously we waited for five minutes, then father went up the steps leading into the kitchen. The door made a crunching noise when he opened it. There was glass everywhere. Half of our windows were broken, but apart from that the house was all right. The heavy front door was blown wide open. We heard people shouting and crying and the sound of fire engines and ambulances.

What a sight greeted us outside! The peaceful little village was like a battle field. A large crater blocked the entrance to our yard, clumps of earth covered the lawn and the wrought iron gate was doubled up. Fortunately, not many houses were destroyed in our vicinity, but almost every house was damaged. Torn curtains fluttered from broken windows and a cloud of dust lay over everything; even the green lime trees looked grey. Most of the bombs had fallen into the many gardens and streets. Our own garden was untouched. One house was burning and people stood in a long line passing buckets of water. Over the town hung a large dark cloud of smoke.

"I wonder if my house has been hit," said Tante Krueger quietly.

"We will go and see," said father, but somebody took him by the arm and said, "Please come and help us. A family is buried under the rubble and we think they are still alive."

My parents immediately went to help. Tante Krueger and I went off by ourselves. Gewi had gone on his summer vacation the day before, and I wished now that I had gone with him. We took the hand cart out of the shed and pulled it behind us, just in case Tante Krueger's house had been hit and we might be able to save something.

The town was in complete chaos.

"Thank God, the Church has not been hit," said Tante Krueger as we passed it. It took a long time before we reached her house. Buildings were burning and collapsing. People pulled handcarts piled high with dusty belongings. We saw familiar faces; some had been lucky, some had lost everything. I wanted to go home when I saw a row of corpses, charred and unrecognisable, laid out on the pavement. I had never seen anything so awful. Tante Krueger said she would go on by herself, but I could not let her do that.

We were stopped once; the road was sealed off because of an unexploded bomb. We sat on the kerb and waited for two hours. We asked passers-by whether No. 21 Wilhelmstrasse was still standing. Some said it wasn't, some said it was. Tante Krueger's face was very pale, and I could not stop trembling.

Tante Krueger's house was completely destroyed. Everyone who was in the house at the time had been killed.

"I am so very glad you were with us!" I said and hugged her. She just stood there. She did not even cry, but said over and over again the name of her dead husband.

Suddenly, I saw something yellow sticking out from under the broken bricks. I pulled it from the rubble. It was Tante Krueger's large brass soup ladle which always hung, highly polished, above her kitchen stove. Except for a few dents it was undamaged. Carefully I laid it in the handcart, but it was the only thing we could save. I put my arm around Tante Krueger's shoulder and said, "You must now live with us," which she did for the next ten years. She moved into mother's green room, and our friendship became closer every day.

From now on, we, like the mother with her two children, rushed towards the cellar at the first sound of the alarm. From then on until the end of the war we hardly had a day or night without air raid warnings. The first attack on Lehrte was the worst, but others followed, and we lived in constant fear when, day after day, night after night, thousands of planes passed overhead and any minute death could strike. It was this which stretched our nerves to the utmost.

I always spent my autumn holidays with my Godmother, Aunt Emmi, in her small Westphalian village, but after the air raid on Lehrte, my parents insisted that I spent the rest of the summer holidays with her as well.

It was sheer bliss to sleep through the nights, for no bombs fell on this tiny village throughout the war.

Aunt Emmi wanted to speak English with me at meal times. I protested.

"I don't like the Tommies one little bit," I said. "All they do is drop bombs on us. I hate their beastly language."

Aunt Emmi said that they were a very nice, kind race and that she had many friends in England who suffered from our bombs as much as we suffered from theirs, and that Scotland was one of the loveliest countries she knew.

To please Aunt Emmi we spoke English at meal times.

Two of my best friends, Elisabeth and her brother Friedrich, lived in the same village. Their father was the Rural Dean and they lived in the largest and most beautiful old rectory I have ever seen. Their large park-like garden and the hilly wooded surroundings were paradise to me, and the thought of spending the next two weeks without air raid alarms, the Hitler Youth and *Ernte Einsatz* was wonderful.

Two things put a damper on this holiday. There was a mental asylum in the village, a yellow painted building with a large garden around it. It was a familiar sight to us as it was almost next to the rectory. Every time we passed it we waved to the inmates, who sat on the garden benches or weeded the flower beds. We knew quite a few of them by name. They waved back to us with an exaggerated and childlike joyous response. This time, I noticed, the garden was almost empty of patients.

"Where are they?" I asked.

Friedrich shrugged his shoulders, but Elisabeth whispered into my ear, "The Nazis have taken them away to bigger hospitals; there are only a few left now."

We all knew what that meant. Hitler had started to exterminate the Jews, and was now doing the same with the infirm and mentally unstable. Anybody who was a hindrance was quietly 'put away'.

On the third day of my holiday I suddenly had an awful pain on the right side of my tummy. The doctor diagnosed appendicitis and I was taken to the hospital in Osnabrueck. Aunt Emmi came with me in the ambulance but had to return with it, so I was left alone in the two-bed ward with the horrid blue ceiling light. I was scared of the operation which was to be the next morning. I was also frightened in case there was an air raid, Osnabrueck being one of the West German cities which had them almost every night. I felt miserable and homesick.

Once in a while, a nurse looked in for a brief moment; they were all so busy.

"Try and get some sleep," she said, but I was lying awake, imagining all sorts of dreadful things. It was quite late when the door opened again and instead of the nurse, my mother walked into the room. Forgotten was the pain in my tummy. I jumped out of bed and hugged her. Mother had caught the next train to Osnabrueck after Aunt Emmi had telephoned her. All was now well. Mother was allowed to stay the night with me and she was beside my bed when I came round from the anaesthetic the next morning. There were tears when she left in the evening, but she said she would come back the next day. The air raid warning came at midnight. I heard nurses giving orders in the corridor, trolleys being rolled past my door, hurried footsteps and the shuffling of feet; everybody was going or being carried into the cellars. Soon they would come and get me. But nobody came. Soon there was no more noise in the corridors. A hush had descended on the hospital. I began to realise that they had forgotten me. I rang the bell, but no answer. I tried to get out of bed but my tummy was hurting and I still felt weak and dizzy from the operation.

"Please, God, let there be no bombs tonight," I prayed. But God was busy; too many people asked for the same thing.

Bombs fell that night on Osnabrueck. Their hissing nearly paralysed me with fear. Their impact made doors and windows clatter. A dazzling light illuminated my room. I pulled the blanket over my head and tried God once again. I was quite sure I was going to die. Then I thought of the many Jews in their hiding-places who could never go to a shelter for fear of being discovered. I tried to be brave like them. I can't remember how long the attack lasted, but it seemed an eternity before the all clear was given and the corridors filled with voices again. Eventually my bell was heard. The nurse was horrified when she realised they had forgotten me, and was full of apologies.

Mother insisted the next day that she should stay with me for the next two nights, and then took me back to Aunt Emmi, where we stayed for one more week before returning to Lehrte.

⇒•◆•⇐

Whenever the alarm was given during school hours, I sneaked out of the school buildings and ran as fast as I could towards our house. It was a good ten-minute run. My parents forbade me to do this, but I took no notice, and they could not stop me. The thought that they could die in the cellar without me was too much to bear.

Some people thought it safer to take refuge in the ditches in the fields rather than to be buried alive under the rubble. Most of the Polish and French P.O.W.s thought the same, and as soon as the alarm was given a clatter of wooden clogs — that's what all prisoners wore on their feet — was heard, as they ran down the village street towards the fields. Heinrich too, took his bicycle and, ringing the bell continuously, cycled furiously to the small barn which stood in the field where in the summer he milked his cows, and where he now sat all by himself until the all clear was given.

Farms and ammunition factories were given the greatest support throughout the war. People used to say the farmers never had it so good.

There were ample P.O.W.s to help - Polish, Belgian, French and now Russians. And then there was also the Hitler Youth and the

Arbeitsdienst, an Organisation of young girls in blue linen dresses and silver brooches, living in camps and put to work on farms, or into households with more than four children. Twice a week we, the Hitler Youth, worked as *Ernteeinsatz.*[30] Four times a week no homework was given to us. We now only had three lessons per day, sometimes less, it depended on the 'Tommies'.

A horse and cart, sometimes a tractor, driven by a P.O.W. took us, always in groups of twenty, to the fields. In the Spring we freed the young corn from hedge mustard, carefully walking up and down the rows pulling out the yellow flower by its roots. When the potatoes flowered we looked for the dreaded potato beetle, carrying an empty matchbox to imprison the little pest.

"The Tommies are dropping them from the planes," everybody said, but we never found a single one.

In the other fields around us, women in head scarves hoed sugar beet seedlings, Polish and German women side by side. We enjoyed the Summer and Autumn work the most. We picked tender young peas, pulled up kohlrabi, cut off their roots, put them twelve to a bundle, and threw them into the trailers which took them to the markets. When we returned home in the evenings at 6 o'clock, our tummies were full of peas, our pockets bulged with kohlrabi and our arms and legs were stiff and sunburnt

In the Autumn we gathered potatoes. Kneeling on a sack, we crawled in front of the loosened earth and fumbled for the potatoes in the sticky, heavy soil, putting them into wire baskets which were emptied into sacks by the P.O.W.s. It was not pleasant when it rained.

We made bonfires with the tops of the potato plants and roasted potatoes in the ashes. On the days when the farmer or farmer's wife did not come out with us, there was nobody to supervise us except for the P.O.W.s. When that happened, instead of having one stop for a tea break, we had several, sharing our roasted potatoes with the P.O.W.s.

"*Très bien,*" the French said and smiled at us.

"*Serr gutt,*" said the Poles and moved closer to their girl friends. They were kissing and cuddling. The Russians did not say anything; they sat apart and made their own fire and ate their potatoes in grim silence.

---

[30] Labour force

We became very friendly with the French. We could speak a little of their language and we tried to teach them German words like, "*Ich liebe dich*" and "*liebling*".

Sometimes we heard the sirens from the town. As soon as the planes came near and the anti-aircraft guns came into action, we flung ourselves onto the grass or sat in the nearest ditch.

"*Merde,*" said the French and looked scared like us.

"*Nix gutt,*" said the Poles.

"*Scheisse,*" said we Germans, and the Russians huddled together and looked up at the sky with worried faces.

We did not get paid for our Einsatz, but we got double rations; my lump of butter was the biggest in the little dishes, but it was the first to disappear. I was always hungry.

On the days when grandfather came to help father preach, I fetched him from the station. He had a very loud voice and as soon as he had spotted me he shouted, "There she is! There she is!" which made me very embarrassed. I never felt very much at ease with him, especially when he insisted on talking to me in Latin for the first ten minutes. Mostly he gave up with a deep sigh of disappointment in my abilities. Grandfather wore pin-striped trousers and waistcoats. A golden pince-nez dangled from the waistcoat pocket. In the summer he wore a black jacket, and in the winter a heavy black overcoat, always unbuttoned, with a velvet collar and a wide rimmed grey hat. He walked very slowly, taking tiny steps and dragging his feet slightly, always using a stick which had a silver handle.

Most of the people of our town and village knew him and were very fond of him. Every time he was greeted with, "*Heil Hitler,*" he stood still, took off his hat, turned towards the passing person and said in his loud clear voice, "*Guten Tag!*"[31]

My grandparents lived in a residential part of Hannover called Kleefeld, where they had a ground floor flat in a large 19th century house. Lovely old furniture and pictures filled their rooms. In the music room stood the concert grand and an upright piano, both Bechsteins, and a Clavichord which grandmother had bought when she was 75. Grandmother played mostly when she was by herself. Once a week, on the days when grandfather visited us, Professor Werner, a well-known

---

[31] Good Day

concert pianist, then retired in Hannover, came and played duets with grandmother. And sometimes, as a special treat, she played to Gewi and me. Schumann's *Scenes of Childhood* were our favourite pieces. Gewi and I sat quietly on the small embroidered sofa and listened to the Traumerei played softly and dreamily, the *Steckenpferd*[32] followed, happy and lively, and then the sad one called *Sick Child*. Grandmother's favourite composer was Bach, and every year until she left Hannover, she went to the Bach Festival in Leipzig.

Grandmother was a very loving and understanding person. She was very quiet and always looked a little sad, I thought. There was a special bond between my father and his mother. Grandmother once told me that one day, when he was about three years old, she had found him sitting on the stairs in a pool of sunlight, with such a blissful and happy expression on his face as she had never seen on a child before. His large brown eyes were staring into the light. When she lifted him gently into her arms, he whispered, "Mother, I have just seen God."

Once in a while grandmother would lock herself into her sewing room for a whole day. Everybody knew that she wanted to be by herself and no one disturbed her. Father told me that he had seen her one day, after the First World War had been over for two years, sitting bent over a parcel, in one hand a letter, in the other a man's jersey, and tears were streaming down her face. The letter bore the news that her son, who had gone to Buenos Aires the year before, had died of pneumonia. The letter was on top of the clothes which she had just received. The official letter informing her of the death of her son two months previously had got lost. Soon afterwards, a 20 year old daughter died. Two other children had died in their infancy.

Grandmother was one of the many German mothers who were honoured by the Führer with the *Mutterverdienstkreuz*, an iron cross awarded to mothers who had had more than four children. Grandmother had given birth to ten.

Two officials in uniform brought the cross to her house, together with a document signed by the Führer, in which he thanked the mothers for their valuable contribution to the Aryan race, and encouraged the younger ones to give him more blond blue eyed *Nachwuchs*[33] for the

---

[32] Hobby Horse
[33] Rising generations

Lebensraum which Germany was fighting for. It was not difficult to burn the document, but grandmother had to go for a little walk in the wood in order to drop the iron cross into the nearest pond.

Grandfather was not a bit musical. His hobby was reading, and like father's study his also was full of books. He read, lying on the chaise lounge, one hand holding the book, the other under his head. His desk, covered with letters and photographs in ornate silver frames, took up the whole of the large bay window overlooking the square.

Grandfather was writing the family history and so far had traced it back to the 14th century. He wrote with pen and ink in minute and illegible handwriting, and father dreaded the day when he would be asked to type it for him. The wall beside his chaise longue was covered with miniature family portraits. Grandfather was very proud of his ancestors and pointed out to us, not once but many times, that we were descended from one of the oldest nobilities of Hannovaria, the *von Hinuebers* and the *von Papes*. One of the *von Papes*, my grandfather's grandfather, had been a friend of Goethe and had often been a guest in Goethe's house in Weimar. Grandfather still had letters which Goethe had written to him. Grandfather's mother, Justine von Hinueber, married when she was eighteen, and lived with her five children on the east bank of the Elbe on a beautiful estate which became the Ungewitter family seat. She was known as the 'black' grandmother because of her very dark eyes and hair. Everybody in the family talked of this Justine Ungewitter, my great grandmother, with the greatest love and admiration. I wish I had known her. She died at the age of ninety when I was three years old.

Grandfather returned to the estate where he had spent his childhood and youth, together with his brothers and sisters, at least once a year. It was now in the hands of his nephew, the third generation, and would be inherited by his son, Carl Ungewitter, who was fighting in Russia. Usually grandfather went on his own. The flat landscape near the river, with the sharp east wind, did not appeal to my grandmother.

———◆———

Stalingrad, the Elborus in the Caucasus Mountains, and El Alamein were the turning points for Germany in the Autumn of 1942.

For the first time the little swastikas on the map moved backwards.

Allied troops had landed in Algiers and forced Rommel to retreat.

The Red Army broke through the frontier at Stalingrad and cut off German troops. The word Stalingrad was on everybody's lips. 300,000 German soldiers were cut off. At the end of January 1943, Offi pulled out the pin over Stalingrad and told us, "Hitler wants to withdraw his troops to spare them the hardship of another Russian winter." What he did not tell us was that only 30,000 men escaped; the rest were killed or taken prisoner. There had been more bitter fighting for Stalingrad than for any other city during the war, and more letters with the official government stamp were delivered that Christmas than Christmas cards.

Ernst, from next door, came home on sick leave in March. He was one of the 30,000 who had come out of Stalingrad. We hardly recognised him. He looked like an old man and did not want to talk, and for the first week he stayed in his bedroom. Gradually he became more himself again. Before he went back to the Eastern front he came to see us.

"How you have grown," he said to me. Yes, I was nearly 14 years old. "Will you write to me sometimes?" he asked. Of course I would. "It's all blood and mud and it stinks," he told us. "I envy my brother Heinrich who can stay at home."

But poor Heinrich was not at all well. He was still cycling to the barn every night in the deep snow and frost to hide during the air raids. There he sat, shivering and frightened, until it was safe to return home. His nerves had definitely taken a turn for the worse. Sometimes I helped him feed his calves. It was so cosy in the large barn with all the animals under one roof. At one end Marie, the Polish girl, and the French prisoner, milked the 20 cows by hand. It was so quiet in the barn that I could hear the steady stream of milk hitting the foam in the milking bucket. Sometimes Marie would hum a little tune when she sat on the one-legged milking stool with her head pressed into the groin of the animal. The cows chewed their sugar beet pulp contentedly and the cats sat meowing next to the churns, waiting to have their saucers filled with milk. Over it all spread the smell of hay and the sweet-sour smell of beet silage, which clung to my clothes for quite a few hours afterwards.

Heinrich spent all his time with the young stock. I stroked the soft noses of the calves and let them suck my fingers. Heinrich, with an unshaven face and a nervous twitch, stood beside me and watched me.

"What do you think of it all?" he asked me.

"Of what, Heinrich?"

"Of the war."

"Oh, I don't know; it does not look too good."

"They will come and get us, we are losing. Will they come tonight?"

"Who?"

"The bombs."

"Probably," I said. "They mostly do."

"I am frightened," he said, his hands trembling as he cut the string around the sheaf of straw. I tried to persuade Heinrich to come to our cellar instead of sitting in the barn by himself, but he would not hear of it.

My brother finished school at Easter. He was now 17 years old and decided to become a farmer. For the last two years he had spent his holidays on the estate near the Elbe and had become very interested in farming. My uncle had lost his only son at Stalingrad and he liked having Gewi around; they were very much alike in character, and Gewi started to work on my uncle's farm in April. Forty Russians worked on the estate, and my uncle and my brother were the only German males on this isolated farm.

As soon as he left home, his room was occupied by a homeless lady from Hannover and her 25 year old daughter, who travelled to Hannover every night and came back in the morning. Every time Elsa B. went off in the evenings she looked smart and heavily made-up, but when she came back in the mornings she looked exhausted and not nearly so glamorous. We also noticed that she always returned with a full shopping bag. We felt sorry for her; the night shifts must be strenuous and taxing, with the air raids and everything. We asked her mother what her job in Hannover was, but Frau B. said she wasn't allowed to tell. We assumed it was a secret government job. When Frau B. cooked, smells of roasted meat and other delicious things came from her kitchen. Where did she get it from, we asked ourselves. Months passed before we knew what was going on. Her daughter became ill and stayed at home. No more delicious smells came from their kitchen. Finally we were told - Elsa B. was a prostitute and had contracted V.D.

After Easter our school was turned into a military hospital. We moved in with one of the other schools in the town. School now worked in shifts. Twice a week lessons were in the morning, the other three days in the afternoons. Our classes became smaller and smaller. A large number of my classmates came from the surrounding villages, either by train or on their bikes. The air raids made it difficult for them to travel, so as they reached the age of 14 many of them stopped coming.

A lot of subjects were cut out. Geography was combined with History. History concentrated on the Nordic race. We knew nothing about other countries' history but we were well informed about Hitler: born on 20th April, 1889 in Braunau am Inn; *Landsberg, Mein* Kampf, and so on and so on.

Other subjects fell by the wayside. No more Sport, Music, Art. Scripture had been struck off the list at the beginning of the war. Five subjects remained: German, English, Latin, History and Maths.

In May, Tunis capitulated. The Desert Fox was beaten. The pins on the map took a big jump across to Italy, and shortly afterwards American and English troops landed in Sicily. Would Italy stay our ally, we asked Offi.

"Of course," he said, but some of us began to wonder if he really believed it.

At this critical moment a great crisis had arisen on the Eastern front at Kursk. We had lost the bridgehead of the Kuban and the Donezbasin, and there was heavy fighting around Kiev.

Meanwhile in the West, German aircraft bombed English cities. A hideous competition had started between the Allies and Germany to kill innocent people, destroy beautiful things and to lower the morale of the home fronts. German fighter planes, our *Sondermeldungen* blared out, had again sunk thousands of *Bruttoregistertonnen* in the North Atlantic, but we knew this was an exaggeration as our planes did not have the capacity to carry large amounts of fuel, and their fighting area was very limited.

Unless we could prove that we spent our summer holidays on a farm, helping with the harvest, we were not allowed to leave the town. I spent my summer vacation of 1943 on my aunt's farm in Mecklenburg. I had never been there before. I had met Tante Pauline only once before, when I was five years old. She was a very tall, handsome woman at seventy; in her long black silk dress and pearls she had made a great impression on me. I asked her if she was a Duchess. This flattered her and she kept a soft spot for me.

A cousin of mine from Hamburg, who was the same age as me, spent the holiday with me. We met at the station in Luneberg and travelled on to Parchim, a pretty small town in Mecklenburg. The countryside was very different from ours at Lehrte. The train took us through woods of Scots pine, interrupted by clear blue lakes surrounded by soft white sands.

The houses were as different as the landscape, single storey, white washed and thatched. We got out at a tiny station called Domsuehl. There was nobody about except the station master, and an elderly man with a long white beard leaning against a landau, which was pulled by a lovely Trakehner horse. The man turned out to be my uncle Fritz, whom I had not met before. I immediately liked this man with the deep set blue eyes which had a friendly twinkle.

Here there were no cobbled streets or asphalt, only tracks in the soft, white sand, small woods of pine and in between, golden cornfields as far as the eye could see.

"How lovely it is here!" I said.

"Not in the winter," replied Uncle Fritz.

We stopped in front of a long white house with dormer windows and a thatched roof. A wide flight of steps led to the front door. Two low barns flanked the grassy farmyard in which geese were grazing, and again, tall Scots pines surrounded the whole complex like a moat.

Tante Pauline ruled the roost, still elegantly dressed and bejewelled, although nearly eighty years old. With them lived Annemarie, their daughter-in-law, and her six month old baby boy. Their only son, Annemarie's husband, was fighting in Russia. I noticed that Annemarie's eyes were often red and swollen.

My cousin, Ingrid, and I slept in a small room in the attic, the only spare room left in the large house. Two evacuated families from Wuppertal, two mothers and their six children, shared the rest of the house with my relations. At one end of the house were the servants' quarters which were occupied by the Polish maid, Marie, and six other Poles, and ten Russians who came daily from the village camp, but had their meals at the farm. My aunt and Annemarie did all the cooking. The meals were simple but nourishing and a great treat for my cousin and me. They cooked for thirty people every day without getting much help from the evacuated mothers. Everybody in the house looked healthy and well, fed on meat stew for lunch, fried potatoes and scrambled eggs followed by *Gruetze* (a sort of fruit mousse) with creamy milk for supper.

Each day, Ingrid and I helped Marie with the washing-up, which always seemed endless, dug potatoes and scrubbed two buckets of them before 11 o'clock, and picked fruit for the *Gruetze*. In the afternoons we helped with the bringing in of the harvest

For the first few days we were exhausted and we sank onto our beds, nursing our sunburnt arms, not only sore from the sun but from the prickly sheaves of corn we had to stook. We got used to it and really enjoyed our work. We made friends with the Poles and Russians, who were much friendlier than the Russian P.O.W.s I had come into contact with so far.

Marie was our best friend, but soon I fell in love with Dimitri, the youngest of the Russians, not more than 18 years old. Dimitri's black eyes shone like stars and kindled in me my first passion. When we staked the corn we paired up, Dimitri and I, and every time we stacked the sheaves against each other, our eyes met and our hands touched.

"*Nix gutt,*" said Marie and shook her finger at us. Ingrid thought it very bad that I fraternised with our enemy, but I could not look on the handsome Dimitri as my enemy. Dimitri could only speak a couple of German words and I knew not a single word of Russian.

We never got closer than touching hands, except for once when I took a cart horse out to graze in the evening. I sat astride on it and my short skirt left a lot of my thigh exposed. Dimitri had taken hold of the halter and walked beside me. He looked up at me with his large dark eyes and his enchanting smile, his brown hand caressed my bare leg and moved slowly up my thigh. It was the first time I had been touched like this and I liked it.

I was afraid somebody might see us.

"*Dimitri, nix gut,*" I said and pushed his hand away gently.

"*Serr gutt,*" he said and looked disappointed. Quickly I bent over and gave him a kiss on his cheek. Now he was all smiles again, but I shook my head every time he wanted to touch me in that way again.

I shall never forget those summer evenings in Domsuehl. When the washing-up was done after supper, uncle and aunt sat on the terrace reading the paper, Annemarie nursed her baby, crying all by herself in the bedroom, and Ingrid and I joined the Poles and Russians who sat smoking and chatting on the grass, waiting for the guard to collect them.

The trunks of the pines were still warm from the sun. The sun's last rays filtered through the tops of the trees and left a rosy shimmer on their scented barks. Stanislaus fetched his balalaika and began to play. The others got up and started to dance. It was an energetic dance, not unlike the one performed by the Cossacks in our house some years earlier. There was plenty of stamping of feet, and dancing in a squatting position with legs outstretched. Ingrid and I clapped to the rhythm. The dancing got wilder and wilder and suddenly it stopped and the dancers flopped onto the grass.

The balalaika started up again, this time a different tune, slow and melancholic, and one after the other they joined in, looking dreamily and sadly into the distance. How they could sing! We guessed it was a song about their homeland and sweethearts. It was so peaceful it was hard to imagine that there was a war on, that soldiers were being killed and that in England and Germany, thousands of planes were getting ready for their nightly killing of innocent people. Why could it not be as peaceful as this all the time?

The sun disappeared in a large fiery ball behind the golden cornfields, the midges still played in the warm air and the pigeons cooed from the more distant trees. Suddenly Uncle Fritz gave a sharp whistle. He had seen the German guard approaching on his bicycle. Ingrid and I withdrew quickly into the house. Reluctantly the others got up and walked slowly and silently towards the guard.

One night, Ingrid and I were woken up by the distant noise of thunder. For two hours the thunder continued, never coming nearer, never going further away. We realised that it was not thunder but a major air attack on a northern German city.

"I do hope it isn't Hamburg," said Ingrid, thinking of her parents and two sisters. We got up and looked out of the window. Towards the north a wide area of the sky was blood red. "It is Hamburg," said my cousin quietly.

It was Hamburg, the biggest attack so far on a German city, on that night of 23rd to 24th July, 1943. Uncle Fritz had heard it on the radio that morning. Eighty enemy aircraft had been shot down over the city, so the attack must have been made by thousands. Ingrid cried all day. All telephone communications to Hamburg were cut off, and she could only hope and wait. We all felt sorry for her. When the P.O.W.s saw her sad and worried face, they shook their heads and said, "*Krieg nix gutt."*

The next day Ingrid's parents with her two sisters arrived in Domsuehl. Two suitcases were all they had left, but the main thing was that they were alive. Ingrid and I moved out of our bedroom and slept on the floor of the landing to make room for her sisters and parents, who stayed in Domsuehl until January 1945, when they decided it was better to go back to Hamburg than to fall into the hands of the Red Army.

On the day when the largest wheat field was to be cut, Uncle Fritz sent us to the village to fetch Julika, a local woman who was a dab hand with a gun. We guessed what lay ahead. The wild boar had done a lot of damage in the wheat field and Uncle Fritz was getting his own back. They had started to cut the corn in the morning, and when the patch got smaller and smaller, everybody on the farm, except for Tante Pauline and Annemarie, surrounded the cornfield with large sticks in their hands and forced the poor animals back into the corn every time they tried to escape. Uncle Fritz and Julika stood with their guns cocked and fingers on the trigger, ready to shoot. Two wild boar and six hares were the booty of that afternoon. Uncle Fritz and Julika had long drinks from the Schnapps bottle.

The Russians rubbed their hands and were already looking forward to roast boar the following Sunday. Meanwhile they carried the carcasses on a long pole back to the farm. Ingrid and I were near to tears for having taken part in the murder of these poor animals.

There was a certain time in the morning when Uncle Fritz retired to his room and on no account was he to be disturbed. I had borrowed a book from him and wanted to return it. I had forgotten that he was in his room at that time and did not knock. He was sitting bent over his radio and jumped up angrily when I came in. I knew at once that he was listening to Radio London.

"Don't worry," I reassured him. "My father listens to it too." Relieved, he sat down again and we both listened. The situation in Italy had worsened. The fascist regime had broken down and Mussolini was a prisoner on Gran Sasso.

"A good-for-nothing race," said Uncle Fritz. "Always knew they couldn't fight." And he switched off the radio, making sure he had turned it back to the Nord Deutsche Rundfunk position.

My four weeks in Domsuehl came to an end too quickly. I had put on some weight with all the good food, and looked well and brown.

Dimitri and I shook hands. "*Wiederkommen*,"[34] he said.

"I will, Dimitri, next year," I promised.

How different the stations looked from four weeks ago. Homeless people from the cities sat on bulging suitcases, clinging on to bundles of bedding, waiting for the trains, which were mostly already too full to take on any more. So they waited for the next one. Red Cross nurses and Hitler Youth dished out cups of Malt coffee and thin vegetable soup. Soldiers, lots of soldiers, mingled with the crowd. I had to change trains in Lueneburg. The loudspeaker announced, "The D-train to Hannover has been delayed for four hours due to a dive-bomber attack."

Sirens interrupted our waiting. Everybody pushed towards the large, sinister bunker on the station, large enough to take thousands, but everybody wanted to get there first, before it was too late. People fell, children cried but nobody took any notice. People kept on pushing, down the many flights of stairs.

It was the first time I had been in a bunker. I was terrified and thought I was going to be squashed to death. I wished I could have run home. I thought of Heinrich; he would have gone mad in this crowd.

"I am glad I am going back to the front," a soldier next to me said. "At least I can do some honest fighting out there. Give me the trenches any time!"

I got back to Lehrte at midnight, six hours late. As soon as I stepped out of the train the alarm sounded again. I left my suitcase at the station and ran until I reached our house. My parents had been very worried about me because telephoning had been impossible. It was so comforting to be reunited with them and Tante Krueger, and I swore to myself not to leave them again until the war was over.

During my absence some more people had moved into our house. Every night thousands were made homeless and the housing problem got more and more difficult. The whole of the ground floor was now occupied by three different families. We moved upstairs and my bedroom was turned into a kitchen. I moved into the small room in which the Jews used to hide. Through the open bedroom window I could hear Heinrich talking to his animals. More often lately I saw him running to and fro in the garden, always talking to himself, stopping in front of the well, and then running away from it, like a hunted animal. It was obvious

---

[34] Come back again

that his condition had become worse. Herr Busch had heard the same rumours that Elizabeth had whispered into my ear, about the inmates of the mental homes, and he refused to send his son back to the asylum.

———⇒•⇐———

Food had become very scarce. Long queues waited outside every food shop.

"I almost can't remember what an orange looks like," I heard somebody say one day in the queue.

"What is an orange, Mummy?" asked a little four year old girl.

Once a week I put an empty one-litre bottle at the bottom of a canvas bag, put my schoolbooks on top of it, and went to see Gabi. Tante, Gabi's aunt, filled it with milk and she took me by the arm and led me to a dark corner of the cow stall holding a pint measure of warm, foamy milk in front of me.

"Drink it," she said. "It will do you good, you are so skinny." I drank it gratefully, holding my nose, because the sugar beet silage left a nasty taste in the warm milk.

Once in a while Gabi's mother put a piece of ham or some eggs on top of the bottle for me to take home.

Farmers had plenty to eat throughout the war, but only very few were as generous as Gabi's family. People were quite right when they said that the farmers never had it so good; there was all the manual labour they could possibly wish for and exchanged goods of all description on the black market. People from the towns came into the country and brought with them articles which were dear and of sentimental value to them, but they were hungry and food was tempting. Not all farmers took advantage of these privileges, and quite a few helped wherever they could.

My brother and I had been keeping rabbits ever since we were old enough to look after them. We were very fond of our rabbits as they were the only pets we ever had. Since Gewi left to work on the farm, I had taken his into my care. There were plenty of dandelions and milk thistles in the garden, and in the winter I fed them on oats Heinrich had given me.

I was horrified when mother suggested one day that we should kill one of the rabbits for our Sunday lunch. The meat rations had become so small, we hadn't had a Sunday joint for quite some while. I refused to have our rabbits killed, but I weakened. I saw how thin my parents were getting. Tante Krueger, on the other hand, never lost any weight though her appetite was minute.

Unwillingly I put a rabbit into a basket and stroking it all the time, I took it to Opa Lieke, an old man in the neighbourhood who was an expert in killing and skinning rabbits. When he saw my tears, he said, "They never feel a thing." I asked him to wait a couple of minutes until I had run a certain distance away from his house, and with my hands over my ears, because once I had heard a rabbit scream with pain. I waited until he called me back. By then he had already slit its tummy open and was taking off the skin with his bloody penknife. He did not want to be paid, but kept the fur instead. Still crying, I carried back the skinned and, oh, so different-looking rabbit. Never, ever have I eaten even the smallest bit of rabbit. I glared at my parents and Tante Krueger over the Sunday lunch, and if it had not been them, I should have wished they had choked on it.

Gabi and Anneliese had both become leaders in the Hitler Youth. They were the right material and took their duties seriously; whatever they did, they did it well. Inge and I were definitely not the right material and we had not the slightest wish to become too involved with the Hitler Youth. We had, however, become keen members of the *Sing-gruppe*[35], and now that art was no longer taught, we also joined the craft group. The Hitler Youth gave us plenty of chance to learn various crafts; the only drawback was that materials were difficult to get hold of by this time. Inge and I took up fret saw work. Else, who had been our maid some years ago, and whose father-in-law was a carpenter, supplied me with plywood. Inge and I made keyboards, shelves, letter stands and little boxes, painted them in cheerful colours, and took them to the farmers' wives and exchanged them for food.

School started again in September. A lot of adjustments had to be made on the map. Offi soon put us in the picture. We knew perfectly well ourselves what was going on at the fronts, but Offi explained it in his own positive way. Did he still believe we would win the war? I am sure he did, and a lot of my classmates believed it as well.

"Badoglio, the Schweinehund, is a traitor," he shouted.

Badoglio had sworn loyalty to Hitler but was secretly

---

[35] Choir

communicating with the Allies, who had landed a few days ago in Calabria. Italy and the Allies had agreed to an Armistice. American troops landed in Salerno, German troops retired to south of Naples, at the same time occupying parts of Greece which had been in Italian hands before. Some Italian divisions were taken prisoner when German troops took up position in northern Italy as far as the Brenner, and so yet another nationality was added to the P.O.W.s in Germany.

Offi had so much to tell us that the double German lesson turned into a two hour session on current affairs.

On the 12th of September a *Sondermeldung* informed us that Mussolini had been freed by German parachutists.

At the beginning of October we removed the pins from Corsica and Sardinia, and our troops withdrew from south of Naples to Monte Casino.

"We shall defeat our enemies from here," said Offi and stuck the little swastika firmly onto Monte Casino.

A few weeks before Christmas we had a wonderful surprise. The whole family each received a small bag of three pounds of green coffee beans via Switzerland from Father's brother in Shanghai and a parcel with chocolates and cocoa from his sister in New York. Chocolates and real coffee for Christmas, what a treat! Mother never took more than six coffee beans at a time when, as a special treat, she made real coffee, and at the end of 1945 she still had some beans left.

I am afraid the chocolates and cocoa did not last nearly as long. From now on, when grandfather came to Lehrte he carried a small paper bag with coffee beans in his overcoat pocket and took back some ham or butter instead.

My father and his brother decided that my grandparents should leave Hannover and live on the Estate on the east bank of the river Elbe. The air attacks got worse daily; life in the country was definitely safer. Grandfather was delighted, but grandmother left Hannover with a heavy heart. Fortunately father's brother, who had 'connections', managed to get extra petrol coupons, and a large lorry was hired to take the grand piano and clavichord, as well as the silver, most of the pictures, and some other valuable belongings, to the small Dower house which stood next to the manor house in the park. This was going to be their home for the next four years.

⟫•◆•⟪

1944 was definitely the worst year of the war. There was so much misery, hunger, cold and despair. The first refugees from East Silesia arrived when the ground was still frozen and covered in snow and ice.

We thought that the gypsies had returned when we first saw the slow-moving wagons with the snow-covered tarpaulined roofs from which pale-faced children peeped out of. No young men came with them, only women, children, old men and shaggy little ponies which were thin and exhausted. Like tinkers' vans, pots and pans clattered underneath the wagons. The sacks, which had stored grain for the ponies, now hung limp and empty from their hooks.

One of the treks stayed in the village and many more followed until every farm had accommodated a family from Silesia. Other refugees from the east came by train. Our small town was full to the brim.

Frau B. and her prostitute daughter had moved back to Hannover. Their rooms were taken by a family from Breslau, a mother, grandmother and three children. They were nice people and stayed in our house for five years, after which a new house was built for them.

The smallest child, Diddi, was two years old and dangerously ill when they arrived. All we could see of her on that day were two large brown eyes looking at us sadly through the gap in the blanket in which she was wrapped. Our house was full.

We were now sixteen people in our small cellar and during air-raids we sat cramped like sardines. In the winter the cellar was full of underground water. Suitcases and feet were put on bricks, and we sat wrapped in blankets and eiderdowns, taking great care that nothing touched the water. My violin lay on my lap; there was now no more room for my bicycle.

Just before his 19th birthday in 1944 my brother had to join the army. After two months' training he was sent to France without first coming home on leave. We comforted ourselves with the thought that he had been sent to France and not to Russia.

Our swastikas on the map kept on retreating from the Eastern Front. Kiev was back in Russian hands, and the Red Army was in Estonia, close to the Polish frontier. Hitler transferred troops from the west to the east. Trains rolled day and night: transport trains, long and sinister ammunition trains and Red Cross trains. The last came from the east, driving slowly towards the west. Was there anywhere safe for them to go with the constant air attacks on German towns, we asked ourselves.

Sometimes a Red Cross train stopped at our station and the wounded were taken to the military hospital in our old school.

Twice a week the Hitler Youth had 'Station Duty'. We dished out cold and hot drinks to the homeless who crowded the platforms, and when a Red Cross train stopped, we took large jugs with malt coffee or hot soup into the trains, and handed them to the soldiers in their bunk beds. Their blood-stained bandages and the stench made us feel sick, but their sad, haggard faces made us forget our nausea. We tried to cheer them up. The response was varied; some still had some humour left, some eyed us silently but gratefully for the food or drink we had given them, some could not bear the sight of us in the Hitler Youth uniform.

The school we shared since our own school had been taken over by the Red Cross received several direct hits one night. Unless we found a room where we could have lessons, our school days were over. We were determined to carry on and found accommodation in a skittle alley behind a bar. There were no tables so we balanced our books on our knees. The map of Europe and Asia lay under the ruins of the school building, but Offi found a new one and fixed it on top of the score-board in the skittle alley.

There were only ten of us left now, four girls and six boys. We were now the oldest age group; the boys older than us were soldiers and the girls were serving in the *Arbeitsdienst*.[36]

Offi was as confident as ever. He now talked to us about a secret weapon which was going to be put to use any minute now. Meanwhile the Allies marched into Rome and the Red Army into Rumania.

The air raids on German towns became worse and worse. Quite a few of my own relations were made homeless, but we could not take them in as our own house was already too crowded. All through the summer we sent baskets of fruit and vegetables to them to ease the food situation.

Uncle Claus, father's brother in Berlin, lost his lovely flat in which we had stayed, that summer of 1939, but he was lucky as he still had his house in Sacrow.

Everything was changing rapidly, even in our small and unimportant town. We met with unfamiliar faces in the streets and shops,

---

[36] Labour force

people with foreign, East German accents. We were also beginning to wear peculiar garments, as clothes were almost unobtainable, even on coupon. Inge appeared one morning wearing old-fashioned high laced boots she had found in her grandmother's attic. We all laughed, but at least hers were leather boots, whilst ours were made of canvas, with thick, uncomfortable wooden soles.

There was a large camp of Nissen huts surrounded by a high fence of barbed wire on the outskirts of our town. To start with, it had housed Russian P.O.W.s but these were now billeted on farms, and refugees from Latvia and Estonia occupied the camp. The conditions in the overcrowded huts were appalling and many people died of dysentery.

One day, an old white-haired man, dressed in a black coat with a wide collar of astrakhan, carrying a violin case under his arm, came to see my father. He had recently arrived at the camp in one of the transports from Latvia. He had been a professor in Riga and felt desperately unhappy in the camp. He came to borrow something to read and to talk to somebody of his own intellect. The violin he was carrying was a Stradivarius. It was not his own, but it was the only thing he had been able to take with him when they were all herded into the cattle train which took them, without any warning, to Germany. It belonged to a Jewish friend of his, a concert violinist, who had asked him to keep it safe for him, before he had been taken to a concentration camp.

Professor von Kurnatowsky asked if he could leave the violin with us for safe keeping, and from then on I had two violins on my lap in the cellar.

After a while, father managed to get a small unfurnished room for the Professor. On the day he moved into the small, dark room which he called his 'heaven'; he and I pulled a hand-cart to his new lodgings loaded with a bed, a table and two chairs. The Stradivarius[37] was never returned to its former owner because he perished in the concentration camp, and the Professor took it back. I played on it several times, hoping that my playing would be transformed to heavenly notes, but apart from the thrill of playing on such a valuable instrument, the noise I produced was the same. The Professor became our good friend and after the war he taught father Russian, which of course he spoke fluently.

---

[37] The Stradivarius was bought after the war by the well known violinist Wolfgang Marschner who came to Lehrete as a refugee.

During one attack on Lehrte, the major part of the *Siedlung* was destroyed. The *Siedlung* was a new part of the town of about a hundred houses, built in 1935 for Hitler's workers. They were delightful one-family houses, with steep red-tiled roofs and fair sized gardens. Every family kept a pig and rabbits, and some people owned a Volkswagen as well. Hitler had looked after his workers well, but now most of them were homeless.

On the 6th June, for the first time, Offi's face looked worried. The Allies had landed in Normandy. Within six days 300,000 soldiers had landed on the north coast of France, and at the same time we lost Minsk, the last Russian city in our hands.

The invasion frightened everybody. Had Hitler left enough troops at the Western Front? Were we able to continue a war on three fronts after all the heavy losses we had incurred in Russia? My parents and I were horribly aware that my brother was in the north of France.

The 20th July, 1944, was a day I shall not forget. I was having a violin lesson with Fraulein Pook, when suddenly her maid, Emma, burst into the room without her usual timid knocking and stammered, "There has been an attempt on the Führer's life!"

Fraulein Pook shrieked, "Is he alive?"

Emma did not know. Like a mad person, Fraulein Pook ran out of the room into the street shouting, "The Führer, is our dear Führer alive?" She was assured that he was. She came running back into the room. "Thank God he is alive," she said. "Let's play *Deutschland, Deutschland ueber alles*."

I had already put my violin back into its case and said I would like to go home.

"But don't you think it's wonderful that the Führer is alive?" she asked.

"Oh, yes," I lied. "It's terrific." Fraulein Pook was a devout Nazi and I had to be careful what I said.

My parents were shocked and disappointed that the assassination on Hitler had not worked, and worried because they knew what lay ahead for those who had been involved. All our friends were disappointed, as were many more Germans, but nobody dared to express their opinions.

The Führer was only slightly hurt and spoke to his people that same night. We did not turn on the radio, because we could not bear to hear his voice any more. Stauffenberg, who had put his briefcase containing the explosives next to Hitler, was shot on the spot, together with three other officers. 200 others were hanged within days and Hitler had their gruesome executions filmed. The persecution of those involved lasted until the final days of the war, and by then the number of victims had reached nearly five thousand.

Not only Generals and officers had been involved in the attempted murder, but the participants stretched into every class of the German people. Special instructions were given to all the clergy to give thanks for Hitler's survival, but at the same time father prayed for the relations of the victims. This he should not have done.

Offi had not been well lately and a young S.S. man, new to the district, had been sent to help him with his official duties. This young fanatic had heard that father had prayed for the victims' relatives. This presented an opportunity to imprison father at last. He arrived at our house with Offi and two Gestapo officials. Offi completely ignored me when I opened the door. They asked me if my father was in. I nodded my head and they pushed me aside and went straight to his room.

On the afternoon before this happened, I had taken father his afternoon tea, and found him with his head in his hands, sitting at his desk. He lifted his face when I entered, and looked at me. Never before had I seen his eyes quite so tired and sad, and he looked so thin and ill.

I had brought him three biscuits on a plate which a parishioner had dropped in on us the day before. "For Herr Pastor only," she had said. I am afraid I had taken a little bite out of one of them. They had looked so tempting and I had been so hungry. When I saw father's thin face I felt very guilty and confessed.

"I am afraid I have taken a bite out of one of the biscuits."

"Take them all," Father said, "I am not hungry." We shared the biscuits and left one for mother. I massaged his neck, which I often did lately when he had a headache, and put my cool hands over his aching forehead. Father had been offered a small parish in Westphalia a few weeks before, and I had been pleading with him to take it. It would be so lovely to go to the real country, away from the air raids.

"Can't we go, father?" I asked him.

He drew me towards him. "For your sake I should like to go," he said, "but a shepherd does not leave his flock. Can you understand that?" I understood and did not broach that subject again.

The same evening father was called to the hospital to give

communion to a sick woman. On his way, he bought a small bunch of violets and put them into his pocket. Arriving at the hospital, the air alarm sounded, and immediately patients were wheeled into the cellar, the usual anxiety gripping everybody. Father helped with transporting the patients into the cellar but did not stay there himself as a voice inside him told him that he was needed upstairs. He walked along the long, deserted corridors; the doors to the wards were open and almost all the beds were empty. Only a few patients who were too ill to be moved had been left upstairs in charge of a nurse. An uneasy silence brooded over the empty rooms. His ear suddenly caught the sound of a nearly inaudible groan from a private ward. The door was ajar and cautiously he pushed it open and saw a young woman lying there alone, obviously dying. He went to her bedside and saw that she was a stranger, perhaps a refugee. He took her hand and asked if she would like him to pray with her. She nodded her head slightly.

The tense features of the dying woman relaxed and her eyes became more peaceful. Father remembered the violets in his pocket and gently he laid them in the hands of the dying woman. She clutched at the flowers as if she would never let go of them again. Her lips moved slightly, but be could not hear what she was saying. Her eyes looked at him gratefully and a weak but happy smile came over her face. She closed her eyes and died peacefully. Father sat beside her and waited until the 'all clear' was given.

This had happened the evening before they came to take Father away for having prayed for those whom Hitler had condemned.

The young S.S. man said, "I don't think you will be released this time. But you can always pray to your God for a miracle."

He suddenly turned his back on father and, looking out of the window, he said in a quiet voice, "Miracles do still happen. My wife died last night in hospital. Somebody put a bunch of violets into her hands, her favourite flowers. If only I knew who this kind person was who gave her this last pleasure!" He turned round and this arrogant, self-assured young S.S. man had tears in his eyes.

He and my father faced each other for a brief moment, then father said, "I am ready."

Mother and I had hurriedly packed a small suitcase for him, and in the presence of the four men we said goodbye to father. It was terrible. We were sure we would not see him again. I looked pleadingly at Offi who shook his head, but the S.S. man grinned. Father kissed mother and I, then with a firm voice he said, "God will help us." We watched him go down the path towards the car, the Gestapo and the S.S. man on either side of him. Tante Krueger stood behind us and from every window facing the yard people watched him and prayers went with him.

An old parson from a neighbouring village stood in for father, but he was ill and the services had to be cut. Only funerals and weddings took place whilst father was absent. We had also been without any news from my brother for the last five weeks. He had always written to us once a week, and his silence made us fear the worst.

The next time I saw Offi at school he came up to me in break time when I was unwrapping my sandwiches. I did not look at him, for hatred was arising in me towards him. He put his hand on my shoulder and said, "Let me see what you have on your sandwiches." I made no move to show him but he took a sandwich and took it apart; he found a thin layer of jam on the slice of brown bread. "Take my sandwiches," he said, and put his in front of me. I could see thick slices of delicious ham between the bread.

"No, thank you," I said, and pushed them away.

"Please take them," he urged me, but I shook my head. "I am sorry about your father, really I am sorry." I looked up at him accusingly and saw that he did look sad. What should I believe? I was beginning to lose faith in Offi, my favourite teacher, who could be so kind and considerate, but yet he had helped to arrest my father, and at the same time he was offering me his sympathy.

A miracle did happen. My father returned after two weeks. Did Offi have anything to do with it? We never found out. No reason was given for his sudden and miraculous release. Oh, the joy when he stood in the doorway! This time we cried out with happiness and everybody in the house came and shook his hand again and again. If only we could get some news from my brother now. Every day we waited for a letter from him, and we dreaded that there might be a letter from the government instead.

I began to realise that neither of my parents was well. Mother had always suffered from migraines, but recently they had become much more frequent and severe. Father had become so thin and often had pains in his stomach. One day they were so bad that he could not manage to cycle to the distant churchyard to conduct a funeral.

One of the six boys in my class had come with the treks from Silesia and was now billeted on a farm in the village. Once or twice I had been for a ride with him in a small trap pulled by two strong ponies, which had come with him all the way from his home. He offered to take father to the churchyard in his pony trap, and it became a regular thing, several times a week. On the afternoons when I was free I went along too, and whilst father conducted the funeral, Wolfgang and I drove to the Autobahn Lake, close by. We got out and let the ponies graze. There were moments when we forgot all about the war. We lay back in the warm grass and shut our eyes and for a short while we, two sixteen year olds, dreamt of the days before the war when there had been no fear and no killing. Everything around us was peaceful, the skylarks trilled, the pigeons cooed from the wood; it was so quiet that we could hear the fish jump in the lake.

Wolfgang imagined himself back on his farm in Silesia. We both wanted to lead a life without murder, betrayal and fear. We longed for a carefree, promising youth. We wanted to listen to records, to dance, to be happy. Instead fear was constantly in our hearts, and a hate had grown in us, not only towards the Nazis, but towards other nations who destroyed our towns and our inheritance and brought misery and death to our people. We were aware that we also brought destruction and misery to other countries, but at that time we did not know the extent of the dreadful and unforgivable things our own nation inflicted on others. We wanted love to conquer our hate, but something had to happen soon to stop this cancerous seed from spreading.

Wolfgang's father bad been killed in Poland at the beginning of the war. Wolfgang had been fifteen years old when he started on the long six-week trek from Silesia with his sick mother and small brother. The responsibility during this journey had been entirely on his young shoulders. Those weeks of hunger, cold and fear he would never forget.

In the Autumn of 1944, Hitler declared total mobilisation: total war. In his last desperate effort he sent 16-year-old boys to the front and commanded 60-year-old men to form the *volkssturm*[38].

Wolfgang taught me to harness the ponies, so that from now on I could drive father to the churchyard.

---

[38] Home Guard

For the last time we drove to the lake together. The next day Wolfgang had to join up. We sat in silence, both with a heavy heart. At last Wolfgang said, "I wanted to become a doctor. Now I shall be cannon fodder." He was so young, he had not even started to shave. I moved closer to him, he looked at me sadly and put his head into my lap. Softly I stroked his blond hair. Who else was there to comfort him?

The next day Wolfgang and the rest of the boys of our class joined up.

Three months later Wolfgang was killed in action.

⟫◆⟪

Now it was the Allies' turn to lead a *Blitzkrieg*. At the end of July, American troops broke through the German lines at Avranches. Paris was in de Gaulle's hands, and we lost Brussels and Antwerp by September. A bitter battle was fought over Arnhem and Nymwegen on 17th September, when our troops defeated the enemy, but in spite of this, by November, the first German city, Aachen, fell to the Americans.

At the same time the Russian army moved into East Prussia. From all sides the enemy moved in on Germany, and still Goebbels, the little man with the *Grossschnautze*[39], tried to keep up the fast-sinking spirits of the German people and lied to us about the '*Wunderwaffe*'[40] which would bring us victory. The majority did not believe him any more, and knew that the Nazis were making themselves ridiculous.

When Christmas came, the Hitler Youth Choir stood under the Christmas tree on the station platform and sang to cheer up the homeless and the many soldiers who passed through the station; not the nice old Christmas carols, but the new and meaningless Hitler Youth songs. We sang:

> *Heilig Vaterland...* and
> *Wir werden weiter marschieren wenn alles in*
> *Scherben faellt,*
> *denn heute gehoert uns Deutschland und Morgen die*

---

[39] Big Mouth
[40] Wonder weapon

ganze Welt[41]

We hardly dared to sing it. A soldier on crutches came up to us and shouted, "Shut up singing those bloody stupid songs. *Es istja alles Scheisse.*"[42]

Inge and I sang with the Hitler Youth as we were told, but on Sundays in contrast, we sang in the church choir:

Dona Nobis Pacem, Pacem.

More refugees piled into our small town from East Prussia and Silesia, and with them came hair-raising stories about brutal murder and rape by the Red Army. The confirmation of these terrible deeds lay in the faces of those who survived the ordeals of the Winter of 1944 - 1945. Many did not make it. The weak and the dying, mostly children and old people, were left to perish near the roadside in snow and ice; there was no other way. The constant stream of fleeing, terrified human beings pressed forward, and could not give in to sympathy or heartache; nothing was allowed to slow down the endless treks on the small, unsuitable roads. The main roads were occupied by the vehicles of the Red Army, who stopped the refugees in their exodus, took away their warm clothing and food and abused the women.

Christmas of 1944 was the saddest I can remember. A letter arrived a few weeks before to tell us that Gewi was reported missing near Avranches. It could mean that he had been killed, but it could also mean that he was still alive. A few days after we received the letter mother and I went to visit a friend of ours who had lost two sons in the war. The third and last was reported missing. Before we went home she opened the door to her garden and pointed to a small viburnum tree. Its bare brown branches were covered with delicate pinkish-white blossoms and it stood bravely amidst the snow and cold wind, a sign of spring, a long, long way away at that moment.

"Look!" she said. "This little tree gives me hope."

There were hardly any presents that Christmas. It did not matter. The only thing everybody wanted was peace. All the families in our

---

[41] We shall keep on marching, amongst the ruins;
today Germany belongs to us,
but tomorrow the whole world will be ours

[42] It's all shit.

house came to supper with us on Christmas Eve. Potato dumplings with stewed prunes and apples took the place of the usual peace-time Christmas supper of *Carp Bleu,* and the next day another of my pet rabbits appeared on the table for Christmas dinner.

After supper we stood beside the Christmas tree and crib and sang carols. The tree and the crib were as beautiful as ever. The candlelight made the children's eyes sparkle as they knelt beside the crib. The two eldest recited the Christmas story, and father gave a short address.

He finished with the words, "Look at the Christ child in the manger; God has sent him to comfort and help us."

A little voice piped, "But Herr Pastor, it is too small."

"No!" said father, and put his hand on the child's head. "Jesus is so big that he can be in everybody's heart, if only we would let Him." The small boy looked at him and could not quite understand.

The grown-ups fought back their tears. I counted myself as a grown-up now. Everybody in the room, except for my parents and me, had lost their home. The husbands of the two young mothers were in Russia, and as for Gewi, we did not know where he was, or if he was still alive. And why did Wolfgang have to die so young? The Professor sat by himself near the stove, and I was just going to join him when the front door bell rang. I went to see who it was.

A tall woman I did not know asked to see father. From her voice I could tell that she was a refugee. She looked cold and unwell, and I was sure that my parents would want me to bring her upstairs into the warm room, so I asked her to come in. Snowflakes hung from her hair and head scarf, and clumps of snow stuck to her boots. With trembling hands, swollen from the cold, she tried to unbutton her overcoat. I helped her and brushed the snow from her boots. All this time she never said a word. She was quite a young woman, but when we climbed the stairs she moved with great difficulty and I had to support her.

Father met us at the top of the stairs. She did not introduce herself. All she said was, "I have lost my child," but it sounded like a cry of pain and a cry for help. When she entered, silence fell upon the crowded room. Father led her to a chair near the stove, where she sat for a while with her face in her hands. Her body shook from her sobbing. In her hair the snowflakes started to melt and, like giant tears, fell onto the carpet. When she became more quiet, she told us her heart-rending story.

A few weeks previously she had left her village in East Prussia with her 18 months old baby and the other villagers. The child was taken ill, and needed medical attention, so she broke the journey and stayed for a few days in a hospital until it was well enough to travel again. The train, like all the others, was cold and overcrowded. She got out at a station on the way to get some warm milk for her baby and left it in the care of a woman unknown to her. Whilst she was waiting in a long queue on a different platform, the train moved on. In desperation and almost out of her mind, she ran after the train until it was out of sight.

Telephone communications did not exist anymore. Nobody knew where the train was going to, or when the next train was coming. She had to wait two days before another train took her to the next big town. She enquired at all the Red Cross centres, but nobody had handed in her child. Two days before Christmas she had arrived at the transit camp outside our town.

"Please help me to find my baby," she pleaded, and clung to mother's arm. We felt only her grief; we forgot our own. The children had stopped playing and stared at her. She suddenly noticed two year old Didi asleep on her mother's lap, the small wet thumb hanging limply from her half-open mouth. The woman got up and went over to the mother and child. She stroked Didi's hair with a trembling hand and with the other she wiped away her tears lest they might fall onto the sleeping child.

I could not get to sleep that night. The woman's story was too much on my mind and I could hear my parents and Tante Krueger talking to her in the next room. I thought of Gewi, of Wolfgang, and I thought of the flowering viburnum tree. Once again I heard the little boy saying, "But, Herr Pastor, the Christ child is too small."

My parents' faith was so strong and unshakeable, and because I loved them and believed in them, their faith transmitted itself to me. I was still not yet sure if the Child in the manger was really big enough to help us all.

The woman stayed with us overnight. On Christmas morning, we found her bed empty. She had left very early to continue the search for her child. We never heard from her again, and all our enquiries about her remained fruitless.

Soon after Christmas we received our best Christmas present ever.

It was a letter from my brother telling us that he was a prisoner of war in Texas and that he was well. These moments of relief, like when the letter arrived, or each time father had been released by the Gestapo, made the love we felt for each other even greater. From then on we received a letter from my brother once a month.

Our school days finished at the end of January. In peacetime, we should have passed our 'O' levels by now, and would be preparing ourselves for the *Abitur*. We had learned next to nothing during the last five years. All the schools were closed, there was no coal to heat the makeshift classrooms and the temperature was about 15 degrees below freezing.

"We will resume teaching in the spring," said Offi, who looked very ill. In fact schools did not start again until the autumn of 1946.

Keeping ourselves warm was a great problem. There was still plenty of coal and food in Germany, but the transport system had broken down as there was no petrol. The only form of transport was the railway, but as railway tracks and trains were continually bombed, a lot of the food and coal remained in large stores all over the country. Sometimes a wagon-load of coal arrived at the goods station. The word spread fast, and in no time at all people arrived, waiting in long queues for hours for a few buckets.

The wooden handcarts were our most useful form of transport. In the autumn, when the large chimneys of the sugar factory billowed out yellow steam, day and night, for three or four months and the sweet smell of beet pulp spread all over the town, horse-drawn farm wagons piled high with sugar beet queued up outside the factory, and our handcarts stood beside them on the pavements. We begged the P.O.W.s, who were in charge of the wagons, to throw down some sugar beet. They always obliged, and after a couple of hours the handcart might be full.

The beet was then scrubbed and cut up, and after hours and hours of boiling the pulp, we were rewarded with a couple of pounds of dark treacle. It was all done on our small range in the kitchen upstairs. We were only able to keep two fires burning. The kitchen range burnt wood, and, so that they should last longer, we put briquettes wrapped in damp newspaper onto the stove in father's study.

On sunless days the house was like an ice palace. All through the winter the frost never left the window-panes. Even when the sun shone it could not melt it, but then at least a golden light filtered through the pretty, icy patterns.

A few of us suffered from chilblains because of our inadequate footwear. One of our refugees told us of a very effective remedy, though it did not sound at all nice. All the same, we tried it and one evening all chilblain sufferers sat with their feet in buckets full of horse manure and hot water. The smell of ammonia was overpowering and the short bits of straw tickled our toes, but it cured the chilblains. Rubber hot-water bottles were unobtainable; instead we heated bricks on the stove and wrapped them in newspaper before we put them into our beds.

Though my schooldays had come to an end, I was never bored. There was so much to do. Tante Krueger and I did most of the shopping whilst mother cooked and did the housework. Shopping took all day. Buying a loaf of bread could take anything up to three or four hours. Very often, after we had queued for a couple of hours, the air raid warning sounded, and however quickly we got back to the shop after the all clear was given, another long queue had already formed, and once again we had to join the end of it. I also did the shopping for Oma Thiele, our neighbour, who had become very ill, and as before, she rewarded me with a very thin slice of smoked sausage.

Dina and I cut down old apple trees in the garden for firewood. We pushed the saw backwards and forwards through the trunk and I chanted: *Ein volk, Ein Reich, Ein Führer, Goebbels ist ein Luegner.*[43] Dina laughed and nodded her head. Dina was not stupid.

Several times a week I drove father to the churchyard. The organist was in the army, and the old man, who had until recently played the organ, had died. There was no one else to take his place, except on Sundays. Father now wanted me to play my violin at funerals. This I did, very reluctantly, because it made the funeral services even more mournful.

On one cold February afternoon, father conducted a funeral for a Russian soldier. The Russians always buried their own dead and I can't remember why they had asked father to do it this time. Nobody attended the service except the grave digger, my father and myself. We did not even know the name of the dead man, except that he was a young Russian soldier. I lit two tall white candles beside the coffin, and father conducted

---

[43] One people, One nation, One leader, Goebbels is a liar

the service in the same way he did for everybody else. He prayed for those who missed him in Russia, and he prayed for peace.

Quietly I played a hymn on the violin whilst father and the grave digger knelt beside the coffin. Then we carried it to that part of the churchyard where plain wooden crosses marked other graves of foreign soldiers from the camp. Slowly and laboriously we walked towards the open grave with the coffin on our shoulders. The grave digger was old, my father was not well and it was the first time I had carried a coffin. With great difficulty we lowered it into the grave. The heaped-up earth around it was frozen hard and the old man used a pickaxe before we could shovel it on top of the coffin. It started to snow and soon soft snow lay like a white blanket over the new grave. The grave digger stuck a wooden cross, which said, 'An unknown Russian soldier' at its head. I was shivering; father put his arm around my shoulders and held me tight.

"You are my good comrade," he said.

⇒◆⇐

I had become good friends with the P.O.W.s of our neighbour, Herr Thiele. They were housed in dark little rooms above the stables. Every Saturday I took them their 'Sunday treat' as mother called it. I gave a soft whistle - their rooms faced our garden - and out of every window popped a smiling face. They were so bored in their spare time, that combing their hair was one way of spending it, and I could smell the brilliantine from below. I threw apples and pears up to them and they leant out of the windows in a most alarming way to catch them, shouting thank-you's and other things in three different languages. Communications between us and the P.O.W.s, at least in the farming community, had become much more relaxed. I knew them all by name now; there was Emil, Henry, Paul, Stanislaus, Joseph and Serge, and they called me Renatta.

The air attacks on North West German cities became less severe from March onwards. Most of the cities were severely damaged and Hannover was one of them. *Flach*[44] was the expression for these cities.

East Prussia was now completely cut off from Germany and

---

[44] Flat

Breslau was in Russian hands. The suffering of East German people fleeing from the Soviet troops were beyond any description. To names such as Belsen, Treblinka, Auschwitz, cruel words symbolising the degree of evil of which humanity is capable, should be added — Dresden.

Masses of refugees waited in this city for transportation to different parts of Germany, on the night of 13th to 14th February, 1945 when Allied bombers transformed it into a sea of fire, and 80,000 people lost their lives.

March 24th brought the last phase of the war on the east and west fronts British and American troops crossed the Rhine at several places and Soviet troops marched into Hungary.

"*Deutschland kaputt*," the P.O.W.s told me. I had never seen their faces so pleased. Yes, Germany was *kaput*, Hitler's last idiotic effort; 60 year old men in the *volkssturm*, and 15 year old Hitler Youth, could not stop the advancing Allies, but tragically many of both the old and young gave their lives in the last days of the war.

On the first of April we heard artillery fire for the first time, but we did not know whether it came from the German or the English side.

The last air raid on a North West German city was on the beautiful mediaeval town of Hildesheim, 40 miles south of Lehrte. It happened four days before the Allies moved into our own town and Hildesheim was completely destroyed. It was the only time I have ever seen my father cry - when he heard that this ancient town, with its many Romanesque and Gothic churches, had become a victim of the R.A.F. Lancasters.

A large army supply depot in Sehnde, a village 20 kilometres from Lehrte, opened its doors to the population when the Allies stood in front of Hannover and the artillery fire had become more than a rumbling. The warehouse was full of cognac and bales of tobacco. An exodus started towards this small village. Some walked all the way pulling their handcarts, but most of them cycled furiously towards the tempting goods. I am afraid I was amongst them. I did not go for the cognac but I wanted to surprise father with the tobacco. I went secretly because my parents would never have given me permission to go that far at this critical time. I was not a bit concerned about the artillery fire; the only thing that frightened me was bombs.

Henry, the French P.O.W. from next door, cycled beside me. I think there were more P.O.W.s than Germans on the road. Though they had not been officially released, they refused to work any more and nobody made them do so.

The inside of the warehouse presented a sad and debauched sight. It seemed that nobody could wait to drink the cognac. Many people had already passed out and lay in a stupor on the floor. Others climbed over them and stuffed their bags with bottles. Drunkenness and fighting were well under way. The other side of the warehouse, which housed the tobacco, seemed slightly more civilised, but even here fighting had broken out and I did not dare to get involved in it. To my horror I saw that only a few bales of tobacco were left, and I feared that I had come too late.

I saw two men arguing over a bale, their fists lashing out at each other. They fell onto the ground and continued their fighting. Quickly, I got hold of the bale they were fighting over. It was not heavy, just cumbersome. I put it across the handlebars of my bike and, steadying it with one hand, cycled away as quickly as I could. I was thrilled with my luck, and the thought of presenting the tobacco to my father made me light-headed. Just as well, because the return journey was rather hazardous.

I have never seen so many drunks in all my life as there were that morning in April, on the road between Lehrte and Sehnde. The Poles were definitely the worst. Some drank the cognac whilst they were cycling, and with uncontrolled steering they drove all over the road, upsetting other bikes. Even the sober ones had difficulty steering, as a bale of tobacco did not make it easy, nor did the heavy bags full of bottles hanging from the handlebars. Some lay in ditches near the road, drinking and throwing the empty bottles amongst the passers-by, and some had passed out completely. The Poles and Russians definitely celebrated their imminent deliverance, whilst the French were slightly more controlled, and we Germans just wanted to be back home as quickly as possible.

Suddenly, two low flying aircraft came towards us. They were flying so low that we clearly saw the blue, red and white rings on their wings. Everybody took shelter in the roadside ditches, leaving the bicycles with their wheels still spinning, on the road. I had taken the tobacco into the ditch with me. I wasn't going to take the chance of having it pinched. The Tommies directed their machine-gun fire towards the goods train thirty yards away from us.

When I came home and presented my father with the bale, his face showed displeasure and so did mother's and Tante Krueger's. Rumours of the chaos in the warehouse had reached them, and somebody had told them that they had seen me there. But in the end father was pleased. It was excellent tobacco. We cut the bales into sections and hid them in the loft. Quite a bit of it we traded in for food.

Hannover capitulated to the 9th U.S. Army on 10th April, 1945, and on the following day the first Army trucks, packed with gum-chewing soldiers, most of them black, rolled into Lehrte. It was the first time I had seen black men, except for the elephant keeper at Hannover Zoo.

There was no resistance. We had lost the War, but we knew it was better this way than to have the Nazis win, ruling not only Germany but Europe.

All the nice large houses of the town and village were taken over by the Army. A lorry and a jeep drove into the yard and a Captain with six men took residence in our house. Everybody was told to move out within one hour. When the Captain realised that father was the only clergyman in the town, he relented, and let my parents and I stay. We smuggled Tante Krueger in and they never noticed. They allowed us to keep the kitchen and father's study.

We were surprised at the noise seven soldiers could make.

They were fairly friendly, but most of the time they ignored us.

It was not quite so easy to ignore them. They had spread themselves all over the house and brought in large amounts of food. One of them started to iron his shirt on the shiny surface of the old mahogany table, making a large burn mark with the hot iron. Mother took him the stand for the iron and showed him how to use it. He called her 'a cute little momma'. Two soldiers never moved from the harmonium and played *Chopsticks* all day long. There did not seem to be any order or discipline, and they never stopped chewing gum. For days after they left we found small hard balls of it stuck in the most unlikely places.

They were completely foxed by the old fashioned range in the kitchen downstairs. Also, the temperamental bathroom boiler was not what they had expected. They came to 'Momma' for help, and we were kept on our toes all day long with heating up food and bath water. Our store of wood and the precious briquettes disappeared rapidly.

Our knowledge of the English language was not great, but their pronunciation beat us. It was definitely different from that which I had learned at school.

Later that day a group of four soldiers arrived with a metal detector, to search our garden for weapons. We had a clean conscience and, amused, we watched them from the window. All the same, something must have made the needle on the instrument move up to the danger mark. Suddenly they were digging like fury, only to unearth a rusty old garden hoe. All afternoon they practised baseball on the lawn, crushing the clumps of the first spring flowers with their big army boots.

After a week they moved out and everybody else was allowed to move back in again. One more refugee couple was squeezed into the house. Herr Mueller, in his sixties, was a tall, quiet man, a bundle of nerves; his wife, small and much younger, looked like a china doll with her ginger hair and white complexion. She talked non-stop in a twittering, rather annoying voice. Frau Mueller told us she had been an opera singer in Breslau. When she gave us a demonstration of her singing we were quite sure we would not be able to stick her for very long. Her husband must have thought the same. He shot himself the next day in front of the town hall. His wife was desolate and for once she was quiet. She surprised us when, a week later, she appeared in a new outfit, her face beautifully made-up and her hair freshly styled. She had exchanged her husband's clothes on the black market for her new bright red suit and shoes. From then on she twittered and sang again all day long.

Heinrich was in a bad way. Ever since the Americans moved in, he had been hiding in a dark corner of the barn. He could not understand what was going on. He screamed every time anyone came near him; not even mother could help him. Herr Busch decided to send him to the asylum, but Heinrich drowned himself in the well in the garden the day before he was due to go. His poor tormented soul had found rest at last. For quite a while I kept the curtains of my bedroom window closed, because I could not bear to look on to the well below.

Hitler's suicide on 30th April in Berlin only brought relief to us.

The war in Europe ceased on May 8th. Church bells rang in the peace and mother played *Now thank we all our God,* on the harmonium. We were all grateful that peace had come at last, that the killing was over, that justice and humanity would hopefully rule from now on.

Meanwhile, the Military Police were kept busy controlling the looting. Russian and Polish P.O.W.s took revenge on those who had not treated them well during the war. The population of the camp demanded better housing, and they were hungry. A curfew was instituted; nobody was allowed outside their house after 8 p.m. All weapons and knives of a certain size had to be delivered to the town hall. House searches took place and those who had kept weapons wished they hadn't.

Three armed soldiers marched into Oma Thiele's room and looked for weapons. Of course she didn't have any, but seeing the chickens in the farmyard, they demanded some eggs. She did not know a word of English but she thought she understood, and went to fetch a large axe, which was immediately confiscated. Oma Thiele had meant no harm, but eggs and axe do sound similar.

An American padre came to visit father. Half an hour after his arrival there was a commotion at our front door and a soldier pointing his rifle at us demanded entry.

"Where is the padre?" he wanted to know. I pointed upstairs and showed him the way. When I opened the study door I could only just see father for all the cigar smoke, and the padre, who, like my father, sat in an armchair with a big fat cigar in his mouth, had his legs on the table. He burst out laughing when he saw his driver with the rifle. He had come to check if he had been murdered, as his visit had taken longer than he had said it would.

For one month after the surrender there were no telephone communications, nor were we allowed to send any letters. We were worried about my maternal grandmother in Schleswig Holstein. Passenger trains had not been made available to the German population, but goods trains were at our disposal. Mother and I decided to travel north to see if grandmother was all right. The only goods train we could get to Hamburg was a coal train.

Beggars can't be choosers, and we climbed into the open wagon and sat on top of the coal. It was an exceptionally slow train; we spent ten hours on top of the coal, whereas normally a train to Hamburg took three hours. Stiff, tired, black and wet because it had rained during the night - we arrived at my grandmother's. She was in better shape than we were. She had been well looked after by Dolly, her maid, but like everybody else she was very short of food. We had brought her some butter, coffee beans and my last rabbit.

During the first night I was woken up by a peculiar noise coming from the street outside my bedroom window. It sounded like lots of people walking by, only it was more like a shuffling of feet. I got up, and saw below me in the light of a pale half moon, a long column of German soldiers walking slowly and silently along the road. Some supporting each other, some limping, some with bandages on their heads and arms. The line seemed endless. Their silence was unbearable. Above all, lay the heavy sweet scent of the flowering lime trees. I almost thought they must be phantoms.

Another long column came past the next day in the midday heat. Again the silence, and everybody else looking on was silent. Their faces told us that these soldiers came from the eastern front. We would have loved to have given them a cool drink and an encouraging word, but the Military Police did not allow such things. We had lost the war, we had to remember. Mothers and wives went up to them holding photographs of their sons and husbands in front of them, and their eyes asked, "Have you seen him?" The soldiers shook their heads. They had seen too many dead, they could not and did not want to remember.

One of the largest *Auffangslagers*[45] for German soldiers was near Segeberg and throughout the three days we stayed with grandmother, German soldiers kept passing by.

The military hospital in our town needed voluntary help. As mother had a young girl again to help her in the house, I volunteered. I still had a horror of hospitals but hoped I might overcome it. The overall administration of the military hospital lay in American hands. They had their 'office' on the ground floor and kept a strict eye on the inmates, mostly German wounded, but also Russians, Poles and Serbians. Food supplies for the entire hospital came from the Americans. For the first time I saw their white loaves and tasted real butter again. I wore the Red Cross nurse's uniform without the cap and worked in the hospital with ten other volunteers for three months. We had one day off a week and worked from 7 a.m. until 8 p.m.

It was odd to see my old classrooms as a hospital ward. All in all there were about 400 wounded. Our jobs varied from rolling up bandages, dishing out food, spoon-feeding the very sick, fetching bedpans, holding someone's hand whilst his wounds were dressed, or just sweeping the floors.

Those who had come from the Eastern Front, and whose wounds

---

[45] Collecting Camps

had not been dressed for weeks, were in very bad shape on their arrival. I did not faint, as I had thought I would, at the sight of their wounds, or the nauseating stench: what I could not stand was the fright in their eyes as they waited on the stretchers outside the operating theatre for their turn, holding out a trembling hand for comfort. Drugs and ether were not in abundance and they knew it. Some of the soldiers who had been so brave in battle now completely lost their nerve. Nurses were too busy, but we could sit beside the stretchers, holding their hands and talking soothingly to them, as best we could.

After the first month, the pressure lifted and fewer and fewer wounded arrived. Recovered soldiers were taken away to the *Auffanglagers* to be discharged.

One day there was a small revolt in the Russian ward. Because there was a shortage of staff in the kitchen, potatoes were always boiled in their skins. The Russians demanded that they should be peeled, but when this wasn't done they took the hot potatoes and threw them at us. When they ran out of potatoes they took anything they could get hold of. The Military Police had to be called in with their rifles to restore order.

I was always pleased when it was my turn to sweep the officers' ward. There was a good-looking young officer amongst them, tall, blond and blue-eyed. One day I had a terrible disaster in this ward. I had overlooked a bottle of urine under one of the beds, and with my broom I sent it flying across the room, its contents spilling in all directions. I stood, bright red with embarrassment, not knowing where to begin clearing up the mess. Everybody thought it was very funny except for the handsome young officer, who walked toward me with a slight limp and led me out of the room. He asked me where he could find a bucket and mop, and insisted upon clearing it up himself.

Lieutenant Joachim Ude and I spent a lot of time together from then on. Although curfew was from 8 p.m., it did not affect the school grounds. It was not the most romantic of places, but we held hands and kissed and suddenly life was beginning to be wonderful again. Joachim never told me anything about his time in the army. Whenever I asked him, he shook his head. I guessed his experiences must have been so awful that he didn't want to talk about them, so I did not ask any more. Soon afterwards Joachim was taken, not by a truck, but by an M.P. jeep to be tried in Hamburg. I did not know that he had belonged to the

Waffen S.S. I never heard from him again.

After Joachim went it wasn't nearly so nice. A few Italians from the camp who suffered from bullet holes in their behinds, had been admitted. They had been caught by the Military Police stealing plums in the many allotments outside the town. They were told to come out of the trees, but when they took no notice, they were 'shot down', and now we laughed at their sore backsides.

More and more soldiers were being discharged and at the end of September there was no more work for us. Before we volunteers left we gave a small variety performance. I don't know how I had the nerve to perform as Marlene Dietrich, but there I was, sitting on a high bar stool, my legs crossed in precious nylon stockings - donated by the Americans and dyed black by one of the nurses - wearing father's black top hat and a dinner jacket which I had smuggled out of our house, and holding a long cigarette holder. I sang with pursed scarlet lips: *Unter der Laterne, vor dem grossen Tor,* in the deepest and huskiest voice I could manage, hoping that my parents would never hear of my performance.

———⇒◆⇐———

When I met up with my friends and classmates again, most of us were at a loss as to what to do next. It was obvious that school would not start for some time yet. All the boys, except for Wolfgang, had survived the war. We decided to look for temporary jobs. We also decided to take dancing lessons. It was time we had some fun.

Fear and hate were leaving our hearts, but something else took their place. It was guilt for something we personally had not done. Yet we belonged to that nation, from which a small group calling themselves Germans, had done unforgivable and inhuman deeds, for which the soldier and the ordinary German was not responsible. Until the evidence of Dachau, Buchenwald, Treblinka and others was discovered, millions of Germans did not know the extent of the horrors committed in the concentration camps. We discussed if it was right to enjoy ourselves when there was still so much misery around. I think all of us, through our own individual experiences throughout the war, were more mature than we would have been at 17 in ordinary times. We would never forget the heartaches the war had caused, and was still causing, through Hiroshima and Nagasaki. The future offered us plenty of chances to contribute towards a more understanding and civilised world, even if it was, for the time being, only clearing away the rubble from bomb sites in our towns.

In October the Americans left Northwest Germany for the occupation of the western and southern regions and the British army took over. The 224th battery of the 94th Wessex Field Regiment moved into Lehrte and one part of the town became the army quarters.

My brother had been writing to us regularly once a month, but since the occupation we ourselves were stopped from sending letters abroad. The new English Town Commander had taken up residence in the house of a friend of ours. She told us that he was very nice indeed, the perfect gentleman, not like the American Commandant who had refused her entry to her own garden to pick fruit and vegetables. She suggested that he might help with sending a letter to my brother. As my English was better than that of my parents, I was the one elected to ask him.

I remember the afternoon well. I was terribly nervous when I reached the house with 'Out of Bounds' written on its front door. I did not know what that meant, and walked in. A Sergeant immediately stopped me and said, "Sorry, you are not allowed in here."

"Could I see the Commandant?" I asked him. He looked at me, amused, and asked if I had an appointment with the Major. I did not know what sort of an appointment he had in mind; I certainly looked innocent enough with my pigtails. Mostly I wore my hair in a ponytail now, but sometimes I still had my plaits. I told the Sergeant that I had no appointment but that I should like to see the Commandant. Reluctantly he went into the next room to find out if he would see me.

Meanwhile I tried to rehearse what I was going to say to him, but I was so nervous that I could not remember a word. The Sergeant came back and said I could go in. I had imagined the Commandant to be an elderly man, and was very surprised when I saw a youngish man get up from behind his desk at my entry. He offered me a chair and sat down again himself. He had such a nice face; what struck me most were his rosy cheeks and his kind eyes which looked inquisitively at me from behind his glasses. I fumbled for words and eventually told him, in my worst English, the reason for my visit. He seemed to get the gist of it and, smiling, he put out his hand for the letter we had written to my brother. He said he would send it to England and ask his mother to post it to the States. He really was a kind man. He asked me what my name was and where I lived. I told him that father was a parson. I got up to go and said, "Thank you very much for your great kindness," and after the German fashion held out my hand to him.

He got up from his chair and shook it and said, "I hope I shall see you again."

The next time I saw the Commandant was when I was painting the newly-repaired wrought iron gates to our yard. A jeep drew up behind me and he stepped out.

"I am a painter, too," he told me. So, he was an interior decorator. "I paint pictures," he explained. "Mostly horses." So, he was an artist.

He had come, he told me, to ask my father if his troops could use the church on Sundays. He stayed to tea and we liked him very much. He had told us his name, but we did not quite catch it, so we just called him 'the Major'.

The second time he came, Tante Krueger opened the door to him. When she saw the Khaki uniform she had a mental block and for a second, she thought he was an S.A. man in the Nazi uniform and saluted with a *Heil Hitler.* Seeing the surprised look on the Major's face, she suddenly realised what she had done. In her distress she said, *"Oh, bitte vergessen Sie es doch!"*[46] I am sure, that had it been anybody else but the Major, she would have been in deep trouble. His kind smile showed her that he had not taken it seriously. In fact, I know now that he thought it was very funny, and of course Tante Krueger thought the Major was wonderful.

⇒◆⇐

We had not dared to tell my grandparents that, because they had now been absent from their flat in Hannover for more than two years, it had been confiscated. We were sure that for the moment they were much better off on the Estate by the Elbe than in Hannover, especially as it was in American hands. My grandparents did not think so and without telling us, decided to come back. My uncle and aunt tried to persuade them to stay but they were determined to return to Hannover. Telephone communications at that time were only permitted in a thirty mile radius.

---

[46] Oh, please forget about it!

We could not even warn them that they would be refused permission to enter the British Zone. My uncle took them as far as the ferry across the Elbe and from there they struggled with their heavy suitcase as far as the next town, only to be told that they had to return. It must have been such a disappointment to them when they had to turn back into 'exile'. Worse times lay ahead for the old people. Of all the family, my grandparents suffered most.

In Berlin, Father's brother Claus had been taken away by the Russians, despite the fact that his wife was half Russian. They had brutally pulled him from his sick bed - he had pneumonia at the time - and all they allowed him to take was his toothbrush.

Tante Clarutschka was driven out of their house, not being permitted to take anything at all. She had great courage and soon afterwards started up a beauty parlour in West Berlin, which was under Allied occupation. Eventually she built up a new home, where for the next seven years she waited for her husband to return. In all this time she was without any news from my uncle. Finally, Adenauer went to Moscow to negotiate with Krushchev about the 50,000 German prisoners still in Russian captivity, taking with him a list of the handful of German scientists who were missing, my uncle amongst them.

Thus, after seven years, my aunt was told that her husband had died from a heart attack soon after he had been captured.

Some more sad news came from my aunt and uncle in Mecklenburg. Annemarie and her baby had got away before the Soviet troops had reached their farm, but the old couple had stayed on. The Russian P.O.W.s were taken away and when the troops looted their farm, they tried to pull the diamond rings from my aunt's fingers. When she struggled they cut off her fingers and shot her husband, who tried to protect her. Aunt Pauline died soon afterwards. It was hard to imagine that this peaceful farm of two years ago, amidst the golden cornfields and the scented pines and all its lovely people, was now witness to such cruelties.

Through a friend of my parents, Lieselotte N., I got a job with a school for the British occupation forces in Hannover. Lieselotte, who spoke English perfectly, helped with the teaching of the six to nine year olds. My job was pretty boring, but at least I could practise my English when I escorted the children to and from school on the buses. It was not a paid job, but I got my meals, and that meant English army rations, which were so plentiful that I could take half of them home every evening.

Food rations remained inadequate for nearly two years after the war. On the black market anything was obtainable, even extra ration cards and clothing coupons. Small wooden huts popped up like mushrooms in towns, selling cheaply made textiles and household goods. Everything was badly made and of the poorest material, but at least it was there again.

We enjoyed our dancing lessons, and every Saturday went to the 5 o'clock tea dance in the Parkhouse. On other days it was used by the British officers and was 'out of bounds' to the inhabitants of Lehrte.

We danced the tango, the fox-trot and the waltz to a small orchestra. In between dances we sat at small tables, smoking the American cigarettes somebody had managed to get on the black market and eating foul tasting cakes. One of the violin players came over to our table, and full of emotion, he played and sang:

Bitte, bitte lieber Geiger mach Musik fuer mich

Bitte, bitte lieber Geiger, dafuer lieb ich Dich

Gibt es auch viel schoene Frauen, wo Dein Mund

fuer lacht,

Bide, bitte lieber geiger, spiel fuer mich heut Nacht.

Many of the discharged German soldiers came from East Germany and had no home to go back to; some did not even know if their families were still alive. In the last two years the population of West Germany had doubled, and because of all the chaos in the months immediately before and after the war, it was almost impossible to keep records of everybody who had sought refuge here.

The river Elbe now divided Germany in two. The Allies occupied, with a few exceptions on the east bank of the river, all the land west of the Elbe, and the Russians ruled over the rest of Germany, east of the river, which was eventually called the D.D.R.[47] Berlin, Germany's former capital, was divided into three sections, the American, British and Russian sectors.

All foreign P.O.W.s (with the exception of a few Russians who

---

[47] Deutsche Demokratische Republik

Copy of a letter dated 3 Aug 46 showing the
Regulations in force at that time.

"Subject:- German Women - Travel to UK for Marriage

There is no Directive at present but the following

procedure is suggested:-

The applicant should forward the following
documents:-

 (a) Form 226 in triplicate
 (b) Appx A to Form 226 in triplicate
 (c) 3 Full and 2 side face photographs
 (d) PSS Clearance
 (e) A Statement from Mil Gov or other responsible
   British Authority that she is a suitable
   person
 (f) An Invitation from the prospective husband
 (g) A Witnessed statement from the prospective
   husband that:-
    (i) He is free to marry X
    (ii) He will marry her within two months
    (iii) He can support a wife (statement
      from Bank of Employer)
    (iv) he has accomodation for a wife.

Copy above made
by :-

E. A. Lowder
HQ 503 Mil Gov Det.

Burgdorf.
9 Aug 46.

*Document for German brides marrying English soldiers.
(Probably one of the first ones issued after the war)*

preferred to stay in Germany, but were later forced to return by their own people) had been repatriated within the first few weeks after the war. Released German soldiers went back to their former jobs, if they still existed. Some, whose homes had been in East Germany, chose to stay in the West and hoped that their families, if still in the Russian section, would soon be able to join them.

In this transitional stage of the post war years, any soldier without a home and work took on any job that was offered, provided it gave him accommodation and food.

Ernst, Heinrich's brother, came back at the beginning of July. Three years of fighting at the Russian front had left their mark on him. He returned just in time for the harvest. His father had grown old, his mother and Heinrich were dead. Many ex-soldiers, still wearing army uniform, the only clothes they possessed, were helping in that first peace time summer to bring in the harvest.

I stayed at the school in Hannover for only two months. Lieselotte gave up her job in November and not liking the daily journey to Hannover in the cold, overcrowded train, I stopped going too. Lieselotte started to give private English lessons and I became one of her pupils. I enjoyed my private lessons more than I had ever enjoyed any lesson of the previous years. Lieselotte was an excellent teacher and I caught up with some of the lost lessons of my schooldays.

Lieselotte not only taught me English literature but also German literature. We had missed out on so much during the war that my ignorance was alarming.

The best help I had with my English homework was from the Major, who now came at least twice a week to see us. At last we had cottoned on to his name and knew that he was called Greenshields, but he had asked us to call him Tom. At first I found it rather difficult to call him by his Christian name. He was so much older than I was, and as a rule we Germans had to know somebody for quite a while before being on Christian name terms. I found myself looking toward to his visits, so that when for some reason he could not come, I was disappointed and missed him.

On some afternoons Tom took me to the riding stables in Kolzhorn, a small village about 15 miles from Lehrte, where a dozen horses, mainly Hanoveraners, were stabled for the officers. I had not dared to tell him that I hardly knew how to ride, as I very much wanted to go with him.

Rather timidly I asked for a very quiet horse, and Sergeant Thompson, who was in charge of the stable, gave me the most docile bay. Tom's horse was a grey thoroughbred called 'Danny Boy'.

"It's the Major's horse and only the Major rides him," Sergeant Thompson explained to me.

Tom soon realised that I could not ride. Patiently he showed me how to hold the reins, how to sit correctly and how to rise to the trot. When on the way back to the stables the horses began to get too lively, he fastened a leading rein onto the bridle of my horse to keep it under control so that I could arrive back at the stables with dignity.

Whenever we went riding, Tom fetched me in his armoured scout car from the end of our garden. I sat hidden in the back of the car, which was most uncomfortable and dark. We had to take care that I was not seen fraternising with the British, and the same applied to Tom. Somebody, unfortunately, must have seen me climbing into the armoured scout car, because one day a note about me was fixed onto the large notice board outside the town hall. The notice board was the greatest source of information during this time, and hundreds of people gathered daily in front of it. This particular note read: 'The daughter of Pastor Ungewitter is fraternising with a British officer who has made the child pregnant. Cut off her hair and give her the punishment she deserves!'

As soon as I heard of the note I pushed my way through the crowd in front of it and tore off the ridiculous bit of paper. Nobody said a word, nobody stopped me, and I am sure that whoever put the note there wasn't worth knowing. All the same, it was better to be more careful from now on. It did not matter that Tom came to see us, but we thought it wiser that I did not go riding with him for a while. My parents and I, and of course Tante Krueger, had become very fond of Tom, and I think the homely atmosphere in our house made a nice change for him from the army quarters.

It was made compulsory for us Germans to carry our identity cards with us wherever we went. A couple of times Tom arranged spot checks in Lehrte. Everybody in the street was stopped and asked for their identity card, and those who failed to produce them were locked up for six hours in a large garage in the town. During one of these checks, a woman leading a billy goat to serve her neighbour's female goat was stopped. Of course, she had not thought of bringing her identity card along as well. She and her billy goat were locked in the garage. She was not very popular with her fellow inmates and when they were released, after six hours, every one of them smelled strongly of billy goat.

Apart from these little incidents no hardship was put upon us by the British occupation. The curfew was extended to 10 p.m. and after a while abolished altogether.

Christmas came, the first in peacetime. Diddi's father returned from the war just before Christmas, but the other young wife in our house was still waiting for her husband. Father's colleague and the organist also returned. At last, we thought, Father could begin to relax. During the war the population of Lehrte had risen from 12,000 to 24,000 and Father was at the end of his strength. On Christmas Day he collapsed with severe stomach pains. The doctor diagnosed ulcers and Father had to stay in bed for nearly four months before they healed. He became even thinner during his illness, and at the beginning of the new year we feared for his life.

A frequent visitor to our house was the English padre, Captain Merton. A rumour had reached him one day that father had died. He came immediately to see us. When I opened the door to him, he embraced me with tears running down his cheeks, and said how very sorry he was that father had died. When he realised that he had not, he embraced me again, this time with tears of joy. He visited father almost every day and supplied him with food he was supposed to eat, that we were unable to get ourselves.

Father had constant visitors all through his illness. It was touching to see how devoted his parishioners were to him.

As soon as Tom's jeep pulled up beside the gates, I ran into my bedroom, brushed my hair once again, put on some scent and rouge, but no lipstick - he had told me he hated lipstick - and waited at the top of the stairs until he rang the bell. I realised that I was falling in love with him.

The first snowdrops were out in the garden. I picked a bunch for Tom. He was so pleased when he saw them, and said that of all the flowers these were his favourite. He told us of the wild primroses in the Devon lanes in the south of England where his home was, and of the Bluebells along the roadside and in the woods. He told us of his parents and brother and sisters, and of the farm he was going to work when he got released from the army.

"Do you like farm life?" he asked me. I said I did. It was true; I liked being with animals and the summer in Mecklenburg on Aunt Pauline's farm had been wonderful.

At the beginning of March, Tom asked me to marry him. I loved him very much but I had not thought of marriage. I could not imagine myself leaving Germany, living in a foreign country, away from my parents and friends, bringing up my children in a language I had not mastered myself. And anyway, I was only seventeen and a half, much too young to get married. Tom laughed and said it would be much easier than I feared.

When he asked my parents' permission, my father gave him the same answer that my great-great-grandfather had given when his future son-in-law had asked for his daughter's hand. "She is too young and unruly." My great-grandmother, Justine von Hinueber, was also only eighteen years old when she married and, like me, was thirteen years younger than her husband. She became a farmer's wife and, like me, had five children.

My parents loved and trusted Tom and gave their consent. They suggested that I should spend a couple of years in Switzerland to complete my education, but Tom said he wanted to marry me as soon as possible. They left the decision to me.

I decided to carry on with my lessons with Lieselotte in the evenings, go and work on a farm to gain some practical experience, especially in cooking, and to marry Tom as soon as permission from the British Government could be obtained.

The spring of 1946 was the happiest of my life. Tom and I spent as much time together as his job allowed, until he was due to be demobbed at the end of May. We thought it wiser not to tell anybody about our engagement for the time being, but of course Tante Krueger and Lieselotte knew and they were delighted.

I still hid in Tom's armoured scout car when we drove to the hills near Hildesheim and had walks in the woods, with their budding leaves and carpets of anemones and wild violets. Tom offered to bring along the food for the picnics, but when after our first picnic I realised that four tins of oily sardines and a loaf of bread was going to be all, I saved up my butter rations and, with mother's help, because I was not very domesticated, made some little cakes and sandwiches for our next picnic.

The first time Tom took me sailing on the Steinhuder Meer, a large lake near Hannover, he dropped me off in his car at the far end of the lake where I could not be seen from the Officers' Clubhouse, but when he came to pick me up with the sailing-boat, the water was too shallow for the boat to come close, so I waded out to it fully clothed and got soaked. We found a remote spot where we could take the boat right to the edge of the water, and lit a fire to dry my clothes. Tom never got worried about anything, and was always cheerful. I liked that.

Once, on the way back from one of our excursions, we found a large carton of 50 slightly damaged Persil packets. We shoved them into the car, Persil being a real rarity. As I had to sit on top of the packets, I sneezed all the way home for 40 miles.

At the beginning of May the 24th Field Regiment got transferred to Westphalia, and at the end of May Tom was demobbed and left for England.

We had applied for permission to get married and now it was a case of waiting. Quite a few German girls had got engaged to English and American soldiers, but in Lehrte, I was the first one.

Meanwhile I got myself a job on a farm together with my former school friend, Anneliese. It was thanks to Anneliese that I stuck to the job. Had I been on my own, I should have left after the first week.

The farm was a large modern one on the outskirts of Lehrte. Anneliese and I had applied for the job there because Frau B. trained young students in domestic science, and we hoped to get a good training in cookery. Instead, we spent most of our time milking cows and working in the fields. I got up at 5.30 every day, including Sundays, and walked to the farm as I preferred to live at home. The only thing that cheered me up at that time in the mornings was my walk through a large cherry orchard where the grass, at the beginning of June, was covered with blossom from the trees, and the song of blackbirds, interrupted by the sound of the cuckoo, filled the early morning air.

Our first job was to milk three cows each, by hand. It nearly killed me to start with. Anneliese was so much better at it than I was. She had incredible patience, and she was also very funny. We had many good laughs which annoyed Frau B. She did not give us a minute's peace. As soon as we had washed-up the breakfast dishes, we set off with a horse and cart to the asparagus field, and for the next four hours we walked in between the raised asparagus beds, and dug the long, thick white stalks out of the warm sandy soil. By 10 o'clock it was boiling hot and we continued to work in our 'bikinis' until noon. Half an hour's rest after lunch, then back to the fields, hoeing and thinning sugar beet plants, hay making, anything but cooking. I hoped that being a farmer's wife in England was not going to be like this. Thank God it came to an end after two months. Frau B., whom I had not told of my engagement to Tom, was told about it by somebody else. She said she disapproved and gave me the sack. I was only too glad to leave.

Everybody now knew that I was going to marry an Englishman, and all our friends were nice about it, except for Inge who had been my best friend for so long. She refused to see me any more and I have never been able to make contact with her again. I minded very much because I had been very fond of her.

The original inhabitants of Lehrte, my father's devout parishioners, all wished me well, but the newcomers, the refugees, stayed away from the Sunday services. I minded for my father's sake. I knew that he was hurt, though he never said a word about it. What made me really sad was that once again it was as a result of my doings, just like at the beginning of the war when I had joined the Hitler Youth orchestra. Neither of my parents ever said a word of reproach to me and they never even mentioned the half-empty church. Instead they let me feel their pleasure at my happiness.

By and by, the church filled again and gradually more and more people accepted the fact that the parson's daughter was going to marry an Englishman.

Tom's letters were illustrated with delightful pencil drawings of his dog and horses, of the farm and the house in which we were going to live. I had written to his parents and grandmother and they had sent welcoming letters back to me.

———⟫◆⟪———

The Estate on which my grandparents stayed had, at the beginning of the occupation, been in the hands of the British. This particular patch of country near the Elbe was given over to the Russians in exchange for another part of Germany at the end of the Summer. Conditions after the new take over changed rapidly for the worse. My uncle was driven from the Estate by the Russians and my grandparents were also made to leave their house. They found refuge with the schoolmaster of the neighbouring village. Later the Estate was divided amongst Russian farm workers, and soon the land and buildings deteriorated.

When the Russian army moved in, the Russian P.O.W.s were still working on the farm. They had always been well fed and well treated by my uncle. The Russian soldiers gathered all inhabitants of the Estate into the farmyard and the officer in charge asked the P.O.W.s if they had anything to complain about during their stay with my uncle. Nobody complained except for one P.O.W. who had been a lazy so-and-so and had once, when my uncle had ticked him off for being too slow with the horses, given a disrespectful and objectionable answer, whereupon my uncle had boxed his ears. This he brought up in front of the officer. The officer took his pistol and gave it to the P.O.W.

"Shoot him!" he said. The P.O.W. shook his head and, handing back the pistol, asked permission to box my uncle's ears, which he did. He then shook hands with his former employer

My uncle, his wife and two daughters did not feel that it was safe to stay on and escaped at night, across the Elbe to the western zone. My poor grandparents were now on their own, accommodated in a minute attic room in the schoolmaster's house. There was no food, no coal, no wood. The Russians had confiscated everything, including their piano and most of their clothes and possessions, except for a small suitcase with some family silver and grandmother's jewellery, which the kind schoolmaster kept hidden for them in his loft. Grandmother wrote pitiful letters to us asking for food and warm clothes. We were not allowed to send anything, even our letters did not always reach them.

Grandmother pleaded in her letters that we should come and fetch them. She did not know that anybody trying to get into the Russian Zone from the west or the other way round, was shot on the spot by the Russians.

Eventually, towards the end of November, a hair-raising undertaking was planned between my uncle, who now lived in a village opposite his former farm on the west side of the Elbe, and my father. My uncle still had connections with the schoolmaster with whom my grandparents stayed. On a dark November night, a villager took my grandparents across the Elbe in his rowing boat for a large sum of money. The suitcase with the silver and jewellery was all they had with them. My father and his brother waited on the other side of the river with a car. As soon as they had lifted my grandparents ashore, and before they had a chance to reach for the suitcase, the boat pushed off again; whoever had taken them across extracted a high price for his services. There was nothing they could do about it as everything had to be done in complete silence and in darkness. They were lucky not to be discovered and shot.

It was almost too much for the old couple. For the next two weeks they were compelled to stay in a transit camp without warmth or comfort. My father and his brother were not allowed to stay with them, and it was only when grandmother had a stroke a few days afterwards that they let my mother join them. Grandmother did not recover from her stroke and died in the camp.

Grandfather survived the ordeal and lived with my parents until he died four years later at the age of 92. A few months before he died I flew to Germany with my one-year-old daughter, my first child, and his first great-grandchild. He put his trembling hand on her head and blessed her.

On the tenth of December, on the same day that my parents came back from the transit camp near Lueneburg with my grandfather, I received the document which gave me permission to marry Tom. With it came the visa and the date of the crossing from Cuxhaven on 18th December.

Though I loved Tom and wanted to marry him, and I had been waiting for this document to arrive, suddenly everything seemed to be happening too soon. In just over a week, I had to leave.

Grandfather looked so sad and forlorn without grandmother, and my parents looked very tired, especially mother who had stayed with grandfather since grandmother died. It had been bitterly cold in the transit camp. Already we had a lot of snow and the temperature was well below freezing. It was going to be another severe winter. Dina and I had been busy cutting down more apple trees and the woodshed was well supplied with logs. Had it not been for the reassurance that Tante Krueger was there with her everlasting love and devotion to help my parents, I should have decided to stay until the Spring.

The last week before I left for England did not count as the happiest of my life. I was happy that soon I should be with Tom, but the circumstances of that particular time threw a great shadow upon my feelings and the old and dreaded homesickness was already creeping up inside me. Doubts, which I had tried to suppress up till now, came up anew; how would I cope with all the things expected of me? I was just

18 years old, but I was sure that for an 18 year old girl I knew too little, and how could I explain to the English people that the war was partly to blame for my ignorance? Mother had tried to teach me to cook after I had left the farm, but it was all in theory; the materials had not been there for practice. Tom had told me that his mother and sisters were excellent cooks and very good at almost everything. I wished that I had more time to learn.

I said goodbye to my friends, to Gabi and Anneliese and all my other former classmates. They were back at school now - an extra two years had been tagged onto their school years, to catch up with all the lost teaching time. They would be twenty years old by the time they sat their *Abitur* (A level).

I went to say goodbye to Offi. At the end of the war, he, like all other Nazi officials, was taken prisoner and sent for trial. He had been released a month previously on the grounds of ill health. Offi had cancer and had only a few months to live. A smile came over his bony yellow face when he saw me; he held out his thin hand to me and said, "I am sorry, Renate, for what I did to your father. We were made to do things we did not want to do."

I took his hand and sat beside him. We knew we should not see each other again, and when I said goodbye, we parted as good friends.

There were so many people to say goodbye to: Lieselotte, Oma Thiele, Herr Busch and Ernst, and the shoemaker and many others, and finally to Tante Krueger and my old grandfather.

On the morning of 17th December, just before my parents and I set off for Cuxhaven, the postman brought two letters. One was from Tom, saying that our wedding had been fixed for 6th January and that he would be waiting for me at Tilbury. The other was from my brother, telling me that he had been transported to England and was now a P.O.W. in North Wales near Ruthin and working on a farm. He was hoping I would come to see him soon, as he was not permitted to go further than three miles from his farm. It was a most comforting thought for my parents and me to know that my brother was in England. (My brother stayed in England for another 18 months before he was released, but he was given permission to work near us on a farm in Devon. My parents were allowed to visit us after two years.)

It was a beautiful winter's day when we left Lehrte for Cuxhaven. The flat landscape of North Germany was covered with a thick blanket of snow which sparkled in the brilliant sunshine and was almost too bright to look at.

We arrived at four o'clock. Cuxhaven itself was a dismal place. I had to report to block 501 at the army headquarters where I was given a boat ticket. The *Empire Halladay* was sailing to Tilbury the next morning at 8 a.m. Meanwhile I was to go to barrack 68 to await further instructions. My parents were not permitted to come with me, nor was I allowed to leave the barracks until the next morning. There was no chance that my parents would be allowed near the boat to see me off. All we could do now was to say goodbye. I would rather not write about it, nor of their lonely journey home in the cold overnight train. I had been a lucky girl, with such loving parents, but now it was 'Good bye'.

Fifteen brides, all waiting to go to England the next day, huddled around the *Kanonen ofen*[48] in the barrack to keep warm. Before supper we were told to line up for a medical examination by a very brusque army doctor, whose main concern was to insure that we had neither lice nor V.D.

"I don't know what they think we are," one of the group said, and we all thought the same.

We were given two army blankets each, and we shivered on our straw mattresses on the iron bedsteads throughout the night.

It was heaven on the boat the next day, so warm and comfortable, with plenty to eat.

All fifteen of us were accommodated in one large cabin. Erika, who talked so much about her fiancé, who was apparently absolutely *phantastisch* and owned a large factory, kept us entertained with all the new *Schlager*[49] songs she knew: her favourite was an old one by Zarah Leander. '*Ich weiss, es wird einmal ein Wunder geschehn, und dann werden alle Maerchen wahr.*'[50] It was a very catching tune, and soon all of us were humming it.

Most of the group were going to live in towns, in Manchester, Liverpool, London. One went to Aberdeen. I was the only one going to live in the South of England. They were all over twenty years old; I was

---

[48] The iron stove
[49] Hit song
[50] I know a miracle will happen and all fairy tales will come true.

by far the youngest.

"*Mein Gott,*" they said. "Why do you want to get married so young?"

Towards the end of the evening we became rather quiet and Erika stopped singing *Schlagers.*

"Why don't you play a carol on your violin?" they asked me. I played and they sang. Halfway through *Silent Night* their voices petered out and I stopped playing. This song stirred too many memories; it was too close to Christmas, which we all wanted to spend in Germany.

Suddenly Erika, our cheerful companion, burst into tears. She did not want to go to England at all and confessed that her fiancé was a very small man of five foot five inches - Erika was five foot nine inches and very large. Besides he was not a factory owner but a vicar in Manchester. I must say, it was difficult to imagine Erika becoming a vicar's wife. We exchanged addresses and promised we would keep in touch with her.

When we were told by the steward the next morning that we were approaching Tilbury, a few of us went on deck.

It was a dark, grey morning. In front of us lay the coast of England, and the cranes of Tilbury Dock resembled inquisitive giraffes looking over a wall, as their tops emerged from a thick layer of fog. Faint lights, here and there, twinkled a welcome to us; all around the water was dark and unfriendly. An unfamiliar dampness, like a fine broken rain - I was soon to learn that it was called 'drizzle' - descended on us. Suddenly I felt cold, frightened and very lonely. I went back to the cabin to pack.

An hour later I stepped ashore. My new and very different life had begun.

———⟫◆⟪———

A Bit of Time

ENGLAND

1946 - 1952

For my grandchildren,
Karl, Alex, Jessica,
Zoe, Elsie, Max
and Sofia.

On the 19th of December 1946, a dark and wet morning, the *Empire Halladale* arrived in Tilbury from Cuxhaven. When the ship's engine stopped a brief silence descended on the passengers, then the babble of excited voices and the running and shuffling to and fro started again.

Our little group of German war brides sat huddled in a corner of the upper deck waiting to disembark. Our fellow passengers were English soldiers, male and female, from Germany, either on leave or for demobilization. Nobody during the crossing had spoken to us, apart from the orders that we were not to leave the ship before everybody else had disembarked. We sat in silence, in unease and anticipation. It seemed apparent to us that we were not going to be welcomed in England.

When it was our turn to leave we staggered down the gangway with our heavy suitcases. I had one in each hand and my violin under one arm. A group of men, our prospective husbands, stood at the end of the gangway, each of us recognised a beloved face amongst them, and as soon as they saw us they came running towards us, disobeying the order not to. Suitcases and violin were dropped, there were hugs and kisses everywhere and worries about hostility were momentarily forgotten. There wasn't much time to say goodbye to the other girls but we all had exchanged addresses and promised to stay in touch with each other.

Out of uniform Tom looked different in his tweed jacket and corduroy trousers, but I was not quite sure about his pork pie hat.

It had been an expensive day for Tom so far. He had put two first class tickets from Waterloo to Axminster into the rim of his hat (one of his many funny habits) and when he had taken his hat off to embrace me they must have fallen out. The taxi from London already showed an alarming fare, having waited for more than three hours for us to come off the boat.

I did not take much notice of the drive from Tilbury to London. It was a miserable rainy day and I was happy sitting close to Tom. London looked sad and gloomy with so many buildings in ruins from the air raids, scars everywhere from the war, but that was not an unfamiliar sight for me. My own town in Germany showed the same signs. Tom took me to his father's club, 'Whitehall Court'. A lovely hot bath, eating

buttered toast and to sit in comfortable leather armchairs in front of a
fire, was sheer bliss after our uncomfortable and stark accommodation
on the boat.

It was late afternoon when we caught the train from Waterloo to
Axminster in Devon, where I was to live from now on. A man reading
the paper was the only other traveller in our compartment. Suddenly,
talking to Tom, I became very conscious of my German accent and my
inadequate English. What if our other passenger hated Germans? He
must have realised where I was from. I reduced my voice to a whisper.
After a while he put down his paper and smiled at me. Relieved, I smiled
back.

The nearer we came to Axminster the more my anxiety about
meeting Tom's family grew. He always spoke so proudly of his family's
abilities, but I could not boast of one single talent. Tom was aware of my
nervousness. He put his arm around my shoulders and said in a reassuring
voice, 'Don't worry, duckie.' But I did.

We were the only passengers getting off at Axminster, a small
deserted station, completely silent apart from the station-master's whistle
and the hissing of steam from the departing train.

Suddenly a tall elegant woman ran onto the platform and,
stretching her gloved hands out towards me, shouted, 'You must be
Renate.' It was my prospective mother-in-law. I could not see her face
properly in the dim light, but I shall always remember the big brown fur
gloves she wore.

It was raining hard when we drove the six miles from Axminster
to Westhay, Tom's home, of which he had told me so much with love
and pride.

The windscreen wipers went furiously back and forth. All I could
see was darkness and broken ribbons of rain in the light of the headlamps.
We were completely enclosed by thick fog, but Tom assured me that on
a clear day the sea could be seen from this road. I remember going down
a steep hill and turning sharp right up a smaller hill, with tall trees whose
massive trunks appeared ghostlike and silvery in the quick passing lights
of the car. 'This is called Westhay Cross, ' Tom's mother said, 'and this
is Westhay.' As we turned into a gravelled drive, I saw the dark shape of
a house with lit windows in front of us. A tall white-haired man came
down the steps of the porch. Shaking my hand with a friendly smile he
said, 'Welcome to Westhay.' I recognised him from photographs as Tom's
father. On top of the steps stood two of Tom's three sisters. They shook

my hand and said formally, 'How do you do?'

My first impression on entering the house was of utter cosiness. Sofas stood in front of a blazing log fire, a desk lamp with a green glass shade, a striking oil painting over the fire place of a girl with dark hair in a white dress. We had supper in the warm and cosy kitchen and Tom's parents' friendly conversation during the meal made me feel at ease. Tom's sisters, one four years older, the other three years younger than me, were not very talkative.

The first evening did not end as I would have liked. I had always kissed my parents goodnight and did not know that this was not done in the Greenshields family. When I kissed Tom's mother goodnight, she did not respond with a kiss but bade me a friendly goodnight. Likewise his father. His sister, Gillian, stood up before I could inflict her with my German habit and said, 'Don't kiss Virginia and me', but she wished me a good night and smiled. I was very much aware I had already done the wrong thing on my first night. When Tom came to my bedroom to say goodnight, he saw that I was upset. 'The Greenshields are a non-kissing and undemonstrative family', he explained, and he gave me an extra big kiss.

Lying in bed after Tom left, I wondered if all English families were like this. In spite of them being so friendly and welcoming, I would miss the physical warmth and love of my own family. When I left Germany my father had said to me, 'Don't change but adjust.' I would have to do just that.

There was no sound in the house. It was still raining and I could hear the wind. Our garden in Germany was already covered in deep snow, but although everything outside was silent, the house inside would still be filled with noises from the various families living in it. Children would be crying, doors banging and voices heard till late into the night. Thinking of my parents, Tante Krueger and my old grandfather made me cry. The dreaded homesickness was welling up inside me. 'Please God, not now, not already, let me be brave', I prayed. Finally I went to sleep.

There were no dreams to remember from my first night at Westhay. The house was still silent when I got up and pulled the curtains apart to get a glimpse of my new surroundings. The rain had stopped and bright sunshine made up for the gloomy day of yesterday. I looked down onto a lawn, half enclosed by a laurel hedge. I was struck by the dark green colour of the grass. Beyond the high brick wall surrounding the garden, I saw fields and fields of the same dark green. This colour in the middle of winter seemed strange to me. Straight ahead a little summerhouse divided the wall, and beyond, white smoke rose from chimneys belonging to a group of thatched cottages. Just visible to the left of the summerhouse was the dark brown thatched roof of a much larger house and, very close to it, even larger roofs rose protectively above the thatched one. 'That must be the farm, ' I thought, and I was longing to see it.

I had not realised, till Tom told me the previous night, that he was now employed by his father till he had gathered enough experience to become a tenant of the farm and be his own boss. Tom had joined the British army at the beginning of the war. War wounds had left him with a slight limp, and manual farm work would not be easy for him. Tom was now thirty-two-years old. I was just eighteen.

On my first day at Westhay Tom was given time off to show me around till milking time in the afternoon. I was so relieved when he came to my bedroom to fetch me for breakfast. I had been sitting on my bed trying to pluck up enough courage to go downstairs on my own. I was also relieved that only his mother had breakfast with us. I felt less nervous with fewer people. Cornflakes were completely new to me, and, topped with stewed pears and cream, they made breakfast into a feast.

A large cream-coloured cooker with silver lids warmed the kitchen. 'This is called an Aga, ' Tom's mother explained, 'and it is the best cooker in the world.' This was also what my mother said about her cooker, which was called a 'Grude', it was the same principle, but my mother's was slightly more old-fashioned. Apart from the Aga the kitchen was very much like a German kitchen, except that I could not see a sink for washing-up. This was done in the scullery next to the kitchen, where there was a large ceramic sink with a plate-rack above the draining board. Next to the scullery was the pantry, with another sink and cupboards for glasses and china. Grey rectangular flagstones covered the whole of the ground floor.

By the time Tom had shown me all of the house I felt muddled and totally lost. I think my favourite room was the dining room with its large polished walnut table and leather chairs and sash window that reached down to the floor, letting in ample light and gave a good view of the garden. On the oak mantelpiece stood a group of painted wooden figures of Austrian peasants in their traditional costumes carved by Tom's father. They looked so familiar to me that I immediately felt attached to them. Two large portraits in heavy gilded frames of his grandmother, Isabella Greenshields, with her smiling face and rosy complexion and her husband, seated and smoking a cigar, brought the room alive with their presence.

Westhay was a substantial Georgian house. Small paned sash windows made all the rooms light and airy. A circular staircase with a thick sage green Wilton carpet wound itself gracefully up the stairwell, it was topped by a glass dome, which on rainy days released a constant drip from its weak lead seams.

I had been longing to meet Tom's old dog Tan, a brown and white spaniel, who followed him everywhere. When I knelt down to stroke him, he gave me a lopsided grin and rolled onto his back with his legs in the air, asking for his tummy to be rubbed. I took it that he accepted me and was thrilled when, later in the afternoon, he followed me without being called. Tom's sister Virginia, fifteen years old, was back from school in Sherborne for the Christmas holidays. She was a pretty girl with long dark wavy hair. Tom took me to the stables where she was grooming her Welsh mountain pony called Greyling. 'Why do you call him grey when he is white?' I asked her. 'All white ponies are called grey, ' she explained. I was puzzled.

Next to the loose boxes was a small room with a tiny fireplace and a glass cupboard full of rosettes in faded colours and with bridles and stirrups hanging from brass hooks on the walls. It smelled of polish and leather, a very evocative smell, which reminded me of Heinrich's stables in Lehrte.

On my tour of the house I had been introduced to Mrs Trott and Violet. Violet worked partly in the house and partly on the farm, helping her husband, Charlie, with the milking. Tall and blonde, more German-looking than myself, she took an instant dislike to me. A nod of the head was all she managed when I offered her my hand, which she ignored completely. Quite the opposite was Mrs Trott, a small motherly figure, who shook my hand and said, 'Pleased to meet you.'

Tom wanted to show me the immediate surrounding countryside so he decided on a picnic. I loved picnics when it was dry and warm, but it was December, and although the sun was shining, it was cold and damp. Tom was, however, quite oblivious of weather conditions when it came to picnics and loved them even in rain and snow. (Family picnics have always been enjoyable occasions, taken seriously. We find just the right sheltered place with a perfect view, and weather conditions play a minor part. We still keep up the unusual tradition of a Boxing Day picnic. We eat our turkey sandwiches and left-over mince pies shivering with the cold and reviving ourselves with apricot brandy.)

The little hamlet of Westhay with Westhay House, the farm and its six cottages lay about one mile from the village of Hawkchurch, surrounded by its own fields and woodland. From the first day I fell in love with the hilly Devon landscape. Oak trees were the main feature. They stood majestically in fields, ancient or in their prime, their brown bare branches silhouetted against the blue watery winter sky. High hedges protected the sunken lanes from the wind. Here and there a pale blue periwinkle braved the winter weather. Little droplets, left by the recent rain, dangled in rainbow colours on invisible threads from leaves and branches. Gurgling rivulets, ran busily downhill each side of the lane towards the ford at the bottom of the hill, where a larger stream came out of the wood. Together they made their way under a wooden bridge into a little waterfall. Tom called this stream 'The Schwarzwassergebirgsfluss'. It was called the Blackwater and eventually ran into the River Axe. Part of the wood was planted with Christmas trees and, although the trees were still in their infancy, their delicious scent was strong enough to transport me to the Christmas markets in Germany, at their busiest at this very time. I stood still for a moment and inhaled their scent deeply. We walked further into the wood. Massive beech trees stood on the banks of the stream. and we sat and ate our sandwiches on their protruding roots. Huge rhododendron bushes grew around what had once been a millpond and boating lake. The dam had long been broken, now willows with weeping branches grew out of the almost dried up lake, and clumps of rushes looked like upturned witches' brooms.

At supper that evening I learned that our wedding was to be in two weeks' time on the 6th of January, in the old church in Hawkchurch. Almost everybody in the village was invited. Much to my horror it was going to be a big wedding. I had hoped for a small one and that my brother would be there. Neither would happen. My brother was in a Prisoner of War camp in North Wales. He had arrived in Liverpool two months previously with thousands of German PoWs from Texas, where he had spent the last three years in a PoW camp. Tom and his father had visited him soon after his arrival in the camp which was near Ruthin. They received a hostile reception from the camp commandant, who refused to let them see my brother, let alone allow him to come to my wedding. At least I was allowed to write a letter once a week to him. To my parents I wrote in great detail every other day.

The wedding preparations meant a lot of work for Tom's mother. I had not even thought of a wedding dress as I had assumed the wedding would be small. A kind person from Axminster, Mrs Pearce, whose husband was employed by a local engineering firm, lent me her wedding dress and Tom's sister Virginia was going to be my only bridesmaid, but I had a feeling that she was not very keen. I understood her predicament and felt for her. A German pilot had killed her brother and it was difficult for a fifteen-year-old to forgive. Her good manners won through though, and she was kind and polite to me.

On the morning of the 24th December two large boxes arrived for me from my Aunt Luise in New York, my father's sister. Her wedding present to me was a complete new wardrobe of suits, dresses, skirts, jerseys, pyjamas and everything I needed, even riding breeches, and two dozen nylon stockings, something very rare and in great demand, and useful for Christmas presents. When Tom was demobbed he had taken several trunks of linen, embroidered and hand initialled by my mother, back to England, but the wardrobe I brought with me was scanty. Aunt Luise must have guessed how difficult it was to get anything in Germany at this time. Suddenly I had more clothes than I had ever possessed. Just before the wedding I received another parcel. This time it was from my father's brother in Hong Kong. It was a lovely silk dress in mandarin style, a perfect fit.

What I had read in my school books about the English Christmas I now experienced. On Christmas morning a stocking with presents hung at the foot of my bed. For Christmas lunch there was turkey, and silver charms and sixpence pieces in the plum pudding. The Christmas tree was laden with coloured balls and tinsel and electric lights. (Our German

tree was always decorated with straw stars, Lametta and honey candles.)
A bunch of mistletoe hung over the drawing room door under which
everybody got kissed, but only Tom kissed me.

At the Hawkchurch Church service, holly and ivy were tied to
every pillar and hung from the eagle's wings of the lectern in front of the
Greenshields' pew. I had a shock when suddenly the congregation fell
to their knees in prayer. Having been brought up in a Lutheran Church,
this was almost papish. Thank God father can't see this, I thought, as I
sank onto a beautifully embroidered kneeler, representing a leaping trout,
which without doubt belonged to Tom's father, a keen fisherman. After
the service in a draughty porch, the Reverend Ludlow shook everyone's
hand. He was an old man of at least eighty and his face was blue with
cold. I was introduced to a lot of Hawkchurch inhabitants whose names
I did not catch and whose faces I forgot for the time being.

The only names and faces I remembered so far were connected
with the farm, like Percy and Renee Hallett and their pretty daughter
Esme. Percy drove the tractors and was in charge of anything mechanical
on the farm. He was extremely clever and reliable. He started work at
Westhay when he was fifteen as a boot boy to Tom's grandmother. His
wife was the daughter of the gardener, Mr Cregor, now in his seventies,
who turned up every morning in a freshly starched white collar and had
great trouble in controlling his set of false teeth.

Mr Amor, a very small man, to my amazement looked after the
massive cart horses. When harnessing them he never bothered to walk
around them but walked upright underneath their bellies. He liked his
cider and every evening without fail his small figure was seen walking
across the fields on a well-trodden path to the pub, returning not always
sober to an angry Mrs Amor who waited for him with a broom to beat
him with if he was drunk. She was not much bigger than him, but as
round as a barrel, whereas he was just a wisp of a man.

Percy Hallett's brother, Bill, lived in the big farmhouse with his
wife Edna and their three children. Bill did not get on with his brother
and Edna did not get on with Tom's mother. I never discovered why this
animosity between them existed. Every morning first Percy then Bill
came up to the house to get their daily instructions from the Colonel, as
they called Tom's father.

Mr Smith was the expert ditcher, hedge layer and pig man. He had
been Tom's father's groom in the army and had been kicked by a horse

so badly that he walked with a limp. He married Annie, the cook, who never smiled. They had two boys, one serious like his mother, the other cheerful like his father. Mr Smith was the only employee on the farm who ever wanted to know about my home in Germany. Then there was Charlie, married to Violet. He shared Violet's obvious dislike of me. It infuriated Tom that they ignored me, and as soon as Tom took over the farm, Charlie and Violet got the sack.

When I saw the farm for the first time it reminded me of a little fortress. It was completely enclosed on four sides by solid farm buildings, except for the entrance and the high archway, which gave a view to the east to the distant hills in Dorset. Pilsdon Pen, the highest hill in Dorset, and the Devil's Three Jumps were clearly visible through the arch. Legend has it that the Devil, after unsuccessfully tempting a local farmer, took three jumps in defeat and desperation, and landed in the sea at Charmouth, leaving behind three clumps, now covered with beech trees, a distinct mark in the Dorset landscape.

The old farm buildings of local flintstone gave a feeling of security. Two massive sandstone pillars supported an open barn on one side, and in the centre of the cobbled farmyard stood an oblong stone water trough. In each of the cowstalls either side of the arch lay thirty cows contentedly chewing their cud. They were red Devons with large horns and of a rich dark red colour. Alfa Lavel milking machines had been bought before the war, but it was the first time I had seen them. The milk from each cow was pumped into a collecting bucket and carried to the thatched dairy for cooling. Until the beginning of the war Cheddar cheeses weighing five kilos each were made here. They were hoisted into a large loft for maturing and sold in Harrods in London. In a low, derelict building next to the dairy clotted cream was once scalded in flat bowls that now stood abandoned, full of dust and cobwebs. These cheeses and clotted cream had been taken daily by pony and cart to Axminster to catch the 5 a.m. morning milk train to London.

I wish I could have spent more time on the farm with Tom, but there were other more important things to do for the moment. One was to get myself registered in Axminster so that I could get a ration book. Two elderly ladies, the Misses Cuningham, had run the food office voluntarily ever since the beginning of the war, except for Wednesdays, when both went hunting with the Cotley Hunt. They greeted me most warmly and took down the many details needed for the registration, many more than I had needed for my permit to come to England. My six Christian names: Renate, Emma, Margarete, Frieda, Arnoldine, Ethelinde, presented a slight problem. They were too many to put onto the cover of the ration book. We cut them down to two.

Tom's mother introduced me to everybody we met as 'my new daughter-in-law'. She did not say I came from Germany, but people either guessed or knew already. I met the grocer Mr Harris, the butcher Mr Chick and his apprentice Philip, and the lady with bright red hair and a long fringe who ran the sweet shop. She wore a necklace of large red and yellow wooden beads which looked like gobstoppers. In every shop there was the same smell I had noticed at Westhay, a smell I did not like and which gave me a slight headache. It came from a small portable paraffin stove, and seemed a popular possession of every English household. I saw and smelled it wherever I went. It might have been efficient in heating a room but it was a very temperamental little stove, and had to be handled with the utmost care. The slightest draught turned the blue flame, visible through a small window, into a dangerous yellow one, exuding toxic fumes and covering everything with soot and black cobwebs. I loathed these little monsters and was terrified of them. The word paraffin caused me much distress and many tears in my married life.

After Christmas Tom took me to meet his ninety-year-old grandmother who lived with her two unmarried daughters in a large Victorian house in Parkstone near Bournemouth. Their house became a second home to me.

Tom's mother, Edmée, was Beatrice van Goethem's eldest daughter. When she came back from India, soon after the beginning of the First World War, she was not only pregnant with her first child, Tom, but was just recovering from bubonic plague. Her husband, Tom's father, served as an officer in the Royal Horse Artillery, and was sent from India to Mesopotamia at the beginning of the war. Tom was born in Parkstone. The birth was difficult. Edmée was still very weak from the plague and the baby was not expected to live, but both survived under the loving care of Tom's grandmother and the aunts.

Everywhere in the house hung watercolours by Tom's grandfather, Edouard van Goethem, who died in 1925 'I will tell you about him one day,' Tom said to me. 'He was a very gifted man but rather peculiar.' Granny was now old and frail. With a shawl over her shoulders, her feet resting on a round embroidered footstool, she sat upright in her chair overlooking the large garden, either knitting or reading.

On my first visit, Tom's grandmother took me aside and asked me if I had a bank account in England. If not, she would like to open one for me. I got mixed up with the meaning of account and counterpane, and thought she meant to give me a bedspread. I told her that somebody had just given me one as a wedding present and that it was a very big one. She seemed very surprised and asked Tom who it was that had given me a large bank account. They were very amused about my muddle. I always called my first English bank account my counterpane account.

With the years I became very close to Tom's Aunt Elsa. Her love and wonderful letters helped me through many a difficult time. She was a very good artist, but devoted her life to looking after her mother and ailing sister Aline, who had a great sense of humour and was just as loving.

The 6th January drew closer. The wedding dress arrived, it was too short and had to be lengthened. Granny van Goethem lent me her precious veil of Brussels lace. Wedding presents arrived from people I did not know, but Tom took careful notes of names and gifts. It was a difficult time to buy presents, and some had obviously been kept in cupboards for years, but the people who gave them to us were all so nice and slightly apologetic about the not so useful presents. Among other things, we were given twenty-four vases, twelve saltcellars, eight butter knives and ten teapots, but quite a few useful presents as well.

Aunt Elsa arrived two days before the wedding. Granny was too frail to come and Aunt Aline stayed to keep her company. I met Tom's brother, Graham, for the first time, but he hardly spoke a word to me. He was very shy and had a bad stammer, so he did not talk much to anybody.

Tom's other brother, Henry, was twenty-two years old when his plane was shot down over Calais by a German pilot in the Battle of Britain. When Henry realised that his Spitfire would crash into the houses of a French village, instead of ejecting, he stayed in the cockpit and headed for the canal. The plane burst into flames and Henry was killed. Tom's parents, or Tom, never talked to me about him. Soon after my arrival, Tom's mother saw me looking at a photograph of Henry. I wanted so much to express how I felt for them, but all I was able to say was, 'I am so sorry'. She took the picture from me, put it back onto the desk, and said in a quiet sad voice, 'He was such a lovely boy'.

I was very much aware how difficult it must be for them all to accept me into their family so soon after the war. Not a word about the war and their bereavement had been mentioned. Everybody was concentrating on the forthcoming wedding. Three parsons were going to officiate. The Rev. Ludlow from Hawkchurch, the Rev. Sanders from Axminster, and the Rev. Lapage from Wootton Fitzpaine. I was afraid I would mispronounce the wedding responses and embarrass Tom so I practised them daily. My six Christian names were not going to be cut down to two this time and I hoped that in pronouncing them the clergy would be presented with similar difficulties to mine.

I was developing a cold on the day before the wedding, most likely the result of nerves. All the same, I was packed off to bed early and when Tom came to say goodnight I was in floods of tears. I was frightened of the lengthy Church service, of the crowd of, to me, unknown guests, and though I did not like to tell Tom, I wanted my mother. I felt so miserable I told him I was going to run away in the morning. Yes, I had made up my mind I was definitely going to run away. Tom calmed me down and reassured me that it did not matter at all if I got the responses wrong, he would be right beside me.

The 6th January was a cold but sunny day. Tom's mother and sister, Gillian, had worked hard to cater for the many guests. I had contributed very little, apart from making dozens of meringues. There were enough eggs from the hens and cream from the cows and the sugar ration had been saved up for the last few weeks, as had a lot of other things, for sandwiches and cakes. A local farmer gave us a barrel of cider for a wedding present.

An old mimosa tree in the conservatory had been coaxed with extra warmth and it provided enough blossoms for my wedding bouquet and to decorate the church with its delicately scented flowers. Percy Hallett drove my father-in-law and me to the Church in the Standard 12, decorated with a wide white ribbon across the bonnet. As I was getting into the car my veil came unstuck. Mrs Trott, who had stayed behind to supervise the food, took a large hairpin from her bun and stuck it firmly into the lace. I trembled at the thought of the damage this might do to the precious heirloom.

Getting into the car I heard the Church bells ringing. My father-in-law looked at me and said, 'Nervous?' I could only nod. I walked up the aisle on his arm towards the altar where Tom and the clergy were waiting. The Church was packed. It was the first large wedding in Hawkchurch since the war. Tom, to please me, had chosen two hymns with German tunes. The first was, 'Praise to the Lord, the Almighty', mine and my father's favourite. The other was 'Praise the Lord, ye heavens adore him', which had the tune of the German national anthem, which I hoped would not cause any ill feelings.

My responses were a little less clear and loud than I had intended, but I did not falter. The clergy however cheated, calling me Renate Margarete and leaving out all my other names.

The thought that none of my own family or friends were among all the guests present was almost too much to bear. I tried hard not to cry and focused my thoughts on the embroidery of the ornate altar cloth. I wished with all my heart that my father could have officiated at my marriage. I had always envisaged that it would be he who would place his hand in blessing on my head. I had pictured little bridesmaids in pastel coloured dresses leading us to the altar and scatter petals from their flower baskets in the German tradition. And after the ceremony, coming out of church, there would be children holding a rope in front of the couple, stopping them, till the groom, well prepared, dug deep into his trouser pocket and threw handfuls of pennies amongst them As a child I had been strictly forbidden ever to take part in this custom, but many a time I managed to sneak in amongst them and then spent whatever money I collected in the nearest sweet shop. Leaving the Church I clung tightly to Tom's arm. He put his hand over mine and his loving, happy and reassuring smile gave me courage to face the many unknown wedding guests.

At the reception Westhay House was crammed with guests. Children sat all the way up the stairs eating jellies and dropping sticky bits of meringues. I can't remember any faces or speeches except for one white-haired elderly man, Trevor Watson, an old family friend, who came up to me and said the church service had moved him to tears. When we left for our honeymoon twenty soldiers from Tom's battery, in great form after several glasses of cider, fixed a rope under the bonnet of our car and pulled us, with deafening cheering, the length of the drive.

We had meant to spend our honeymoon in Scotland but only made it as far as North Wales. The weather changed for the worse and the sunny day gave way to rain and sleet. After thirty miles the windscreen wipers packed up and had to be worked by me. Tom had booked a hotel in Bath for the first night. We discovered on our arrival in the dark and in pouring rain; that the hotel had been bombed in the war. Tom, booking by post, had not expected an answer. We found another hotel but unfortunately were immediately recognised by an elderly friend of Tom's parents, who was staying in the same hotel with her husband and another couple. They insisted that we eat with them and so, instead of a romantic wedding-night supper, we shared it with four elderly people who were complete strangers to me.

The two old ladies took a very motherly interest in me. Seeing that I had a cold they told me I had to go to bed early and firmly escorted me to our room. 'You must not worry, dear' they kept on saying. I did not know why I should be worried anyway. I just wished they would leave me alone, though I am sure they meant well. A couple of times they came and knocked at the bedroom door, enquiring if everything was all right, and to give me aspirins. I had visions they would be doing this all night, but finally they left me alone.

They joined us again for breakfast. The two ladies leant across the table and whispered to me, 'How do you feel? Did you have a good night?' 'I feel much better, thank you, and I had a wonderful night', I reassured them.

Slowly we drove to North Wales in sleet and fog and found a small hotel at the foot of Snowdon. I was delighted that I would soon see my brother and not as planned on our return from Scotland.

A few elderly people were the only other guests in the hotel. They spent their day reading the papers in front of a small coal fire. Dark oak furniture, heavy velvet curtains and complete silence from the other guests during mealtime did not lessen the gloom this place exuded. Our waitress never smiled. Her sad red face was covered in tiny blue veins, which spread over her cheeks like the Nile delta. We said nice things about the awful food and tried to have a conversation with her, but no response.

On the second day of our stay we visited my brother who was now working on a farm near Ruthin. Because of the bad weather conditions and the distance to his work place, he was allowed to stay the night on the farm. We had great difficulties in finding the isolated farm of the Edmund family at Penymaes. Dense fog did not help and the Horse Shoe Pass was steep and narrow.

It was almost dark when we arrived. Mr and Mrs Edmunds and their three small boys welcomed us warmly and said that George had just come in from milking and was changing. It was strange to hear my brother referred to as George, to me he would always be Gewi (short for Georg-Wilhelm). It was now four years since we had seen each other. When he came into the room he looked very different from four years previous when he had joined the army at eighteen. Before me stood a young man in a brown PoW uniform with short blond hair and a thin and serious face. A slight smile crossed it when he saw me. When I put my arms around his neck and hugged him, I felt his body stiffen, there was no response. I pulled away from him and looked into his face. There was an unbelievable sadness in his eyes. Three and a half years in a PoW camp in the Texan desert had taken their toll. I was shocked to see such suffering in his face and found it hard to continue a cheerful conversation. Tom came to my rescue. It was the first time he and my brother had met. Farming was an easy subject to talk about, and one that interested everybody. Mrs Edmunds had made a wonderful spread of home cured ham and home made bread and cakes. We sat at the large kitchen table by the light of an oil lamp. The Edmunds family spoke Welsh amongst themselves; it sounded pleasant and melodic. Gewi and I of course spoke German to each other. Gewi wanted to know about our parents and home in Lehrte. I told him that Tom's father was trying to get him transferred to Hawkchurch so that he could live with us and work on a farm in the village. Gewi thought it was better to wait till Tom and I had a home of our own. He was happy with the Edmunds, he said, who treated him as one of the family, though they were not supposed to fraternise with the PoWs.

My brother was treated badly at his camp in Ruthin by the camp commandant, who was a real bully. Gewi did not want to talk about it. He said that the commandant was Jewish, and who knows what the Nazis had inflicted on his family. The Edmunds told me they were glad to have Gewi's help on the farm, but were worried that he was too quiet and withdrawn.

After four long years of not seeing each other, our visit was too short. There was so much I wanted to ask and tell him. After our goodbyes I could not contain my tears any longer. I felt his palpable loneliness and I wanted to stay with him. I hoped that the bad weather might continue so that he could stay on the farm and not have to suffer any more ill treatment in the camp. It was a comfort to know that he had the warmth and affection of the Edmund family.

Fog and rain kept us indoors for the next few days. I wrote a long letter to my parents telling them about our visit to Gewi and about our wedding day. Tom wrote thank you letters for all the wedding presents and made a beautiful drawing for my parents of the wedding cake. Eventually the sun appeared and a lovely landscape of hills and mountains and valleys unfolded out of the fog, with Snowdon right in front of us. 'Let's climb it, ' Tom said, so we set out in our walking boots, without maps or walking sticks or instructions of which was the best and least dangerous way to ascend.

After a two-hour climb we sat down and ate our sandwiches. Far below us was a lake, dark and lonely in a stark, rocky landscape. The sun had disappeared and menacing clouds indicated that more rain or snow was not far off again. We did not meet another soul on the whole of our climb. I suggested we return to our hotel, but Tom was all for going on.

After one more hour of climbing I had had enough. By now a freezing fog enclosed us. My bun had come undone and I had plaited my hair into pigtails, which had frozen stiff and stuck out at right angles from my head. We were parallel with the little railway, that laboured up the steep slope to the summit in the summer months.

Tom took my hand and carefully we descended hoping to reach the wider, safer footpath before long. By the time we reached the hotel it was dark and sleeting. We were glad of the ample hot bath water the hotel provided. I have to admit this was not a climb I had enjoyed.

To give us some privacy at Westhay, Tom and I had our bedroom in the old servants' quarters, a Victorian addition to the main house. It had not been used since the beginning of the war. Though newly painted it still smelled musty and was sunless and bitterly cold. Below us was the games' larder, dank and dungeon-like, with grey uneven flagstones stained from the blood of pheasants and other game that hung from the rusty hooks in the ceiling. This part of the house gave me the shivers in more ways than one. I did not like it at all.

Ever since I arrived in England I had been cold, however many jerseys I put on. I could not understand at first what made me so cold, till I realised it was the dampness. Invisible particles of moisture settled on shoes and clothes in a thin film of mould and crept into my bones. I stood in front of the Aga to warm my hands on the warm lids on the top of the stove . I spent too much time sitting in front of the log fire, mesmerised by the flames licking the logs, and watching small sizzling bubbles appear on the sometimes wet wood. I avoided the oil lamps which gave me a headache, and I was glad when the wet weather turned so cold that the dampness made way for a dry and icy spell like a northern continental winter.

The winter of 1947 was one of the coldest in northern Europe. It hit England hard as nothing was prepared for such unusual freezing conditions. Pipes froze, roads became blocked with snow, and transport came to a near standstill. When the snow stopped falling the temperatures dropped even more.

With the first snowflakes I felt happy and hoped for more. Little did I know the chaos it would bring. Everything looked pretty and everybody seemed to enjoy the sparkling white landscape. Woolly hats and long scarves came out of cupboards. Tom and I waxed the old skis, last used in Kitzbuehl in 1938, and skied down the slopes in the hillier fields, children from the village joined us with home-made sledges or tin trays. I longed for my old sledge from Germany (which eventually made it to England and was used by my children and grandchildren). But the snow kept falling, the road conditions worsened and vast numbers of animals were stranded in deep snow or buried in it. My brother wrote from Wales that they were completely cut off and they remained so for the next two months. On the farm, though the animals were under cover, the problem was how to get the milk to the factory in Chard Junction when we were surrounded by deep lanes full of snow . Tom and Percy Hallett set out on the grey Ferguson tractor with two shovels, thermos flasks of hot coffee and ten milk churns in the trailer. They dug through the virgin snow and slowly progressed to the milk factory eight miles away. There was no wind protection on the tractor and they returned in ·

the dark, frozen and exhausted. This journey continued daily for the next three weeks.

Newspapers reported the hardship this severe weather caused in Germany where people died from lack of food and lack of shelter and fuel. Calories were down to a thousand a day, less than at the end of the war. It was a comfort to me to know that my parents had enough firewood to keep them warm and I hoped they had enough to eat. I sent them parcels regularly, mainly with coffee and tea which they could exchange for butter and meat. When I thought of so many Germans sitting hungry and freezing in their ruined houses, I felt sad and guilty for not sharing the hardship with them.

Tom's third sister, Hazel, returned from Switzerland at the end of January. She was cheerful, witty and closer to me in age, and I felt more at ease with her than with Tom's other two sisters.

The language barrier was my biggest problem. It was frustrating not to be able to express myself as well as I wanted to, and I shied away from any lengthy conversation. I only felt relaxed with Tom, but I saw too little of him. He appeared briefly at mealtimes. The unaccustomed farmwork was tiring for him and most evenings he fell asleep in front of the fire when everybody else was listening to the radio. 'ITMA' was a popular evening programme, but I understood very little, it was all too fast and I did not get the jokes. There was this silly voice at the end of the programme which said, 'It's being so cheerful as keeps me going.' Well, it did not me.

Gillian and Hazel were, like my mother-in-law, good cooks. The few dishes I had learned in Germany were from wartime recipes, and not very exciting. My mother-in-law began to teach me some basic English dishes. The most important one was porridge. I still cannot understand why the English are so fond of it. 'Haferbrei', as it is called in Germany, is only given to the sick. In 1947 a lot of food like meat, butter, cheese, bread, sugar and sweets were still rationed, but compared with Germany there was more than enough. Living on the farm we had plenty of milk, cream and eggs, and the occasional pig was slaughtered. Quite a few dishes like curry, steak and kidney pie and kedgeree were new to me, also some puddings like bread and butter pudding, apple charlotte and one very peculiar dessert called junket. Mrs Francillon's cookery book had been given to us as a wedding present by Mrs Leech from the village, who was 101 years old. I still use it regularly. Cooking on an Aga with its four ovens, each perfect for roasting, baking and keeping food warm, was a great help. I hoped I would have one when we eventually had our own home.

Because Martin had been on sick leave, I did not meet him till we came back from our honeymoon. Martin was a German PoW in a camp at Honiton, ten miles away, and worked on the farm. A group of German PoWs were taken daily from the camp to their work places in the Axminster district. I had looked forward to meeting Martin but had not realised that this would be a difficult situation. When he came to the kitchen door at lunch time to get his food, I was not able to ask him into the warm kitchen to share it with us. It was not only a question of class, fraternising with PoWs was still forbidden and I was not mistress of the house so I could not ask him inside, which I would like to have done. I was the first German woman with whom he had contact after three years of imprisonment in England. He had fought for my country, and was still separated from his wife and three small children, two years after the war had ended. I felt ashamed and followed Martin to the cold potting shed where he had his lunch. I explained my situation but my excuses felt hypocritical. Martin shrugged his shoulders and I knew what he was thinking. He accepted the restriction put upon him, the difference was that I was not British, I was German, like him.

Lunch time was the only chance I had to talk to Martin and whenever I could I shared my lunch with him in the shed. I told him about my brother's time in the PoW camps in Texas and North Wales. Martin had had the fortune of staying in England throughout his three years of being a prisoner and had been treated well. The Red Cross provided the camps with cigarettes and chocolate, and they were not short of reading materials, though Martin did not read books. He was worried about his family who lived near Magdeburg in East Germany in the Soviet Zone. He had no wish to be under a communist regime when he was released, and wanted his wife and children to defect to West Germany, which meant giving up their smallholding and starting again from scratch. An uncertain and hard future lay ahead of him. To my relief, he was released in late summer in 1947. Hopefully there would be enough time left for his family to escape to the West before the borders were closed. Towards the end of 1947 most PoWs were repatriated, though some were not released till December 1948. Many friendships were formed, some lasting till today. My brother, after 59 years, is still in contact with the Edmunds family in North Wales. The farm is now run by one of their three sons, who was a small boy of three when Tom and I visited them in 1947.

Tom and I were frequently asked out to tea or drinks by friends and neighbours. I learned to respond to the 'How do you do' without going into details about my health, and I became aware that the weather was a very important topic. Some of the people I met had been in the army in Germany. Not many of the English stationed there had made the effort to learn the language. Occasionally I was greeted with 'Guten Tag', once even with 'Gruss Gott'. They had heard that my father was Austrian which he was not, he was only born there. Everybody was friendly and welcoming, but what they really thought of a young German girl coming to England so soon after the war and marrying a popular bachelor, I did not know.

My first English tea party was with Dr and Mrs Briscoe. I was greeted with a warm hug by May and a delicious smell of freshly baked scones. At the kitchen table sat their two little girls of eight and nine years old, they stared intently at me and murmured an inaudible 'Hello', and throughout tea did not take their eyes off me. When their mother asked them what the matter was, they asked, 'Is she going to shoot us?' They had obviously been told at school about the barbaric Germans.

Another tea party that sticks in my mind was with the eccentric eighty- year-old Lady Pinney of Race Down, a large red brick house where Wordsworth and his sister Dorothy had once lived. Tom and I, with a few other guests, sat in a freezing dining room eating small triangular pieces of bread sandwiched together with a – to me – strange brown substance called Marmite, and nibbling hard rock cakes. Lady Pinney sat in comfort in front of a roaring log fire next door and demanded that her guests came to see her, one at a time. I timidly stood in front of her. She did not reply to my 'How do you do?' Instead she poked her walking stick so hard into my chest that I fell into the chair opposite.

'So you are Tom's German wife they are talking about', she barked.

'Tell me, what do you think of the English sandwich?'

I certainly did not like the ones I had just tasted, though I did not dare to tell her so, but I had eaten some very good ones at other parties, and I told her I liked them.

'Rubbish', she shouted, 'they are disgusting. Can you cook?'

'I am learning', I replied.

'Well I hope you are going to be a good housewife to Tom', she said, and with that I was dismissed.

Lady Pinney's husband, General Pinney, forbade his troops in the First World War to wear steel helmets because he said it weakened hair growth. One of their daughters, a doctor in London, had one silent day a week in protest about some political cause. On one of her silent days her pet python escaped, and, because she had to remain silent, she pinned notices all over Hampstead about the reptile, which was found eventually.

Another Pinney family lived nearby in the Jacobean Manor of Bettiscombe. The house was known for the screaming skull, which belonged to a slave brought back from the West Indies by one of the Pinneys from his sugar plantation. When the slave died he was refused burial in consecrated ground, and was buried outside the churchyard. Screams from his grave were heard during the nights and did not stop till the skull was removed to the manor.

My father had many friends who were eccentrics, and their stories always fascinated me. One of my favourite was of the parson who milked his goat during the church service. He gave his congregation an extra long hymn to sing, so as to have enough time to milk the goat and rush back into the pulpit. One Sunday, during the inflation after the First World War, he stuffed millions of marks, all of the collection money, into his surplice. The goat found the money and ate the lot while being milked.

Another eccentric friend, an absent-minded professor, came with his wife to lunch at our house. When he started to eat the soup with his fork, his wife suggested a spoon, whereupon he replied. 'What a most ingenious idea, my dear'.

Captain Owen Bragge lived in Glebe Cottage in Hawkchurch. He could also be called an eccentric, but I did not think he was a very nice person. He was a huge man with a loud voice. A few limp strands of hair stuck to his bald head, but from his nose and ears sprouted a healthy growth of hair. He spoke to me with mocking politeness, but when it was just him and me, he ignored me. He employed two maids, one with a loud voice, who he called 'screech', the other, rather grubby one, was called 'slut'!

One Sunday in church a boy with severe hiccups sat in front of him. The Captain leant forward, tapped the boy on the shoulder and whispered, 'Open your mouth wide and look up to the ceiling'. He then sat back smugly and waited for the result, which soon came. It was the loudest resounding hiccup ever heard. With a smile of satisfaction Owen Bragge folded his hands over his vast stomach and went to sleep for the rest of the sermon.

The Norman church tower of Hawkchurch nestles on the northern slope of a hill facing Somerset, and coming from Chard, can be seen from miles away. In 1894 a rose-loving Rector of Hawkchurch gave everybody in the village a rose to plant and the pretty little cottages lining the village street greet the visitors to this day with rose blooms and their scent, and Hawkchurch is known as the 'village of the roses'. The church in the middle of the village is dedicated to St John the Baptist. Grotesque but amusing images of human and animal faces, skilfully carved by Norman masons, look down from the scalloped capitals of the pillars in the north and south aisles. The church's charm and simplicity reminded me of the little village churches of lower Saxony in which my father preached from time to time. These small atmospheric churches breathe a comforting reassurance of a divine presence, which I also felt when I entered Hawkchurch church for the first time.

In the old rectory next to the church lived General Goddard and his family. His nine-year-old son was very proud of his father and told everybody that he was a general. When Major Watson, the old gentleman who had cried at my wedding, came to lunch at Westhay, together with the General and his family, he was told beforehand about the precocious little boy. 'Leave it to me, ' he said. 'I know how to deal with him.' When young Geoffrey on shaking hands was just about to boast about his father, Major Watson forestalled him and said, 'My father is a Fieldmarshall, what is yours?' The boy was speechless.

Opposite the church was the village pub with its cobbled courtyard, and next to it was the village shop and bakery owned and run by Mr and

Mrs Hayball. Mr Hayball called at Westhay twice a week. In his large wicker basket he had freshly baked bread and delicious doughnuts, all sugary and stuffed with jam. Mrs Hayball in her seventies, tall and thin, her grey hair severely brushed back into a bun, was in charge of the shop, which was small and low ceilinged, filled with the mingled smell of apples and chocolate and soap and cheeses, and the ever-present smell of the dreaded paraffin heater in the winter months.

On entering the shop a little brass bell above the door tinkled and Mrs Hayball, wiping her hands on a tea towel, appeared from her kitchen next door, greeting the customer with, 'And what can I do for you today, m'dear?' On a slab of grey marble, ham and cheese were skilfully cut into thick or thin slices with an alarmingly large knife. Chelsea buns and rock cakes lay temptingly under a glass dome on the counter. There was no till, let alone a calculator, to add up the bill. A sharpened pencil rested behind Mrs Hayball's ear and before adding up the groceries it was briefly licked. I much preferred to shop here than in Axminster. Mrs Hayball's motherly instinct soon found out that I was homesick, and whenever there was nobody else in the shop, she'd say 'Stay a while, my dear, let's have a little chat. It takes a bit of time to get used to another country.'

The winter of 1947 seemed endless. Snow covered the ground till the end of March. I helped my mother-in-law in the kitchen in the mornings, but the afternoons were long and lonely. I read books recommended to me (Georgette Heyer, Ryder Haggard) which I did not like. I loved Thomas Hardy. It was slow reading as I had to look up so many words I did not know. I wrote long letters to my parents and hoped that their frequency did not reveal my homesickness. I waited for the evenings when Tom finished work and I could be with him. I began to long for our own home, but nobody had so far mentioned anything about it. Tom seemed content to continue living under the same roof as his parents and sisters, and I think he thought that I was as blissfully happy about it as he was. I was not ungrateful for Tom's parents hospitality towards me, but I wanted to have Tom to myself sometimes. I think Tom did not realise how homesick I really was. I tried hard not to burden him with it, but one night when, in our freezing bedroom, he lovingly covered my cold shoulders with the blanket and tenderly pulled me towards him, I burst into tears. He understood that I felt homesick, but was surprised that I felt the need of our own home. He kissed away my tears and promised to do something about it.

At the end of March, when the snow had finally gone and spring appeared almost overnight, Tom and I were told we would soon have a house of our own to move into. Mullins cottage, built of local flintstone, stood on its own between two fields. In the winter Westhay House was just visible through the bare branches of the oak tree in the cottage garden. In the summer there was not a sight of a house anywhere, except the isolated farm on the far hill.

The Charlesworth family owned the Westhay estate together with several farms, from 1880 till 1912, when Tom's grandmother, Isabella Greenshields, bought it from them. Jack and Eileen Charlesworth rented Mullins cottage from my parents-in-law and they had lived there with their two children Mary and Aidan. for the last 15 years. It was for Tom's and my benefit that they now had to leave, and we felt very dismayed about it. Tom had hoped that we could have moved into the farmhouse, which would have been more convenient for him, but the decision was not up to Tom and me, and so it was decided that we should move into Mullins cottage at the end of April.

Before they left Mullins the Charlesworths asked Tom and me to lunch. On that day I saw my first primrose which Eileen had dug from the hedge and planted in a small pot that stood on the dining room table. When I saw this small pale yellow flower, which up till now had only been a legend and promise to me, it was a very special occasion, and the memory of it has remained with me throughout these years.

I was amazed at sixteen-year-old Mary's easy and friendly chatter. With sincerity and a genuine interest she asked questions about my home and country. Her twelve year-old-brother was quiet and shy, and let Mary do all the talking. Mary, like her mother, was beautiful with dark hair and deep blue eyes. They were a lovely family and they never let on how difficult and sad it was for them to leave their home.

A busy time lay ahead of us. Mullins cottage needed decorating and Tom and I were asked to do it ourselves. I was surprised that a professional decorator was not called in, but as I had nothing else to do and needed more physical exercise, I threw myself enthusiastically into the job. I had never painted anything except garden furniture. I soon learned to apply emulsion paint to walls and undercoats and gloss to doors and windows. It was monotonous work, day after day, but in my mind I worked out the furnishing of the rooms (with furniture we had not yet got). I envisaged a new cream-coloured Aga in the kitchen, and a warm and cosy bedroom. Tom was given more time off from farming to help with the painting. Progress was slow and to paint eight rooms was daunting.

It was now the middle of April and spring had well and truly arrived. A year ago Tom and I had enjoyed the spring with picnics in German woods full of anemones and lily of the valley. Now an abundance of primroses and bluebells made us put aside the paintbrushes and, in our Standard 10, we set out for Dartmoor and the Teign Valley, to Dorset and Maiden Castle, Hardy's Monument and Abbotsbury, and wherever we went the yellow of the primroses and the blue haze from the bluebells surrounded us. The landscape was forever pleasing with its rising and falling hills, and farmsteads safely tucked in the coombs, the sea never far away. To live in such beautiful countryside was surely a privilege, which soothed my homesickness for the time being, and I was confident that, with all the kindness I was receiving and our new home to look forward to, I would soon be rid of it.

Before Tom and I moved into our own home we spent a couple of days with his grandmother and aunts in Parkstone. When Tom was at prep school in Swanage and later at Sherborne, to be taken out by Aunt Elsa and Aunt Aline was not just a big treat but a great comfort in his misery and dislike of boarding. Granny and the aunts simply adored Tom as he adored them, and I benefited greatly from this relationship. Tom's grandfather, Edouard van Goethem, died in 1925. Tom vaguely remembered him but his presence remained in every room of the house through the abundance of his paintings. The images of children and animals he captured gave a vivid feel of everyday Edwardian life, and his woodland scenes and landscapes conjured up an atmosphere of spring hopefulness in contrast to his sometimes melancholic sunsets over Poole harbour.

Edouard van Goethem was born in Brussels of an Irish mother and a Belgian father. He married Beatrice Lafone, who was of Huguenot descent, in 1889. They moved with their four children from Brussels to Parkstone in Dorset in 1905. He was a frail man and never in the best of health. He detested money and refused to sell any of his paintings and left all financial matters to his wife, who fortunately had a very generous father, Henry Lafone, who supported them throughout their married life, and paid for the education of their children. E.v.G. swapped his work with other artists. Henrietta Ronner lived in Brussels at the same time, and three of her cat paintings hung in the dining room in Parkstone. Undisturbed, Edouard painted in his studio, a large wooden hut in the garden, all day long except for his daily one-hour solitary walk. On Sundays his wife and children were allowed to accompany him. He loved his family but did not encourage them to bring home any of their friends. On the few occasions his wife asked some of her friends to tea, he showed his disapproval by turning his chair away from them and drinking his tea in silence. Nearby, in the New Forest, lived the artist Augustus John with his family. E.v.G. admired his work but did not approve of his bohemian lifestyle. The children of both artists attended the same Sunday school, but Aunt Elsa and her siblings were not allowed to talk to Augustus John's children. I began to think that Tom's grandfather had not been a very nice man, but I was assured that he had been kind but rather strange.

Tom's grandmother did not have an easy life. She met Edouard in Morocco, where he was painting and she was on a visit with her father. In a letter to her sister Lilian (letters I recently found in an old suitcase) she writes of meeting an artist, delicate in appearance, speaking good English with a French accent. And later, after she had become engaged to him, she again writes to Lilian, 'I think I may be more in love with his paintings than with him.' She admired his paintings but did not share his love of music. When taken to the opera by him, she sat with her knitting throughout the performance, her attention focused on not dropping a stitch. Beatrice was not happy living in Brussels and finally persuaded her husband to move to England. Her father, Henry Lafone managed the huge Butler's Wharf in London. He was loved and respected by everybody he employed. In the great London strike of dock workers in 1896 he gave his employees three shillings a day throughout the strike, and fought for better wages for them. After the strike he received the testimonial of an album inscribed with the name of every worker at Butler's Wharf. They dedicated it to the 'peacemaker'. Cardinal Munnings and the Mayor of London, Lord Brassey, presented the album to Henry Lafone and praised his help and loyalty towards the workers. The workers themselves insisted on being present at the speech and presentation. A London newspaper reported, 'A shed was erected and lighted on purpose with electricity. Speeches were made and the men cheered lustily.'

Henry Lafone's son, Alexander Malins Lafone, brother of Beatrice, was awarded the Victoria Cross for his bravery when defending hill 720 in Palestine. In a regimental dinner speech Lord Allenby referred to Alexander Lafone as one of the bravest men who ever lived or died, and they drank to him upstanding and in silence. Beatrice's only son, Harry, was killed in a flying accident in 1919. Through her faith and lack of self-pity Tom's grandmother radiated a warmth and serenity in old age lovingly looked after by Elsa and Aline, and took a great interest in what went on in the world, but especially in her own family.

Fairly recently, in October 1946, Beatrice's sister, Lilian, had died. She had also lived in Parkstone and she left her entire estate to her and the aunts. Another sister, Ella, had been married to Fieldmarshall General Sir Arthur Barrett, who was stationed in Poona. They were childless, and in 1913 they invited Edmée, Tom's mother, to stay with them in India. Entertained by dashing young bachelor officers at fabulous dinner parties and dances, Edmée had a wonderful time. A little silver trophy stands on our mantelpiece, a proof of Tom's mother's excellent marksmanship in a shooting competition in Simla. During her stay with the Barretts she met her future husband, David Greenshields.

Before we returned to Westhay, Tom and I were invited to choose whatever we needed from Aunt Lilian's house. We chose practical things like beds and chairs, but Tom's grandmother also gave us a boulle cabinet.

Tregarthen, her house in Parkstone, had a large garden with gravelled paths edged by red bricks on their side and at a slight angle, similar to a chevron design. The paths led through small glades of rhododendrons and azaleas to a shed at the end of the garden, in which stood a Rover car. Since the day Aunt Aline accidentally drove over her beloved dog, the car stood idle. When they visited Westhay or needed a car, the Aunts hired Mrs Bailey from the local garage, who chauffeured them at thirty miles an hour and at great expense in her Daimler. Neil, the gardener, came on three days a week. He was fussed over by the aunts and showered with nourishing food planned days in advance. His lunch and tea were meticulously and lovingly arranged on a tray at precisely one and four o'clock.

After his death Edouard van Goethem's studio in the garden was left untouched. Easels, paint brushes and palettes were as he had last used them. Paintings of children paddling in the sea and mothers in wide brimmed hats sitting on the beach, covered every space on the walls and were propped against easels and chairs. Tom was captivated by sketchbooks full of exquisite drawings. In amongst all the paintings was a self portrait of the artist with a bowler hat and a pointed beard, his piercing eyes looking straight at you from under his high forehead. Unfortunately, Tom's grandmother, with her Victorian attitude, did not approve of his nude paintings and burnt every single one of them. His prolific and beautifully executed paintings and drawings are a treasure to his grandchildren and their children, and will be loved and cherished for years to come.

⸻⬛⬛⬛

On the first of May, a warm and sunny day, we moved into Mullins cottage. I shed tears of disappointment when, instead of a cream coloured Aga, I saw a curious stove of bright blue. How was I supposed to cook on this old-fashioned, dangerous and, to me, alien monstrosity? A large glass jar, filled with paraffin, was attached to the side of the stove. A black box perched on top next to two burners. Knobs for regulating the heat stuck out in front of the stove like gear levers of a vintage car. Whenever I became nauseated by the fumes of the paraffin and opened a window, the burners flared up and the flames came alarmingly close to the paraffin jar. Every time this happened bits of greasy soot settled on furniture and food. I hated this stove more than I can say. I swore at it, I kicked it, I cried over it. Why could I not have an Aga like my mother-in-law? The answer was simple. Our kitchen did not have a chimney.

But it was wonderful to have a house to ourselves. We had enough furniture to make the drawing room and bedroom cosy, and for the time being we did not need any more. I thought it odd that the name tapes my mother-in-law had given me to sew into sheets and towels had, instead of my initials, Tom's, and all my letters were addressed to Mrs T.L. Greenshields. On the farm and in the village I was called Mrs Tom. It made sense of course, it was practical and saved confusion, but somehow it took away a fraction of my own identity. Something else I had to get used to were the blankets on our bed. Why not have a lovely continental duvet? Tightly tucked in blankets and sheets might give a feel of security, but they were difficult to get out of when nature called in the middle of the night, and letting in cold air annoyed the person sleeping with you. Tom did not like the blankets tucked in at the end of the bed, but I did. Fortunately it was the sole disagreement between us.

I had been looking forward to cooking on my own and to surprise Tom with the dishes he liked best. But the surprises turned into charcoal mixed with tears. The oil stove and I did not bond. The flames of the burner had a will of their own and turned my new shiny white enamel saucepans black.

An old Lister engine powered the generator to supply Westhay House and the farm with electricity. At the back of the stable yard, next to the smithy and saw bench, every morning Percy topped up large batteries with distilled water for the Lister engine, which chugged away all day long till at 11 p.m every light was switched off. It was not till 1950 that all of Westhay and the cottages were connected to the mains supply.

Until then our little house had no electricity. The only source of lighting was candles or Tilly lamps, fuelled by paraffin. At the slightest touch, the delicate lace-like mantle in the cylinder disintegrated, and the smallest hint of a draught extinguished the flame. The lamp released a constant hissing, together with a bright white light. I can't remember how our water was heated, but there was enough for one bath a night, which Tom and I shared. The ironing was slow and tedious. I heated a flat iron over the flame of the burner and, because it became covered in soot, it was put into a metal shoe before touching the clean laundry. The telephone was another archaic entity, and looked like a hearing aid. The receiver resembled an ear trumpet and was hooked onto a slim stand like a microphone. When dialling you had to hang on to both to stop them toppling over. We shared a party line with Westhay House. Not only was this inconvenient for both sides, at times, but it could also be tempting to listen to the conversation of the other. Luckily we trusted each other not to do this.

Every Wednesday evening Tom went to Bridport to Territorials. Sometimes I went with him, and he dropped me off at the cinema on his way to the drill hall. In the summer, when the weather was fine, we stopped on the way home for a crab sandwich at the Anchor Inn in Seatown, and went skinny dipping in the sea.

A few weeks after we moved into Mullins we invited the farm staff and their families to a little party in our new home. It was the first party I had hosted and I was terrified of entertaining so many people, but Tom promised to do all the talking. Two attempts at making rock cakes were spoilt by the wretched oil stove. When I was taking the third batch out of the oven, Tom came running into the kitchen telling me he had just remembered a very important meeting with his colonel in Bridport that evening. He absolutely had to go. It was one hour before the guests were due to arrive. 'You can't go.' I yelled, 'I can't do it by myself.' But Tom was already rushing upstairs to change into his uniform, and after five minutes he was gone. How was I going to entertain eighteen people when I could not even speak their language properly? I stared at the slightly burnt rock cakes, and the sardine and egg sandwiches. I was sure they would not like them. Mrs Smith and Mrs Hallett were excellent cooks and would no doubt be critical about my cooking. I felt angry with Tom for the first time.

The guests arrived on the dot and, like a coach party, all at the same time, which threw me completely. In my confusion I asked them to take off their clothes instead of coats, which they declined to do, and they held on to their coats throughout the evening. I explained about Tom's absence. Mrs Smith said, 'Mr Tom can be very forgetful at times.' The sandwiches and rock cakes went down well, and alarmingly quickly. The wives did not touch the sardine sandwiches. They said sardines repeated themselves. I filled their glasses with cider. The children were well behaved and sat in silence sipping their orange juice. After the food, a lull in conversation set in. Up till now I had done most of the talking, but my repertoire was exhausted. How could I possibly keep them happy for another hour? I suddenly thought of my photograph album of my childhood and home. It did the trick. They showed great interest and laughed about the chubby little naked baby, which was me. They stayed longer than I had anticipated, but perhaps that was a good sign. I was still angry with Tom when he came back, but coping on my own had given me a little more self-confidence.

Tom, 1952.

Renate, 1949.

The Empire Halladale.

Our wedding, Hawkchurch, 6th January, 1947,
Tom's father and sister Virginia, and brother, Graham.

Tom's parents.

Tom and Gewi on visit to Wales in January 1947.

Tom and Renate in Mullin's Cottage garden, 1947.

Mullin's Cottage.

Renate and Annie,
one week old, 1948.

Gewi in PoW uniform, 1948.

Aline, Renate, Granny van Goethem, my parents, Summer 1948.

Renate's father on visit to Westhay 1948.

*Renate and Annie
on Charmouth Beach, 1950.*

*Renate and Annie
in Lyme Regis, 1952.*

Rectory Lehrte, 1950.

Rectory Garden, Lehrte, 1950.

Renate's grandfather and her mother, 1950.

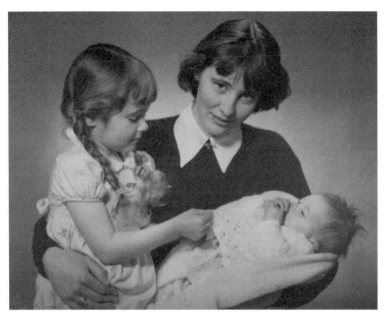

Renate, Annie and Janie, 1951.

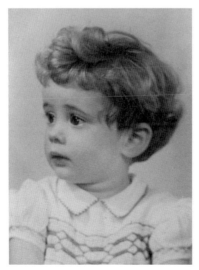

Janie, 2 years old.

The cowstall, Westhay, 1947.

The farmhouse, Westhay, 2006.

I went to Axminster once a week to do the shopping, usually on Thursdays, because it was market day. I was learning to drive but, till I had passed my test, I went with my mother-in-law. I was now in charge of our own ration books. This was no problem as I was used to them from Germany. Meat was rationed to 16 ozs a week and butter to 6 ozs. Sugar, bread and sweets were also still rationed. Marguerite Patten's postwar cookery book was very popular with its sympathetic recipes using the limited foods. Whale meat was highly advertised, so was a fish called Hoek from South Africa, which was very salty, and Tom and I hated it. The change from the decimal German measures, weights and currency to the English inches and ounces, pounds, guineas, half crowns, threepences and farthings was difficult at first. Shopping at the greengrocer was easy. I pointed to the fruit and vegetables I wanted to buy. Groceries were more complicated, but everybody was most helpful. Mr Chick, the butcher, knew exactly what I required when I asked for 'cow, pig or sheep', and produced the right joint plus a few extra ounces.

The shop that intrigued me in Axminster was the haberdasher and outfitters of Dawkins and Sons. It was run by Miss Shepherd, a tall, middle-aged woman, immaculately dressed in matching outfits with a wide brimmed hat of the same colour. The only let-down to her wardrobe was her sheepskin slippers. She greeted her customers like long lost friends, and kept a sharp eye on all her assistants. What really fascinated me about the shop was the overhead paying system. The bill and money were put into a wooden capsule which was fastened to an overhead rail. Pulling the cord it then whizzed across to the pay desk at the other end of the shop. A cashier unhooked it, checked the money and returned it with the change and receipt. It was still in use when the shop closed thirty years ago.

In contrast to the misery the oil stove gave me, the garden was a pleasure. Old photographs showed a lovely cottage garden before the war, but now old and crippled cabbage stumps decayed in the once colourful flower beds, which had been turned into a vegetable plot during the war. I have always loved gardening and, inspired by our beautiful rectory garden in Germany, I was determined to restore our small garden to some of its former prettiness. At the back of our cottage I started a kitchen garden with lettuces and herbs, which we shared with rabbits and deer till we fenced it in. I was happy working in the garden and looked forward to Tom's lunch break and our time together after supper.

I did not always wish to accompany him on his daily evening visits to his parents. Living in such close proximity with my parents-in-law, I saw a great deal of them during the day and did not feel it necessary to spend the evenings with them as well. I often felt a pang of jealousy and inadequacy when I saw Tom happy and content, adored and adoring amongst his sisters and parents. Would I ever be able to make him so blissfully content and happy, I asked myself? Would he ever like my cooking, my rice puddings, as much as his mother's? It would have been a comfort to hear my parents' voices once in a while, but telephoning to Germany was not permitted in 1947. From time to time I phoned my brother, who was now staying on the Edmunds' farm all the time. His monosyllabic conversation was of no comfort to either of us. I urged him to apply for a transfer to Devon and come and live with us. He said he would after the harvest.

I was never bored, but I was lonely. There was plenty to do in the house and garden. There were books to read and to learn from, letters to write and my violin to practise. I had started violin lessons with Nora Ford in Lyme Regis, a brilliant violinist and a strict teacher.

Since the farm staff party I had gathered a bit more confidence and had begun to ask people to tea. I invited the Rev. Ludlow and his wife, May Briscoe and the two little girls, who were not frightened of me any more, and a dear old lady called Da Adams, who played the organ in Hawkchurch. Most of my guests were in their seventies and eighties, except for May who had just given birth to a third daughter she called Cordelia. When I was holding her baby I longed to have one of my own.

At the end of July I knew I was pregnant. I was longing to tell Tom, but when I did, he already knew. His mother had told him. I was disappointed. I had not told anybody. How was it possible that she knew? Because I was looking pale in the mornings and had been feeling car sick when we went shopping in Axminster, my very experienced mother-in-law, who had given birth to six children, drew her own conclusions – and, of course, she was right. But Tom was thrilled when I confirmed this marvellous news. Tom's mother sympathized with my morning sickness and recommended sucking barley sugar sweets first thing in the morning. It did not help, on the contrary, it made me sicker, and even now, fifty-six years later, I cannot bear the sight of the sweet.

The latest in bringing up children was a book by Dr Spock, which I read religiously, but I have to confess, after the baby was born, I did not take the slightest notice of it. Dr Spock's advice seemed too strict and clinical for me.

Expectant mothers received extra meat coupons and cod liver oil tablets. I was in the good care of the family doctor in Axminster, Dr Morton, a kind and fatherly man who declared me in excellent health with good child bearing hips. I had never heard this expression before and thought it meant that I would be good at carrying the baby on my hips. 'Where do you want to have the baby?' the doctor asked me, 'at home or in hospital?' I had not thought about it, but as I loathed hospitals I decided at home. My mother-in-law insisted that we hire a midwife for at least one month after the birth. I had read that nannies and nursemaids stayed for years with families and took complete charge of babies and children. I did not want that to happen with my children, and Tom had to promise me that, after one month at the most, the nurse would have to go.

As fortunate as I was with my doctor, I was not so lucky with my dentist. On my first visit he was charming. On subsequent visits I realized that he hated Germans. Sitting in the dentist's chair, my mouth wide open, and stuffed with cotton wool pads, he told me that Germans were 'a God damn awful race', and every one of us deserved to be shot. I could sense his pleasure when, without an injection, he inflicted the maximum pain on me, drilling my teeth. When he told me that my front teeth were rotten and had to come out, when in fact they were healthy, I plucked up enough courage to tell him I had had enough and was not coming back, and slammed the door behind me.

Tom was appalled when I told him and wanted to confront the man, but I begged him not to. I should have confronted him myself, but would he have taken any notice of a young girl from the country he hated, who tried to explain that not all Germans had been Nazis, and that many Germans themselves had suffered under the Hitler regime, and that the ordinary German soldier was not responsible for the bestial behaviour of some megalomaniac Nazis. I would have liked to talk and explain to him, but I doubted that this young man, who had spent the last five years fighting the Germans, and harboured so much hate because of the cruelties he had witnessed, would listen to me. I hoped that one day he would experience kindness and friendship from the nation he hated and thought 'so God damn awful'.

I kept in touch with two of the German girls who came to England with me on the *Empire Halladale*. Five of the other twelve went back to Germany for good. Flamboyant Erika was one of them. She had not married her vicar after all.

To live in Manchester or Birmingham in a semi-detached house was a far cry from the pretty little Westphalian villages some of the girls had come from, and promises made in Germany by their fiancés in the first flush of love, did not always come up to expectations. Ilse's husband was a long distance lorry driver, and she spent lonely days in her small flat in Manchester and was not accepted by his family or by the community. We invited her to Devon, but she never came, and after a while her letters stopped. I realised what a lucky girl I was in Tom's family and the friendly village.

I kept up a regular correspondence with my old school friends. Schools in Germany reopened in 1947. My former classmates, delayed by two years of chaos in the post war period, would be taking their A levels at the same time as I was expecting my first child. Gabi wrote: 'We are having a great time with parties and dances and boyfriends, and are catching up on the fun we missed out on in the last few years.' Did I envy them? No, I did not. I was happy in my new little world, but I did miss their companionship.

I was now preparing myself to take the driving test and was studying the Highway Code. Tom was my teacher, but his instructions were more directed towards soldiers learning to drive an armoured car or tank. Disregarding rules and ignoring his advice, I drove the car to the village on my own before I passed the test. Twice I crashed into a letter box and knocked it off its stand, and one day, when collecting the vicar and his wife for tea, I drove into the ditch and had to be pulled out with the tractor. After that Tom strictly forbade me to drive on my own till I had passed the test, which I did at the second attempt. It gave me a wonderful feeling of independence.

At the beginning of October Tom and I spent a few days in London. Tom had an appointment with his tailor and we had arranged to meet the midwife who was recommended to us by a friend of my mother-in-law.

I wanted to go to Westminster Abbey, because in the Chapel of Henry VII, on a choir stool of the Knights of the Bath Order, was the coat of arms of the von Hinuebers, my grandfather's mother's family. Henry von Hinueber's father had been a tutor to King George III and his siblings, and later, under his reign, became Attorney General at the German Chancery in London. The King and Queen Charlotte were godparents to one of his sons who was called George Charlotte. Henry von Hinueber was in command of the 3rd Linien Battalion of the King's German Legion in the Napoleonic war. He was knighted in 1815 and received the Knight Commander of the British Bath Order (K.C.B.), the British Golden Nive Medaille and the Great Cross of the Guelpen Order. He was married in St Martin's in the Field.

Tom and I stayed at the Savoy, which my father-in-law thought was too extravagant. I had asked Tom to take me to a night club in London, and he promised he would. I was four months pregnant, but my bulge was still small enough for me to fit into my silk Chinese dress. I put on lashings of lipstick and mascara and was looking forward to my first visit to a nightclub, Going down the steps to the club Tom suddenly said, 'I can't take you in there.'

'Why not?' I asked him.

'You are too young and all that make-up doesn't suit you.'

He took my arm and firmly led me back up the steps to a cab. My eyes filled with tears of disappointment. I had come so close to something I had looked forward to. Tom suggested a nice meal at the Café Royal instead, but I refused. We went back to the hotel. I took off my make-up and went to bed in a huff. Next morning I received a bunch of red roses and a card which said, 'You are not only too young, but too precious'. Needless to say, I forgave Tom.

We met the midwife at Veraswamis, an Indian restaurant in Regent Street. I was fond of curry but my pregnancy did not agree with the spicy food. I craved my mother-country food, like herring, potato pancakes and Frankfurters. The midwife, half Swiss and half English, sympathised with me and told us of a place called Schmidt's in Charlotte Street, which sold German food. Alas, when we went next day we found that the German food supply was still very limited and all we could get was a soused herring.

The midwife, in her fifties, was small, round and looked motherly. She talked in Switzerduitsch to me, which was harder to understand than her English. We booked her from the last week in February for four weeks. The baby was due on the 24th February 1948, and I hoped it would arrive in time so that the four weeks did not have to be extended. I was not quite sure that I liked her.

The rebuilding of war damaged buildings was well underway in London. Sounds of men shovelling rubble and bulldozers preparing ground for new houses and shops mingled with the busy everyday traffic. The size of the red double decker buses amazed me, and I admired the incredible agility of the taxis performing u-turns in crowded streets.

Tom's tailor, 'Cooling & Lawrence' in Maddox Street, was a far cry from that of my father's in our little town in Germany. My father's tailor, small in stature, Polish by birth, sat cross-legged on a table in his tiny shop, with glasses half way down his nose, and a tape measure around his neck. When he arrived from Warsaw in 1930, all his belongings were wrapped in a small bundle. Gradually he built up his small tailoring business, but his real passion was bell ringing. Unfortunately he was only five feet tall and could not reach the rope. When the bells became electrically operated he was put in charge and, standing on a footstool he was just able to reach the starting button.

Tom wanted a bright red lining to the tweed jacket he had ordered. When he was in the fitting room the manager came to me and said, 'Can't you persuade your father to change his mind about the colour?' I was very amused and could not wait to tell Tom. I said to the manager that my father was an artist and preferred bright colours.

We went to look at paintings in the Royal Academy and National Gallery, and visited the Victoria and Albert Museum. The last time I had been in a Museum was in Berlin just before the war, when I was nine years old. I remembered from my visit to the Pergamon Museum the thrill of seeing the Ishtar Gate from the Garden of Babylon. My grandmother had given me a book about the Seven Wonders of the world, which fascinated me. To see a piece of this mysterious and romantic world in front of me left a lasting impression.

Tom insisted on a visit to the Imperial War Museum. It lasted four hours and completely exhausted me. I was not the slightest bit interested in tanks and guns, and could not understand why Tom, who hated war, was so nostalgic about these horrible metal objects which brought anguish and destruction to our countries.

I was glad when the train took us back to beautiful, gentle Devon.

I was so pleased when one day I saw a group of German PoWs working on the road near Hawkchurch. Eager to talk to them, I got out of the car. They were incredulous to see a German girl in Devon and bombarded me with questions. When I told them that I had recently married an Englishman they showed their disapproval by turning away from me without another word. I felt stunned and rejected. I did not want them to see my tears and drove to the nearest lay-by, where I sat and cried. I should have learned from my experience with Martin that German prisoners would not take kindly to my marrying an Englishman. I should not have told them, but how else could I have explained my presence in Devon? In my heart and thoughts I was German, and I loved Germany as much as they did. It would have been better had I waited a little longer before coming to England. Wounds of war do not heal overnight. My happiness suddenly seemed premature and selfish, when others still suffered imprisonment and separation from their families. What I had just experienced with the PoWs. I understood, and was the price I had to pay. I sat for a long time in the car and I decided to keep this encounter to myself.

My brother had not been amongst the repatriated PoWs, but finally, five months after our application, permission was given, he could live with us. I had painted his bedroom and everything was ready for him.

A guard accompanied him all the way from the camp in Wales, and on his arrival handed us a piece of paper to sign. We were now responsible for my brother in case he made a dash for freedom. PoW, in bold white letters, stood out on his brown uniform and canvas sack. Gewi shook hands with the guard and thanked him for his company. They had got on well together.

The November day was dreary and not a leaf was left on the trees, but our little cottage looked welcoming for him, with a cheerful fire in the grate and a German apple cake for tea. Now I had two men to look after, both easy, helpful and lovable. Gewi had been allocated to work on Piercehay Farm in Hawkchurch, which belonged to Mr.and Mrs Watts who were kind and friendly to him. Tom and my brother got on well. They shared an interest in farming and a dislike of war. Every time I asked my brother about his time in the PoW camp in Texas, he refused to talk about it. Tom never liked to talk about the war either. He only told us some encounters, like when his jeep was stolen in Brussels with the entire battery pay, and he faced a court martial. Luckily the money was in a leather bag, and was found in a ditch near the town, but the jeep never turned up. Tom was a non-smoker. The only time he smoked was when the stench of corpses in the war overwhelmed him. Tom and my brother did not want to be reminded of the war, and neither did I.

Christmas came, the second for me in England and the first with my brother for seven years. We had our Christmas lunch with my parents-in-law and Tom's sisters in a small pub called 'The Golden Fleece', a few miles from Westhay. Well-trodden stone steps led to the oak front door of this humble looking inn. A handful of thatched cottages encircled the hamlet's green. I had seen this little place before in early spring, when snowdrops and crocuses covered the grass under the old lime tree in the centre of the green. The interior of the pub was equally enchanting. From the ceiling beams hung pewter beer mugs of different shapes and sizes, and highly polished horse brasses decorated the massive oak beam above the large Hamstone fireplace. The smoke from the fire smelled of apple wood, and large trunks, covered with pale green and yellow lichen, leaned against the golden looking stones from the Hamstone quarry nearby.

We were the only customers and were waited on by the local postman's daughter. My brother looked relaxed and handsome. Instead of his brown uniform he wore a pullover and corduroy trousers. It was good to see him laugh. He had tasted the cider in this pub before and taken a liking to it. He had bought himself a second-hand motorbike, an old 'Ariel', and was getting to know the Devon villages and pubs. The people he met were friendly and invited him to their homes. To my great relief he became less withdrawn, and his dormant humour emerged once again.

My parents were relieved that my brother was now living with us. They were facing another winter with no improvement in the food shortage or in accommodation for the 5.8 million refugees in West Germany. At the end of the war a million German soldiers were in prison camps. When released, most of them stayed in the western sector of Germany, so food and housing were a big problem.

In the autumn of 1947 the American Secretary of State, General Marshall, offered financial help for a programme of European Economy Recovery to relieve poverty and hunger, and help towards building desperately needed houses. The Russians disagreed with the aid and forbade any country under their control to accept help from the Marshall Plan. Their animosity was acutely felt by the people in Berlin. Cars from the western sector were refused entry into East Berlin. Trains from West to East were unnecessarily delayed, and arrests were made for crimes as innocent as carrying a western newspaper. But for West Germany, the Marshall Plan was a godsend, and was gratefully received, as were the many Care parcels sent by Britain and the USA.

We kept sending coffee and tea to my parents, and our mutual correspondence kept us in constant touch. My mother had entrusted an English soldier, going back on leave to London, with my lute and some old table silver, which he was to take to friends of ours in London. The lute and the silver were not delivered, and the soldier was never heard of again. My parents did not like to complain, as it had been illegal to ask him in the first place.

The winter of 1947 was not nearly as severe as the previous one but our little house was cold. Without electricity, we relied on the hated oilstoves, which always gave me a headache. I lit the fire in the drawing room as soon as I got up in the mornings and piled on logs throughout the day. I was longing for the end of my pregnancy.

For seven months Granny and the Aunts had knitted for the great-grand baby, and parcels kept arriving with beautifully knitted vests and jackets, smocked vyella nighties, soft little booties in pale pink and blue, and Shetland shawls as light as a feather.

Soon after I knew I was pregnant I had bought an unnecessary amount of baby wool, with the intention of making the best and prettiest outfits ever. I had learned to knit when I was quite young, but not to read patterns. My attempts turned out to be so deformed, they frightened me, and I quickly unravelled everything I had knitted. I did manage to knit a cot blanket, and I lined a wicker wash basket with padding and pretty material. The basket now stood in our bedroom, filled to the top with everything a baby needed, enough for triplets.

When I first saw an English pram I burst out laughing. They seemed so old fashioned to me, with large wheels and the carriage high off the ground. A friend proudly presented us with a pram she had restored with dark brown canvas and pink American oilcloth. It was the ugliest pram I had ever seen. It had no springs, and our baby would have a rough ride unless I padded it with a very thick mattress as a shock absorber.

Everything was now ready for the baby's arrival, even a name was chosen. We did not mind what sex the baby was going to be. Tom had chosen the name for a girl, which was Anne. I liked biblical names like Joshua, Alubi, Malaki, Timotheus or Ebenezer. The shoemaker in Hawkchurch was called Ebenezer Hayball. He was a lovely old man with long white flowing hair, who played the organ in the Methodist Chapel opposite his cottage every Sunday. I chose the name Timotheus, but agreed to Timothy.

The baby arrived promptly on the 25th February at 1 a.m. at the Cottage Hospital in Axminster. The doctor decided at the last minute that it was safer to have it there and not at home. When holding my small but healthy six and a half pound daughter in my arms I was filled with sheer happiness and wonder. I could not believe that this lovely little thing with dark hair was mine. Tom and I could not take our eyes off the baby, and reluctantly handed her back to the midwife who had arrived the day before, and had come to the hospital with me. She was a great help and comfort during the birth, when she had rubbed my back, with soothing and encouraging words.

My mother-in-law came the next morning to see her first grandchild, and I received the first warm hug from her since my arrival in England. I felt like clinging on to her embrace and having a good cry. It would have been such a mixture of tears; of happiness, of childbirth pains, of relief, and of longing for motherly comfort. My mother-in-law put a beautiful golden locket, a family heirloom, on my bed, and the midwife gave permission for her to hold the baby.

The midwife ruled our lives. The brooch of the midwife guild and a silver watch were pinned onto her spotless white starched apron. She took complete charge, not just of the baby and me, but of Tom and my brother as well, and even of Mrs Trott, who had come to do the cooking for a month.

I had no chance to bond properly with my baby, who was handed to me at mealtimes only, wrapped tightly in a shawl, with only her little red face visible. When the midwife was not looking I loosened the tight wrap and freed her hands and caressed the tiny fingers. As soon as the feed was over, she was snatched away, and all my pleading to hold her a little longer was ignored. Whenever I thought it safe, I sneaked into the room where the baby was sleeping in her basket. I put my head close to hers so that her soft breath touched my lips and I could take in the magical smell of a new-born baby.

However much the baby cried during the day, a four-hourly feeding schedule was strictly observed. At night it was a different matter. With the slightest whimper the baby was brought to me several times, and every time I was aware of a strong smell of alcohol on the midwife's breath. Fortunately Tom was a sound sleeper and unaware of what went on, but my brother had noticed the midwife's drinking, and had refused her late night invitations for a nightcap in her bedroom. We now had a very good reason to get rid of her before the agreed date in her contract. Tom and my brother disliked her as much as I did, and she had upset Mrs Trott by criticising her cooking. I breathed a sigh of relief when Tom took her to Axminster station and swore never to engage a midwife again.

Tom and my mother-in-law worried that I might not be able to cope with the baby on my own, but I felt full of confidence, and was looking forward to have at last the baby to myself.

Bath time was nerve-racking to start with. I was terrified I would drop the little soapy and wriggling body, but it soon turned into a social occasion with my mother-in-law, one or two sisters-in-law, and even Mrs Trott watching. The latter kept on saying, 'that dear little soul.'

My father-in-law presented us with a breadboard he had made from Westhay oak. He had carved the letters 'T' and 'R' in the right and left-hand corners, and in the middle of the board a small letter 'A', leaving room for a few more. After fifty-eight-years the breadboard is still in daily use, with quite a few more initials added to it.

A jubilant letter came from my parents ten days after our telegram, telling them of the baby's arrival. Post took a long time in 1948. With it was a note from my grandfather, written in a shaky hand and barely legible. In my parents' letter was the wonderful news that they could now apply for permission to visit us, provided we would vouch for their accommodation and expenses, as German currency was not yet permitted into England.

My mother-in-law undertook to register our daughter's birth in Axminster. We had decided on the name Anne Pauline. Pauline was my mother's name. When I looked at the birth certificate I saw that it read Anna instead of Anne. I knew that Tom's mother preferred Anna to Anne, but it had been Tom's and my decision to call her Anne. Tom thought it was better to leave it with Anna. We agreed to call her Annie, and she has been Annie ever since.

I had been feeling very tired after the birth and was anaemic. The doctor told me to eat plenty of liver and to drink stout, both of which I abhorred. Little Annie flourished and only cried when she was hungry. Her first smile was a wondrous event. I had padded the springless old pram with cushions and pushed it up and down the hilly lanes.

It was now the end of March and Tom was ploughing the fields for the summer barley to be sown. Dressed in an old fur-lined flying jacket and his army hat, he sat on the grey Fergeson tractor, which looked so small in the big ten-acre field. The shiny silvery blades of the plough turned the tired clods of earth into rich dark brown soil, which stood upright and in straight lines, waiting for the harrows to turn them into a fine crumbling seedbed for the next harvest. Seagulls, with their wings flapping, and shrieking greedily at the sight of juicy worms in the damp soil, followed the plough closely. I spread a blanket on the grass of the headland and took a picnic lunch from the basket for Tom and me. Clusters of primroses flowered around us and silver pussy willows glistened in the sun. The March wind played with the yellow lambs tails, full of pollen, swaying from the bare hazel branches. All around us hills and fields waited for more warmth to open up for yet another summer season. White fluffy clouds hastened across the blue sky and threw their shadow onto the earth below. Tom and I felt happy and content. Little Annie, snugly wrapped, was asleep in her pram beside us.

Later in the spring Tom and I were told we had to leave our little house and move into the farm house in the autumn. Bill Hallett had moved to Axminster and the big farm house stood empty. It was the obvious place for us to live, but Mullins cottage, with the oaks and green fields around us, had become dear to us. The farm house and garden were surrounded by a high brick wall and lacked the sunny aspect of our present home. I remembered the farm house with its low ceilings being dark and gloomy. I tried not to think about it for the time being. The renovation of the farm house had already begun, but we did not have much say in it. By the end of September it would be ready to move into.

Meanwhile summer lay ahead and with it the visit of my parents. At the end of May a visa was granted and on the 15th June they flew from Hamburg to Northolt airport. I could hardly contain my joy and excitement, and I cleaned and polished the house till it sparkled. Tom and I went to London to meet them. Northolt Airport in 1948 was not busy. I can't remember any crowds or queues, but I remember watching their plane come in to land out of the pink evening sky. It was not a Boeing 707, but an ordinary forty seater passenger plane. When I ran to the arrival gate I was followed by a newspaper photographer who was intrigued by my excitement, and wanted to know from Tom who I was meeting. My parents were among the first Germans after the war to visit their war-bride daughter. I had been one of the first war brides to arrive in England and was certainly the youngest – three months after my eighteenth birthday. The photographer took pictures of us and wanted to know more details, but we had no wish to get involved with any publicity. We were much too busy hugging and kissing in a good old continental fashion.

It was difficult to imagine that four years previously my parents and I had sat in our cellar, frightened by the impact of English bombs falling around us. Tom was fighting German soldiers in Normandy and my brother was in a PoW camp in Texas. Now we all sat, happy and well, in a cosy kitchen in England with the people we loved most. Thankfully we clinked our glasses of 'Schnapps' which my mother had smuggled through the customs.

My parents-in-law warmly welcomed my parents. They called them 'Mutti and Vati' and they in turn called them 'Ma and Pa'. I wondered what my father and my father-in-law would talk about, both being so different in their interests. My father, a classicist and theologian,

Tom's father, an officer and sportsman. But judging from their animated conversations they must have found plenty of topics. My mother and mother-in-law were keen gardeners, and their conversation never flagged. My parents' English was adequate, my father's better than my mother's, but with her charm she would have made herself understood in any country. On her arrival my mother had handed me a heavy parcel, which again she had somehow smuggled past the customs. I could not believe my eyes when I unwrapped a large joint of beef, a present for my brother and me from our family butcher in Lehrte. Meat in Germany and England was still rationed, so it was a very special present which we shared with Tom's parents. For supper we had German beef and English Yorkshire pudding.

Mr and Mrs Watts from Piercehay farm gave my brother a week's holiday and invited my parents to tea. They were selling the farm shortly, and my brother, who was discharged from being a PoW in April 1948, had to decide if he wanted to go back to Germany or stay in England a little longer.

The June weather was wonderful. The bluebells had faded but azaleas and rhododendrons were at their best. My father took long walks in the mornings, and mother and I fussed over little Annie, who was a cheerful and contented baby, and thrived under our constant attention.

We visited Tom's grandmother and aunts in Parkstone. My parents and my brother received the same warm welcome I had been given. We returned by ferry from Studland, through Corfe Castle and Lulworth Cove. On the road from Abbotsbury to Bridport we watched the sun set on the sea and Golden Cap.

One day we walked to the mill at the bottom of the farm. It had recently been sold by my father-in-law to an old lady who kept goats and white doves. After Annie was born she walked up the lane and presented me with two plucked pigeons. She lived on her own and kept the goats solely for company. Three places were invariably laid on the kitchen table for herself, her dead husband and dead son. Whenever I called on her I found her talking to her goats, feeding and fussing over them. There was no billy goat, so consequently no kids or milk. These were goats personified for companionship and solace in her lonely life. From under her long skirt, held up by binder twine, emerged worn out gym shoes with the big toes sticking out through a hole to relieve her gout. Once a week a metamorphosed Mrs Bartlett was driven in a taxi to

Axminster. Nobody would have recognised the old lady from the mill in her smart outfit.

When Philley Holme Mill was pulled down at the beginning of the century, the flint stones were carted up the hill to build the house Tom and I now lived in. It is said that the first Dorset Knobs were made here, but even authorised opinions vary. The hard crusty little knob is now baked in Morcombelake near Charmouth, and provided one's teeth are sound it is a must to eat with Dorset cheeses.

The frame of the large waterwheel was rusted and the cogs rotted, but we could still hear a constant sound of dripping water from the leat above, and glistening and slimy moss covered the stone walls either side of the wheel. The miller's house still stood, with a little garden and stream where brown trout hid in water weed and under stones. The horses in the summer, as they waited for the sacks of corn to be unloaded, were tied to the old walnut tree, safe from flies, which did not like the acrid smell of the tree. A shallow ford and a wobbly narrow bridge with a crooked handrail permitted a crossing to the other side of the stream. There was another watermill nearby at Sadborow. It was then still in working order. I never failed to go with Tom when he took sacks of barley to be ground for pig feed by the seventy-year-old miller, Mr Foxwell. I watched the big wheel, fed by the leat above, as with a slight groan it churned round and round setting all the different wheels inside the mill into motion. Never before had I seen a watermill. It was all new to me and so much more romantic than the windmills of North Germany.

I was proud to drive my parents in my own car, but felt they were not relaxed because I drove on the left side of the road. On our visits to Axminster my father disappeared first into the tobacconist, and for the rest of the time into a bookshop. I introduced my mother to my favourite shops, like Mr Chick, the butcher, Harris and Son, and of course Dawkins, the haberdashers. Miss Shepherd, the owner, stayed at our side throughout our visit. My mother wanted to buy a small toy for a six year old boy and could not make up her mind between a tractor and a bulldozer. When she eventually decided, she said, pointing to the bulldozer, 'I will have that bugger.' Miss Shepherd could not believe that such language came from somebody as gentle-looking as my mother. I had to explain that in Germany a bulldozer is indeed called a bugger!

I was anxious how my father would react to the kneeling and genuflecting in church. I need not have worried. He remained seated and enjoyed the sermons and the singing of the psalms. He must have looked with envy at the pulpit barely off the ground. In German churches pulpits were often twelve feet high, which presented a great problem for him with his fear of heights. I wondered if he remembered when I, four years old, saw him for the first time in the pulpit, and, frightened he might lose his balance when he leaned over and spread his arms out in blessing, stood up and shouted, 'Father, please hold tight!' (Vater, halt dich fest.)

Over cups of tea my father and the Rev. Ludlow discussed the difference between the Church of England's liturgy and the German Lutheran. They talked about Dietrich Bonhoeffer and Karl Niemoeller, whose faith never wavered when both were imprisoned during the war.

We spent one day visiting Torquay. We sat amongst the palm trees on the promenade, looking on to the shimmering sea under a blue sky, relaxed and happy, as we soaked up the early summer sun. We had our lunch in a small restaurant and were delighted when a German girl served us. We learned that she also had married an Englishman. We were even more surprised when she told us she came from Osnabrueck-Schinkel, which had been my father's parish from 1920 till 1925. When he heard her family name it turned out that her parents had been married by my father. What a small world! Fortunately the restaurant was not busy at that time and we were able to have a good chat. The German girl was happily married and loved being in Torquay. Before we left, she and my father wrote a postcard to her parents, telling them about the coincidence. The German girl and her husband visited us several times at Westhay after that.

On the last day of my parents' stay we bathed in the sea at Charmouth. It was the first time I had seen my father swimming and I was amazed what a good swimmer he was. He always disliked swimming in public pools, and we had never had a seaside holiday together.

The goodbye at Northolt Airport was a contrast to the joyful arrival. The last two weeks had been filled with glorious sunshine and with a loving family togetherness.

By the autumn the farm house was ready for us to move into. I had hoped that with the renovations a slight modernisation would also have taken place, but I was mistaken. I was glad to see the brown and dark green colour of doors and windows gone, and replaced with glossy white paint. The only other redeeming feature was a new cream-coloured Aga in the kitchen, but the sad thing was it took up all the space of the inglenook fireplace.

Over the years the kitchen had been deprived of a stone spiral staircase and a large bread oven, and now another attractive feature, the inglenook, had gone. The old flagstones had been ripped up and lay in a heap in the farmyard. The new quarry tiles were obviously easier to clean, but not nearly as appealing. A black shiny varnish covered every exposed beam in the house, though the cobb walls retained their white lime wash. The scullery, a long lean to and a couple of steps lower than the kitchen, showed no sign of a washing-up unit. An old iron pump and a stone sink stood at one end, and at the other was a large copper with a lid and an oven underneath. The flagstone floor sloped towards the window facing the yard and an opening the size of a cat flap gave constant admission to stray cats and vermin. Instead of a larder, two wooden safes hung on a wall. Three further steps down, the scullery led into the cloakroom, which was connected to the harness room and the stables.

Old and cracked lino, curling away from the walls, covered the floors of the five bedrooms upstairs. The dormer windows were small, the rooms large but dark. A long passage led to a huge freezing bathroom with a water tank in a corner. I saw cobwebs swaying in the draughts that came from cracks in the ceiling. There was the smell of hay from the loft above, and of horses from the stables below. The smell of ammonia penetrated into the linen cupboard, and I put lavender bags between sheets and pillow cases.

There was one room in the house still unrestored. It was the room I liked best. It was thirty foot long and had been roughly treated in the past and was in bad shape. Because of its size it was not a practical living space and had been a store room for motorbikes, bicycles, rabbits, ferrets, potatoes or anything else that needed a place. The room's attractive features cried out to be restored. Two massive oak upright beams supported an even larger beam in the middle of the room. Wooden shutters framed the window and a large fireplace compensated for the loss of the inglenook in the kitchen. A French door led to the garden and, together with the window, gave ample light to the big room. I was longing to restore it and turn it into our drawing room.

I was thrilled to have an Aga. It was such a joy to cook on, I almost forgave it for blocking out the inglenook. For me the Aga was the most important thing in the house. After a while a washing-up unit was installed and a small larder built. The opening in the wall was immediately done away with and no more cats and rats shared the house with us.

To my horror I discovered that all the water pipes in our house were of lead. I knew from my chemistry lessons that lead was poisonous. I urged Tom to talk to his father about it because any change in our house had to have his approval. Tom did not seem to be very concerned about the lead pipes, but I am sure he must have felt the same responsibility towards the health of our child. In the end it was I who asked my father-in-law to have the pipes changed.

Tom never liked to ask his father for anything. A slight uneasiness existed between them. There was not a trace of military manner in Tom, and his gentle and easy-going attitude often annoyed his father. I never really felt at ease with my father-in-law either. I was very fond of him and admired him, but his brusque manners, though always well meant, frightened me a little. I can't remember ever embracing, let alone kissing him, except on my first evening, when it had been a mistake. My father-in-law was a very kind man. He was Deputy Lieutenant of Devon, and chairman of numerous committees, and he took endless trouble to help wherever he could. When I voiced my concern about the lead pipes my father-in-law said that all his six children were brought up with lead pipes and they had not come to any harm. In the end Tom and I replaced the lead pipes with copper ones ourselves.

After my struggle with the oilstove, cooking on the Aga was a relief and joy, but when carrying a large and heavy saucepan of boiling water down the steps from the kitchen into the scullery, I had to be careful that little Annie was not crawling under my feet.

I was determined to make the big neglected room habitable as soon as possible, and every spare minute I scrubbed and painted, till bit by bit, after months of really hard work, it was ready to move into. Two large carpets we had bought at auctions covered the floor, which I had stained with 'darkelin', a popular black varnish at that time. Two armchairs, from the first Ideal Home Exhibition in London, looked forlorn on either side of the fireplace. An old oak refectory table from Tom's parents and the Boulle cabinet from his grandmother added a bit of style.

We had plenty of watercolours by Tom and his grandfather to hang on the walls. Jack Banfield, an excellent carpenter from the village, made bookshelves from Westhay oak along the two end walls.

On the first evening in our new drawing room, Tom and I sat in the armchairs in front of a roaring log fire, drinking a bottle of red wine. Our own small supply of wine was stored in the wine cellar of Westhay House. During the Napoleonic War French PoWs built the high brick wall surrounding Westhay garden, and laid the drainage for all the fields on the farm. Because of their skilful and precise work, the system still works, though from time to time some of the old stone pipes have to be replaced. It would be interesting to know where these prisoners were housed. They might well have stayed on the farm because Tom found a French sword hidden in the roof of the hay loft.

Admiral Domet bought Westhay House in 1797. He extended the house considerably in 1815 when he retired from the Navy. Again French prisoners built the massive vaulted ceilings of Westhay cellars. The wine cellar had neat compartments made from small bricks, for different vintages. Since the time a few years back when workmen, repairing some damage in the cellar, helped themselves to my father-in-law's best brandy, the wine cellar door was kept firmly locked. We had to ask for the key whenever we wanted to get one of our own bottles. My father-in-law kept a strict eye on our little supply of wine, and every time Tom and I asked for the key we felt like children asking for another sweet. Now we had enough space in the farm house. We moved our few bottles and enjoyed a glass of wine whenever we felt like it, and without feeling guilty.

Every day a small middle-aged woman, called Emma Froom, came with her enamel can to fetch milk from the farm. She lived in a thatched cottage which was badly in need of repair, and could only be reached on foot or in a horse and cart, via a rough track across a field and a water splash, which flooded regularly and then cut off the cottage completely. Emma's shrill voice heralded her approach from a long way away. She was not blessed with prettiness, but she had a heart of gold and was always helping people. She looked after her old and ailing mother and shared her cottage with a family of eight children, whose smallholding had been destroyed by a fire in the severe winter of 1947. I remember seeing the flames of the fire on the hill, and no fire engine was able to reach them through the deep snow. Tom and his father fetched the shivering and frightened children on the tractor and brought them to Westhay House, and later the family found a new home in Emma's cottage.

Two little girls always accompanied Emma to the farm. They had such pretty faces and loved stroking the calves. I wished I could have understood their happy chatter, but the Devon accent made it difficult. Emma realised this and she told them 'to talk proper'.

Cyril, in his seventies, lived half a mile from the farm. He also came to fetch his milk in the evenings. When he paid for his pint he took off his hat and fished for the pennies in the rim, and slowly counted them into Tom's hand. One day he needed change and Tom remembered that some money had fallen into his gumboot, through a hole in his trouser pocket. He took off his boot and gave Cyril his change. Anybody witnessing this would have shaken their head in disbelief.

All our cows had old-fashioned names like Maud, Mabel and Joan. Three lots of twins were called after London stores: Marshall and Snelgrove, Swan and Edgar, and Debenham and Freebody. Our Red Devons were beef animals and not suited for milk production. Tom had a penchant for the hardy brown and white Ayrshire cows and his aim was to have a pedigree Ayrshire dairy herd. During the first year of his farming he bought six in-calf Ayrshire heifers from Scotland. When they arrived they looked like sophisticated debutantes, in spite of their advanced pregnancies, amongst the heavy Red Devons. These six heifers were the foundation of the high yielding Ayrshire dairy herd Tom gradually built up.

The farm was mainly a dairy farm, but some pigs were reared for the market. Three cart horses did the farm work, together with a small grey Ferguson tractor. Hay was harvested once a year, as were oats for the horses and barley for the pigs. Every autumn, at the beginning of the turnip harvest, there was a knock on the door and a bearded down-and-out type of person, with a sack tied around his waist, asked for work. Everybody knew him, but this was the first time I saw him. He said his name was 'Happy'.

'Happy' had no fixed abode and had been coming to the farm for years. He slept during the autumn months in a barn in the hamlet of

Hewood nearby. Every morning he turned up at eight o'clock, whatever the weather, and worked till it was beginning to get dark, pulling up turnips and throwing them into the cart. When it rained or it got too cold, he pulled the sack over his head and continued with his work. Sometimes, when on the night before he had had too much cider, he curled up in the ditch and slept it off. Every day after work he came into the farm house kitchen for cake and mugs of tea, sweetened with six spoonfuls of sugar. He never stopped talking, but I found his broad Devon accent difficult to understand. A smile never left his face, and I knew why he was called 'Happy'. The tea sessions became more drawn out, and I had to remind him it was time for me to make the supper. When working or walking 'Happy' hummed a little tune to himself.

Happy reminded me of the many tramps who had knocked on our vicarage door in Germany. They were, however, of a different kind, not honest and hard working like Happy. If you gave them money they spent it on alcohol, and many times they walked off with the spoon or fork they were given with their food. There were a few exceptions who earned some pennies with their skill. There was the trumpeter who turned up once a year. He played the 'Blue Danube' at the farm next door but, in front of our house, he played a solemn hymn.

I loved the organ grinder with the fairground music and his little monkey in a knitted jacket sitting on his shoulder. The dancing bear caused great excitement and every time he performed crowds gathered to see the sensation. One day a boy I knew well stood too close, the bear attacked him and removed half his face. The poor boy was disfigured for life.

Beside the church in our little town stood the asylum for down-and-outs. It was a bleak small building, reeking of urine from the men's urinal next door. For me it was a place of horror. Once, as I was going past, a man stood in the doorway with his penis hanging out, and flashed me.

During the war my grandfather, to relieve my father, held short services in the asylum at Christmas, and I went with him to carry the basket my mother had filled with food. A dim bare light bulb added to the gloom of the room, but was kind in hiding the grime. About a dozen old tramps sat huddled in front of a small stove. At the last Christmas of the war the stove was stone cold. These were people without families and homes, with little food and even less faith. It must have been difficult for my grandfather to find words of comfort, but he always seemed to, handshakes and tears proved it, or were they because of the contents of my basket?

I think Happy could indeed be called happy compared with these poor men.

For my twenty first birthday Tom gave me twelve Leghorn chickens, and four young peach trees which I planted against the south-facing wall of a barn. The chickens took no notice of my calling them at feeding times. They cocked their heads and stared at me. Tom pointed out that I used the wrong language. It had never occurred to me that chickens had their own parlance and could be puzzled by my German calling of 'peele, peele'. They immediately reacted to my English 'coup, coup,' and eagerly ran towards me.

After our move I became much more involved in farm life. During the hay and corn harvest I took sandwiches, cakes and tea to the extra helping hands in the fields at lunch and tea times, and when, in the autumn, the threshing machine laboured noisily up the hill to the farm, I cooked for ten people for a week. I had the help of sixteen-year-old Lorna from the village. She was good looking after Annie, but not trained in housework or cooking.

A farm student with an enormous appetite lived with us. Three men to cook and wash for was a lot of work without a washing machine. The boiler was supposed to produce hot water, but only worked when the wind came from the north, so most of the water was heated on the Aga and had to be carried to the stone sink in the scullery. Dirty shirts and socks piled up next to nappies, and again on the Aga for drying when the weather was too wet, which it was too often. Bed linen and cord trousers I sent to the laundry once a week, together with the milking overalls. Every Friday I handed freshly laundered white milking overalls to the milkers, but before the first milking was finished, they were covered with dung.

A new cowman had taken Charlie's place. He was an ex-public school boy, the son of a bishop, and wished to be addressed as Mr Newman, and not by his Christian name by anybody on the farm. His wife (he said he had married beneath him) referred to him as Mr Newman as well. He was tall, dark and handsome, and a very efficient cowman. At home he was a tyrant and all his five children were scared of him. His two older children, a daughter and a son, also worked on our farm and meekly carried out their father's instructions. Mr Newman did not share his meals with his family in the kitchen, but insisted on a table laid for him alone in the drawing room, with a white tablecloth and napkin. I don't know if the marriage was a happy one, but Mrs Newman never complained about her husband. On the contrary, she seemed to worship him and was very proud of her father-in-law, the bishop, who was also a poet. Once in a while he sent his son one of his new poems which Mrs Newman brought secretly to show me. Handing me the new creation she proudly said, 'Mr Newman's father, the bishop, has written a new poem'. (She pronounced it 'pöm'.) They were very good poems and I enjoyed them.

The Newman family stayed with us for six years. Individually they were a lovely family, but we were relieved when they left. They must have got on each other's nerves, because one day the father, the son and daughter were chasing each other around the large manure heap in the middle of the farmyard, each brandishing a pitchfork. Had Tom not stopped them, they would have surely killed each other.

With all my new tasks I did not spend nearly enough time with my little daughter, who was walking now and had started to talk. I was longing to teach her my mother language, and Tom and I discussed if we should bring her up to be bilingual. It was I who decided against it in the end. I felt that not enough time had elapsed since the war, and that the sound of the German language might cause aggravation. I was eager to please and fit in with my new country, where everybody so far had been kind to accept me. At the same time, I worried that my still inadequate English might impede my daughter's language. Tom laughed about my doubts and, encouraged by him, I read to Annie as often as I could from the delightful books of the flower fairies and Beatrix Potter. In the months before our baby was born Tom had read Charles Kingsley's *Water Babies*, and *Winnie the Pooh* to me. In blissful childlike happiness I had listened, cuddled close to him on the sofa. I hoped that any future children of ours would be brought up bilingual, but at the moment I did not think it appropriate, except for the odd word, which I was bound to sneak in from time to time.

I admired Tom's determination to make a success of farming. It was a completely new life for him. He was trained as an artist and painting was in his blood and was what he was best at. Stoically he stuck to the unaccustomed and hard farm work and never gave in or complained. I knew how much he missed not having enough time for his art, but a sketch book and pencil were always in his pocket, and he never missed the chance of a quick sketch of whatever caught his eye. I admired his even temper and cheerfulness, and his great kindness to anything living.

The only thing that upset him was the word 'Bankmanager'. Not only did he hate anything to do with money, he was utterly hopeless with it. He would much rather give the calf to the dealer than argue about the price. I was not very good with money either but better than Tom, and so I took over the book keeping and money matters, and to start with I made a lot of mistakes.

The Dairy and the Motor Show, and the Summer Exhibition at the Royal Academy were Tom's annual trips to London. On one of these trips I tried to persuade him to buy himself a new hat. His old hat was almost fossilized with grime and a certain amount of cow dung, but it had become rather a pleasant colour and Tom was attached to it and thought it perfectly good enough to wear to London. He did however buy himself a new hat in Jermyn Street, but unfortunately he left it in the taxi neatly and expensively wrapped in tissue paper and in a smart bag. He returned wearing his old hat and I am sure he was secretly pleased he still had it!.

Tom did not like to talk about the war, but occasionally one or two stories came to light. I know that his D-Day crossing was rough. The landing was postponed for two days and there was nothing to eat except tinned salmon and Christmas pudding, with the boats bobbing up and down in the choppy water. In the defence of hill 112 Tom destroyed a German tank which had inflicted heavy casualties to his regiment. For this he was awarded the M.C. At another time when directing his guns onto German Artillery he saw a group of French children walking towards the German guns. He halted the firing, because he could not bring himself to endanger the children. Near Liége he was wounded in both legs.

Tom told us when the Red Cross truck picked him up after he got shot in the legs, it was already full of wounded men. His stretcher was fastened onto the roof of the truck next to a soldier from the enemy line. An extraordinary conversation took place between the two. Tom being Tom started up a conversation with his wounded companion. In broken English Tom was told that the soldier's home was Kitzbuehl in Austria and his father was a ski instructor at Schloss Kaps. Tom replied that that was exactly where he had left his skis six years before to be repaired, but the war had prevented him from collecting them. In their vulnerable situation on top of the truck and amidst artillery fire, Tom was assured that his skis stood in a shed at Schloss Kaps with a label tied to them saying: 'Belong to Englishman'. Before Tom was demobbed he fetched his skis. By then the young Austrian had also recovered from his wounds and was back home. Their second meeting took place in a more comfortable and peaceful situation.

Tom recovered from his wounds in time to take part in the surrender of Bremen in North Germany. He loved describing the Hogarthian scene of British soldiers lying comatose under the open taps of the wine barrels in the cellars of this old Hansa city. He confiscated a smart sailing boat from the sailing club in Bremen and used it throughout his time in Germany on the Steinhuder Meer and the Dummer See, but after he got demobbed he returned it to the club in Bremen, probably the only British soldier who ever returned anything confiscated. Tom liked to boast that I was his only bit of loot from Germany!

Tom's working hours on the farm increased, and there was not much time for leisure after supper. I still had not made any friends of my own age, and I felt tired and often weepy. Tom encouraged me to talk to his mother and sisters, when they were at home, but I found it difficult to talk to them about anything personal. Tom realised that he and I did not spend enough time together, and he thought he had found the solution by getting a horse for me. There had always been a horse for Tom, who was a good rider with an excellent knowledge of anatomy of horses. Before the war he had illustrated a book called, *Two lost on Dartmoor* with delightful drawings of ponies and children. I loved horses but they did not reciprocate my love, and sensed my fear of them. Tom had taught me to ride in Germany and I felt fairly confident about that, but I was never a good or keen rider. Tom promised that my horse, which was called Stodge, was a very docile creature. Indeed, when I saw it I was reassured by its enormous girth and placid manners.

When I appeared in the riding breeches, which had arrived in the parcel from America, Tom and his father threw up their hands in horror. My American outfit was totally unacceptable. The breeches made my hips stand out like large elephant's ears, and the jacket was not the right shape either. A pair of foxy coloured jodhpurs and an old tweed jacket, both Tom's, were sent off to be altered for me, so that in future I would not be an embarrassment, even if it was just for the odd ride in the lanes. The horse, Stodge, knew from the moment I mounted him that I was scared. Suddenly, cantering across a field with Tom, the horse stumbled and turned a somersault. Luckily I escaped his bulk and was not hurt, but it did not add to my confidence in horses. All the same, Tom and I had some good rides together and it made a pleasant change for both of us.

Among the books on our new bookshelves were three novels by the Canadian writer, Mazo de la Roche. In 1937 she had rented the old rectory in Hawchurch for a year and during that time wrote the book, *Under a Norman Tower*. She wrote of the church and the congregation and of the unfortunate weather vane on the church roof, which never managed to predict the wind correctly. The rector, fed up with this useless bird, saved his last cartridge and had a crack at him every time he came back from a shoot and passed the church. Mazo de la Roche was best known for her *Jalna Novels*, a chronicle of a close-knit Canadian family with the red headed and hot blooded Renny as the main character. I defy anybody who has read these novels not to have fallen in love with the handsome Renny.

During her stay in Hawkchurch, Mazo and my parents-in-law became great friends. For a number of years a large tin of Maple syrup arrived at Westhay every Christmas.

One afternoon Tom, Annie and I had tea in the 'Mad Hatter' in Lyme Regis. Next to us two slim and elegant looking women with Canadian accents chatted over their cream tea. A quiet youth of about sixteen sat next to them. When Annie dropped her biscuit onto the floor and Tom, in picking it up, upset the milk jug on our table, both women jumped up and helped with the mopping up. Later that day, while I was giving Annie her bath, my mother-in-law walked into the bathroom with some guests she had asked to supper. She wanted to show them her first grandchild. They were the same two women we had sat next to in the 'Mad Hatter', who were no other than Mazo de la Roche and her friend, and Mazo's adopted son Renny. During the time Mazo de la Roche had rented the old rectory in Hawkchurch, Tom had been at the Slade in London so they had not met before. She insisted on bathing Annie, and kneeling beside the bath blew soap bubbles through her fingers, to Annie's delight. The boy Renny stood awkwardly aside. He showed every promise of turning out as handsome as the Renny in the *Jalna* novels.

Soon after my arrival at Westhay, I noted on a walk through the garden a row of mysterious white objects in a secluded part under a tall yew hedge. My first thought was, 'My God, it's a graveyard for pets'. On closer inspection I could not see any inscriptions on the little wooden structures, which were made up of several frames on top of each other. It was wintertime and an eerie feel enclosed this dark small corner of the garden. How they laughed when I told them about my suspicion of a burial ground, when in fact they were beehives. The beehives I knew from Germany were plaited straw cloches, and stood on shelves under low roofs. I had seen our neighbour, an old man with a long white beard, standing in front of his hives, smoking his pipe, but without any other protection. Every autumn we bought two buckets of golden delicious honey from him.

My great aunt, Helene Artemise, abhorred honey, and watching me spooning lashings of it onto a crisp bread roll, told me, a six year old, that honey was Bienen Be-Be (bee-shit). I did not like Aunt Helene and she in turn did not like children, and lavished all her love on animals instead. She was brought up on an isolated farm near the banks of the river Elbe, the only girl amongst four brothers. When her brothers left for boarding school she was left without any playmates, and her various pets became her constant companions.

After her parents died she, a spinster, went to live in a Damenstift (home for gentlewomen) in Hanover next to the zoo. She spent most of her money on animal charities and during the war bought food for the animals in the zoo, because she was convinced that they were starving. During one of the air raids on Hanover her home was hit. A few of the residents' belongings were rescued from the burning house and my aunt was put in charge of guarding them, but hearing the plaintive cries from the injured animals in the zoo, she deserted her post to help them. The suitcases and everything that had been rescued were stolen and my aunt received a hostile reception when she returned.

She was eighty-five-years old and all on her own. We were not able to have her with us because our house was full of refugees, but eventually my parents found a room for her in Hanover. My aunt spent the last two years of her life as a recluse in a shabby attic room. She spurned the air raid shelters, in spite of heavy and continuous bombing on the city, and refused to have her room cleaned. My mother and I visited her whenever we could, and took her fruit and fresh vegetables from the garden. She cut up the vegetables and fed them to her birds and hamsters, who shared the room with her. Bird seed littered the floor and we were tempted to protect our noses from the smell of the cages. My aunt died amongst her beloved animals. On a November day in 1944, my parents and I, the only mourners, followed her coffin in a hurried funeral that was interrupted by sirens. Her only surviving brother, my grandfather, was too old to travel. He lived at that time on the isolated farm where both had spent their childhood.

My father-in-law offered me his six beehives. After years of handling his bees he had become allergic to their stings. I jumped at the offer. I thought beekeeping romantic and mysterious. I soon thought differently. Westhay bees were particularly vicious and became angry with the slightest disturbance, but for many years I looked after the hives and extracted the golden liquid from the frames in the autumn. The old and cumbersome extractor leaked the precious honey onto the kitchen floor, and my barefooted children licked their sticky fingers and got their feet stuck on the honey-sweetened floor tiles.

I was totally ignorant of beekeeping, but a local beekeeper helped and taught me. My instructor had plenty of amusing and alarming beekeeping anecdotes to tell. Unfortunately he was also a bit creepy, and had the nasty habit of coming too close to me when telling his stories. Sitting next to him in church one Sunday, he got hold of my hand and firmly held on to it throughout the service. When attending to the bees he whispered endearing words to them and to me, but apart from this he was a good teacher.

My parents were now acquainted with my new surroundings and could visualise the places and people I wrote about in my weekly letters. They in turn told me what went on in my old home town and what was happening in Germany in general.

Vast changes were taking place in Germany all the time. The Marshall Plan worked well and huge amounts of aid (in money) flowed into the country. But it needed to be controlled. The black market kept on growing, and something had to be done to stop the galloping inflation. The Reichsmark was abolished and the Deutschmark introduced. A miracle happened overnight. Shops suddenly were full of goods Germany had not seen since the beginning of the war. The black market was finished. The average wage for a German was 200 Deutschmarks a month, and people were happy to know what the money they earned was worth.

The Russians responded to the new currency with hostility, and refused to accept the Deutschmark in the Russian sector of Berlin. They stopped all traffic on roads, rail and rivers from the west, and West Berlin became an island under siege. After a brief euphoric period with the introduction of the new currency and the disappearance of the black market, West Berlin was once again thrown into extreme hardship, which could have ended in utter disaster, but for the airlift of American and British planes. Between June 1948 and September 1949 food, medicines and coal were flown in day and night to West Berlin. The inhabitants, who used to dread the drone of enemy aircraft over their city during the war, now welcomed the sound of every aircraft bringing relief and life-saving supplies. Unfortunately a lot of goods from the air supplies were stolen, and ended up on the black market once again.

The Berlin airlift continued for over a year, and nearly three hundred thousand flights saved the Berliners from starvation. When the blockade finally stopped and the shops were full of food and clothes, West Berlin could once more join West Germany in enjoying a better and more normal life. East Berlin and East Germany remained under strict control of the Soviet Union.

In the late autumn of 1950 I visited my parents in Germany with my little daughter. Four years had passed since my leaving for England. I flew to Hamburg, where I briefly met my eighty-four year old grandmother from Schleswig Holstein. She was so pleased to hold her first great grandchild on her lap.

Our rectory was almost back to normal with only one refugee family left, and my grandfather and Tante Krueger as permanent guests. Tante Krueger, with her rotund figure, was as loving and cuddly as ever, but my grandfather was more frail than when I had last seen him. Little Annie was fascinated by his pince-nez, and tried to pull it off his face.

My old bedroom was newly decorated and my childhood cot, with its brass knobs, stood beside my bed for Annie. The garden looked as beautiful as ever, with colourful autumn flowers and the leaves of the vine on the house were turning red. The lawn was freshly rolled and mown, the rabbit cages and chicken coops gone. The large bomb crater opposite the entrance to our house was filled in and grassed over. Gone also was the clatter of thick wooden soles of wartime shoes, and soft and colourful jumpers had replaced the knitwear made from the coarse yarn of stolen sugar beet sacks during the war.

Almost everything that had been damaged by the war was repaired and newly painted. The larder was full of delicious food, and I was spoilt with my favourite dishes I had been pining for, like Frankfurters with sauerkraut and asparagus and schinken (ham). It was good to be home.

Annie played happily with my old dolls and toys, and took possession at mealtimes of the high chair, which had served eight of my grandmother's children, and my brother and me. Everybody said I had changed. I had lost weight and my long hair was now shoulder length. My shorter hair did not meet with the approval of Tom or my parents, but I had never liked my hair long and decided one day, when shopping in Axminster, to have it cut by Mr Luff, the local hairdresser.

Nearly all the bomb damage our small town had suffered had been replaced by new shops and houses. I was amazed how much had been achieved in the last four years. My mother and I went shopping in Hanover. More than half the city was destroyed during the war, but most of the rubble was cleared, and prosperous and luxurious shops displayed tempting but expensive goods. The patrician houses on the Marktplatz, which had looked like ghosts in their black burnt-out shells, were accurately rebuilt to their former medieval grandeur. Somewhere in amongst the cleared rubble lay a beautiful diamond studded little golden watch, a present from my grandmother to me. A goldsmith on the Marktplatz was engraving my name onto it when the incendiary bomb struck.

We finished our shopping with a delicious cream cake, the first of its kind I had tasted since the beginning of the war, and a hot chocolate in the popular 'Kakao Stube' which, though newly rebuilt, had the same smell and atmosphere and schmalz music as the original one.

I witnessed a great change for the better wherever I went. The German people themselves had taken on a new lease of life. The years immediately after the war had been Germany's worst. Food and housing shortages, and family separations through bombing and escaping from the advancing Russian army, and the disclosure of the atrocities in the concentration camps had brought more misery and low morale to the German people than the war itself. With help from Britain and America, West Germany was now able to help herself. Driven by enthusiasm and necessity, rebuilding what the war had destroyed took place at an astonishing pace, and the Germans showed a positive and cheerful attitude towards the future.

I was proud to show my daughter off to all my friends. Annie, of course, could not understand the language, but it did not seem to worry her. Everybody spoilt her. The butcher gave her a slice of smoked sausage, the baker a biscuit, and the grocer a bonbon. She delighted them by saying, 'Danke schoen', one of the words I had taught her, so far.

Most of my old class mates were at university or had jobs. I missed Gabi most of all, but visited her family, who were as welcoming as ever. Lotti, who had tried to improve my English before I left, had married again. Her new husband had lost his entire family in a concentration camp, and Lotti had lost her husband and only child during the war. It was good to see her build her life again.

Our neighbour, Oma Thiele, had died. When I stood in front of the window through which I had climbed many times to share their lunch, I saw in my mind Oma Thiele sitting at her spinning wheel, with her glasses half-way down her nose, and her sick husband, sitting on the shabby black sofa, staring aimlessly in front of him.

One of the largest and smartest farmhouses in the village now stood empty. Tragedy had struck right at the end of the war when the couple's sixteen-year-old son, their only child, was forced to join the Volkssturm, Hitler's last and ludicrous attempt to save Germany, made up of sixty year old men and school boys. The unnecessary death of the boy, two days before the end of the war unbalanced both parents. The father shot himself and the mother was in a mental hospital. The farm, for generations in the same family, was on the market.

Lying in bed at night, in my old familiar bedroom, which had been mine for nearly eighteen years, I felt a long way from the thatched farmhouse in Devon, and the walled garden with the shrubs and trees I had planted. People and places I had begun to love seemed like a dream, which partly still hovered in front of me, partly dissolved into the distance. But the nagging homesickness had gone, because I was at home. I snuggled deeper into the softness of my bed. I felt secure and comforted, and would have gone to sleep blissfully, were it not for the longing and love I had experienced in the last four years. I missed Tom and could not imagine anymore a life without him. At the same time I wanted to stay right here. I realised that, unless I took a firm grip on my homesickness, my life would be divided for ever. I stretched out my arm towards the cot and stroked my sleeping daughter's soft hair. I was aware of my blessings. I was determined to shake off whatever was hindering me from giving my all to my child and husband. I remembered the comforting and encouraging words Mrs Hayball had said to me in the village shop, 'It takes a bit of time, my dear'. A little time had passed, it should not take all that much longer.

My father was advised by his doctor to take early retirement, and my parents decided to move closer to Hanover and into a much smaller house. It was obvious that they could not take all their furniture with them. We enquired if it was possible to ship furniture to England, and, yes it was. I was thrilled that soon some of the old familiar furniture would find, like me, a new home in our farmhouse, and we would keep each other company.

I loved the cheerful and diverse sound of English church bells, but the deep melodious and resonant German bells made me want to rejoice and weep at the same time, and hearing the bells from the old village church did not make my departure any easier. Again I cannot write about saying goodbye, without remembering the trembling hands my old grandfather put in blessing on little Annie's head. Knowing it would be the last time we would see each other, still makes me want to cry.

I had put four acorns from the oak tree in our yard into a small box to plant in Westhay soil on my return. I hoped that one of the acorns would eventually grow into a strong oak tree, and wondered if it would be the first German oak in the Devon landscape.

Just before Christmas, in 1950, my brother went back to Germany. He had decided to study agriculture and was to start his course at the beginning of the new year. I missed his company and Annie missed her uncle who gave her piggybacks and rides on his motorbike. Before he left, Tom and I borrowed his motorbike to get us to a supper party in Seaton because our car refused to start. It did not have a passenger seat, so we tied a cushion onto the back mudguard. It was very uncomfortable but the ride only took twenty minutes so it was bearable. Our makeshift, and illegal, seat was discovered by the police, and we were summoned to appear at the magistrates' court in Axminster a couple of weeks later. Unfortunately my father-in-law presided as a J.P. and was not amused to see us breaking the law. We were fined £30, but my father-in-law's reprimand was worse than the penalty. We were indeed sorry to have given him that embarrassment.

Our farm student, Stephen, was a nice young man but he caused us a bit of trouble. His recently acquired terrier, Toby, was ruining my new honeycomb woollen blankets. After digging all day for rabbits and rolling in and eating disgusting cow cleanings, the dog ran straight upstairs and slept it off on his master's bed. When I tried to chase him off he growled and bared his teeth at me, and Stephen, besotted by his dog, did not try hard enough to control him. From Stephen's first day on the farm Percy Hallett took a dislike to him. Arrogantly Stephen had called him 'Hallett', which Tom soon put right, but Percy did not forget. The cart horses had sadly been sold in 1949 and another Ferguson tractor was bought instead. Both tractors were the pride and joy of Percy H. But of course the student had to drive too, Percy did not approve. Stephen drove well but too fast, and dismantled the stone gate post at the entrance to the farm, to Percy's glee and satisfaction. The gate post was repaired by Percy himself, only to be knocked down again by Stephen's erratic driving a couple of days later. Percy was convinced he had done it on purpose, and a kind of civil war broke out between them. Percy's black mood affected the whole of the farm. He knew he was invaluable, and, when Stephen became engaged to Tom's sister Hazel soon afterwards, his mood dropped to its lowest and we feared he might hand in his notice.

However, Percy Hallett and Stephen made peace eventually, but unfortunately the engagement did not last and a new farm student took Stephen's place.

Over the years a number of students worked on the farm, mostly Germans who wanted to improve their English. Some of them were farmers' sons with some experience in farming. All of them were hard-working and conscientious, but the downside was their enormous appetite. Having got upset over Stephen's little terrier sleeping on his bed, I was aghast when the next farm student produced a large Pyrenean mountain dog. This time I was firm, and this big but beautiful animal was restricted to the cloakroom.

Another student was fascinated with chickens. We called him 'Chicken Heiner'. When a clutch of chicken eggs were deserted by the sitting hen just before hatching, he transported them to his bed and miraculously three of them hatched and he successfully nurtured them in his bedroom till they were old enough to fend for themselves.

Bernd, a giant of six foot six, was a sad looking young man with a nervous twitch. He loved his puddings and I can still hear him say 'More pudding please', as he asked for his third helping. Sadly one day a sweet little kitten got squashed under his heavy, large-sized gumboots. The children and Bernd were in tears and I found it harder to console the sensitive and sobbing young man than my children.

Dieter was a student from Berlin and had never seen a calf being born. When his chance came, I drove him in the truck to the field where Tom was assisting a cow with a difficult birth. Dieter looked in horror at the blood and slime of the cow's backside and the next minute he passed out and was lying in the grass beside us. We heaved him into the truck and drove him back to the farm and revived him with some brandy.

Years later quite a few of the farm students, now married and with families, visited us and we recalled many funny stories of their student days at Westhay.

For thirty years the carthorses had been in George Amor's care and he must have missed them when they were made redundant. He was now seventy-years-old and smaller and more frail than ever. His retirement seemed appropriate. He performed an astonishingly agile broomstick dance at a farewell party we gave for him and got very merry on too much cider. Sadly his retirement was short lived. Late one evening, when Tom was checking on his cows in the field, he saw some of them gathered around a small bundle lying in the grass. It was George Amor on his way home from the pub, unconscious and barely alive. Tom carried him to his cottage but before he could explain to Mrs Amor that her husband was seriously ill, she started to beat him with the broomstick. Quite a few blows fell on Tom's shoulders too, as he carried the unfortunate husband up the narrow rickety stairs to his bed. Mr Amor died that night. The grass started to grow over his well trodden path to the pub and before long there was no trace left of it.

Of all the farm staff I liked Ted Smith, or Smithy as he was called, the best. As I have said before, he was the only one on the farm who showed an interest in the country I was brought up in and who wanted to know about the German farming methods. Eagerly and gladly I told him about Heinrich's farm next to our rectory and how, as a child, I used to peel off the dried dung from the cows' backsides on Gabi's farm. Smithy, with the help of another cowman, milked the cows twice a day except on his day off. The milking machines were sterilized every day, and once a week the lining of the milking clusters had to be changed. This was a tedious job, the new rubber liners were stiff and needed nimble and strong fingers. Smithy's finger joints were already slightly arthritic, and he was glad of any assistance. I looked forward to helping him. He had a great sense of humour and a very infectious laugh and lots of amusing tales to tell. He loved singing though his voice was not good, but the excellent acoustics of the dairy helped, and I loved listening to his ditties like, 'Lavender's blue, dilly, dilly, lavender's green, when I am king dilly, dilly, you will be queen.'

Once a month young calves and occasionally a cow were taken by cattle lorry to Yeovil market about twenty miles away. It was Smithy's responsibility to be present at the auction and clean the animals before they entered the ring. As Smithy did not drive, I combined these market days with shopping in Yeovil, a much bigger town than Axminster. I dropped him off at the market with buckets and brushes and soap, and whilst I shopped he cleaned the animals and shampooed and combed their tails. The market started early and by lunch time the animals were sold. Smithy was very attached to his cows and sometimes he was upset when a favourite was sold, but more often he was relieved when a particularly troublesome cow with a vicious habit of kicking off the milking sets was got rid of, like 'Hitler' and 'Satan', who both fetched more than the expected price.

On our way home we stopped the car on Hamdon Hill and ate the pasties I had bought in Yeovil. The view down into the flat Somerset landscape below was fabulous. Smithy told me the names of the villages below us; Norton-sub-Hamdon, Stoke-sub-Hamdon and Merriott in the distance, with the typical tall and slim Somerset church towers rising in their midst. The unaccustomed small bottle of beer at lunchtime made Smithy sleepy and invariably he nodded off on the way home.

After the carthorses were sold the harness room was hardly ever used, which was a pity, because it was a large, sunny room with a big window and pinewood panelling. Most of the harness had gone with the horses, though some girths and reins were still hanging from the wooden arms sticking out from the walls, but the leather lacked the softness and shine of George Amor's care. On the wide oak seat under the window I had found a box full of horse brasses with intricate designs. I polished some of them and hung them on the oak beam above the Aga in the kitchen. On one of the breastplates was a brass replica of King Edward VII with a crown either side. In a pine cupboard brushes and curry combs and saddle soaps were neatly arranged from Mr Amor's days.

The medicine cupboard next to it was a mess. It mainly contained medicine for the cows and was a jumble of old jars and bottles with smudgy labels, which read: the lotion, the ointment, the tablets, but never indicated for which ailment or treatment. Smithy and I decided to clear the cupboard out. Some of the bottles and jars we cleaned (after emptying) were so old that they qualified as antiques. We had a good laugh about the rusted instruments we found, like the ancient castration crusher and the elaborate and alarmingly large syringe for enemas. One useful tool amongst all the broken and out of date ones was the still intact trocar and cannula, a most useful gadget to save bloated cows. Only a short while ago I had watched Tom when he had pushed the dagger-like instrument into a bloated cow not far from the hip bone. As soon as it penetrated the skin, the trocar was pulled out of the cannula and the gas escaped. Many a cow has been saved this way, but it does need some strength and skill to perform this operation.

Smithy and I were proud of our newly organized medicine cupboard with efficiently labelled bottles and jars and sterilized tools (for the time being). Sadly Smithy developed heart trouble in his early sixties and had to give up farmwork. Not given to idleness, he took up basket making from willows grown in the Westhay willow garden. For a few more years he was happy making all sorts of useful baskets in the stables of Westhay House. My sister-in-law Virginia found him slumped over his work one day. He had suffered a fatal heart attack. He was sadly missed by many of us.

In my childhood, winter was my favourite season. The same melancholic feeling which befalls some people when summer turns into autumn, I experienced when the first grass appeared under the melting snow and my winter paradise of skating and tobogganing had come to an end for the next nine months.

Since living in England I disliked the dark wet winters. I felt sorry for anybody who had to work in the constant damp and foggy weather. I felt particularly sorry for the postman, Leonard Hayball, from Hawkchurch who, every morning except Sundays, walked ten miles a day to deliver post within the parish, whatever the weather, the week before Christmas this included an extra round in the afternoons. On a particularly nasty day I had offered him a cup of coffee which he gratefully accepted, and from then on it had become a daily habit, come rain or shine. On some days his delivery of letters could be very early, and many a time was I woken up (Tom was already milking at that time) by Leonard's loud shout half way up the stairs of 'Anybody in?' Coming down in my dressing gown and half asleep I would find him sitting at the kitchen table, with a puddle of water at his feet from his dripping oilskin cape on a rainy day, waiting for his coffee. This went on for a number of years till his retirement. Leonard was a keen bell-ringer and his good tenor voice was very evident in the small Hawkchurch church choir.

On 17th September, in 1951, our second daughter was born. We named her Ethelinde Jane and called her Janie. I had been disappointed when my parents, because of my father's ill health, had to cancel their visit to us in the summer. Instead they spent a few weeks in the Harz Mountains which improved my father's health, and my mother was able to come over for the birth. I had the baby at home. Again it was an easy birth, assisted by Dr Morton and the village midwife. Janie was a gorgeous and healthy baby with large dark eyes and masses of hair. This time I could hold my baby as often and as long as I liked, and our household was happy and relaxed without a bossy midwife like the last time.

My mother had intended to stay for four weeks, but after two weeks a telegram summoned her back because my father was unwell again. It had been so comforting to have her with us. Her sudden departure and my father's illness upset me, also I was disappointed at once again being unable to breast-feed my baby. Painful boils on my breasts and arms plagued me, and anaemia made me feel constantly tired. Janie was a contented baby and only cried when she was hungry. Annie was thrilled and gentle with her new sister and was not a bit jealous. I struggled with my various household tasks and was beginning to feel depressed and despondent. My mother-in-law said I was having post natal depression which apparently was quite common, but I had never heard of it. It was different from being homesick, and much worse. I could not see the reason why I should be depressed at all with two beautiful children and a loving husband. I tried to think of all the wonderful things I was blessed with, but it did not lessen the unhappiness and hopelessness descending more and more on my mind and body. Frequently I burst into tears for no reason at all, and Annie, seeing me cry, said one day, 'Mummy, have you got a hurt?' I wished I had a definite pain instead of the constant and oppressive black mood I found myself succumbing to. I took long rests in the afternoon when Lorna looked after the children, but the short and dark November and December afternoons did nothing to help me want to get up again. Tom became worried about my depression but was reassured by his mother that it was a passing condition and normal after a birth. I did not look at it in that way and started to worry that there was something fundamentally wrong with me.

I was longing to talk with Tom about my anxieties and emotions, but I knew that talking about health and very personal matters was taboo. I lacked the English stiff upper lip and was ashamed that I was not able to pull myself together, so I kept everything bottled up. I did not tell Tom about my frequent nightmares of reliving life-threatening and fearful moments of the war, which up till then I had been able to shut out of my mind. But now they occurred again and again, and as vivid as ever. The sound of hundreds of German soldiers shuffling, tired and disillusioned, towards a PoW camp in May 1945 would not leave me. I was haunted again by the complete silence that had lain over the long column, and the haggard faces of our soldiers. I again saw the charred bodies of bomb victims in front of me, and the urge to get out of the confined space of our small cellar seemed to suffocate me.

It was near Christmas and I was completely unprepared. It weighed on my mind that I had not done anything about the customary Christmas presents for the farm families. I had focused all my mental and physical energy on making a tiny dolls house for Annie and writing a letter of pretend cheerfulness to my parents. I can honestly say that one of the worst moments of my life was lying on my bed the day before Christmas in the semi-darkness of the afternoon, hearing the front door close and the crunch of the pram wheels on the gravel below the bedroom window. I knew that my mother-in-law was taking my children to Westhay House because I could not look after them any more. I felt utterly bereaved and deserted. I hated everybody and I wanted to die.

In 1951 drugs to help with post natal depression did not exist. Instead electric shock treatment was used in severe cases. My parents-in-law and Tom took the advice of a psychiatrist, not our family doctor, and decided I should have this treatment. I had no idea what it involved and nothing was explained to me. I remember this treatment in Axminster hospital as something horrific and frightening, and still can't believe I was submitted to it.

Recovering from my first and only shock treatment I remember Tom sitting beside my bed holding my hand, and on the bedside table stood a small jar of the first primroses he had picked for me. Later that day our own doctor, Dr Morton, came to see me. I pleaded with him not to let me undergo another of these terrifying treatments, and he promised that I would not have to. He had not been in favour of it in the first place, he told me. He was like a kind and loving father to me, and I poured out all my gloomy thoughts and anxieties to him. He listened and explained, and reassured me that my jumbled thoughts, cluttered with all the new impressions of the last four years, would sort themselves out and that the balance of my hormones would soon be normal again. I clung to his comforting words. But there was something else he comforted me with. It was faith.

I had never talked to Tom about religion. I had been brought up with it and it was close to my heart. Since I came to England going to church had become more of a custom and not something I needed. Arthur Morton was not only a good physician, he was also a man of faith. Next to me sat a man, my father's age, who folded his hands over mine and said a silent prayer. His sincerity and concern touched me deeply. In him I had found a friend I could trust and confide in till his death many years later.

I went back to the farm the next day and gradually I was able to look after Tom and the children. A strong dose of vitamins and a bottle of Sanatogen, recommended by the handsome chemist MacNamara in Axminster, soon got rid of my boils and put new energy into me. My mother-in-law had been helpful and understanding during my postnatal depression and Tom's sister Hazel had lovingly looked after Annie and Janie. A pretty girl from Hawkchurch called Marion came to help me in the house and with the children, because Lorna wanted to go to college. Complete recovery did not come overnight, but spring lay ahead and with a constant effort and Tom's patience every day brought a slight improvement till I felt my cheerful self again.

At the end of March a large van arrived with furniture from my parents, each piece carefully wrapped in sacking and enclosed with wood. I was touched by their generosity and by the hard work and planning that must have been involved with the shipping. Everything arrived unbroken and without a scratch.

Two large boxes from our attic came with the furniture. They were lined with pages and pages, in my father's handwriting, from his exercise books in Greek and Hebrew. I remember how puzzled I had been when, as a child, I had stared at these peculiar letters and dots. These same boxes, filled with books, had accompanied my father to his universities in Tuebingen, Breslau and Koenigsberg, and later they had protected duvets and blankets from moths in the summer months in the attic of our house in Lehrte. I could still detect the smell of camphor and mothballs as I unwrapped the gold and white bone china dinner service, which my mother had carefully wrapped in tissue paper and blankets, and the green and white Austrian pottery which had been given to my grandfather by the Duke of Cumberland whose children he tutored in Gmunden.

I dusted and polished each piece of furniture and we placed it first here and then there till we found the right place for it. My favourite was the oak dining table. It had been in our nursery in Lehrte, and before that my father and his seven siblings had left their ink stains and carved their initials into the rim of the thick oak top, and I recognized the deep cuts my fretsaw had made when the blade had slipped and became embedded in the oak. My father's mother, shortly after her marriage, had the oak table copied from a table she had seen and liked in a painting, and now it stood together with eight heart-shaped oak chairs in our farmhouse kitchen. We hung the lampshade from our nursery above the kitchen table over which it had hung ever since I could remember. It was no ordinary shade and it was not of any value, but I treasured it. Twelve panels of intricate fretwork depicted stars, birds, moons and suns, and the light inside the shade made the shadows dance on the white ceiling above. It was an unusual lampshade and many visitors remarked on it and admired it. A young man from my father's parish had given it to my brother and me, though originally my parents had commissioned the work. The young man said that it had given him so much pleasure to make he did not want any payment. Sadly he died of tuberculosis at an early age.

It was comforting for me to see these familiar childhood pieces mingle with our own few pieces of furniture. They were part of me, of my parents and grandparents, and would become part of our children too. My father was retiring in two months' time. It was incomprehensible to me that my last visit had been my final one to the beloved home of my childhood and that our lovely house in Lehrte and the garden would soon be a world of the past, but it would be cherished in my mind for ever.

Tom and I passed our love for picnics on to Annie who was as eager as we were to go on our outings. One of our favourite places was Lambert's Castle, a Celtic hill fort not far from the coast at Charmouth. In spring the beeches and oaks, interspersed with larches on the northern slope of the oblong hill, resembled a patchwork quilt in exquisite shades of various greens. The fort's plateau was closely cropped by sheep and rabbits, and sometimes a young bullock jumped up from behind a gorse bush. Apart from the occasional thorn trees, crippled and lopsided from the east wind, the top of the hill was completely bare.

To the south the sea, only a couple of miles away, shimmered like a sheet of aluminium in the sun. On a dull day the sea and the horizon merged into one infinite grey distance. The view to the east revealed the vast basin of the Marshwood Vale, with Portland Bill clearly visible in the distance on a good day. Strips of woodland with primeval oaks interrupted the vivid green of luscious pastures embedding isolated farmsteads. The noise of traffic was completely absent. Instead an almost biblical tranquility spread over the vale. The only sound reaching the summit was the bleating from some lambs, the occasional bark of a dog, and the mewing from buzzards circling high above one minute and swooping down onto their prey the next. I wondered if all these fields had names. I was fascinated by the names of our own fields like Mullins, Westhay Platts, Cowliss, Rick Field, Little Ashes and London (the furthest field from the farm, the closest to London) and many more.

From 1709 horse racing took place on Lambert's Castle once a year. The old racetrack is still clearly visible .Another popular event was the yearly fair on Wednesdays. It attracted people from far away, gypsies included. Sadly no more races or fairs are held, but Lambert's Castle is still a favoured picnic place, and the ditches of the three remaining ramparts give wonderful shelter when the wind comes from the east.

Witchcraft and folklore and secret recipes of blue vinney cheese and cider are closely connected with the Marshwood Vale. The shrine of St Candida in Whitchurch Canonicorum with its healing powers attracts visitors to this day. Shave Cross Inn, where monks shaved their heads on pilgrimage to the shrine, serves blue vinney cheese made on farms in the Vale, and strong local cider from Tom Putt apples, Morgan Sweets and Black Kingstons. People live to a ripe old age in the Vale. Friends of ours were told by a couple they bought their eggs from not to collect them on Thursday evenings because that was their 'Love Night' (they were both over eighty).

There were good and bad witches in the Marshwood Vale. A few good ones still charm away warts on men and beasts, but the bad ones have had their day (to my knowledge). The last died about forty years ago. She was frequently seen squatting in the middle of a lane peeing, her long black skirt pulled up over her knobbly knees with one hand, the other holding a stick to support her. Cars stopped and walkers gasped in disbelief. Anybody disagreeing with what she was doing had a curse put upon them. She lived in a cottage below Lambert's Castle, which was fittingly crooked.

Thomas Hardy wrote that he witnessed as a boy the last public hanging in England at Birdsmoor Gate near Marshwood of a woman who had murdered her husband.

A few of the larger houses in the Vale were clearly visible from the top of the hill. There was the red brick house of Marshwood Manor, surrounded in spring by meadows full of wild daffodils, closely guarded by the owner from pilfering gypsies who, a couple of years ago, had stripped an entire field of its blooms in one night.

There was Bettiscombe Manor, also visible, with the screaming skull that had found peace in the library of the Manor, and Pilsdon Manor at the foot of Pilsdon Pen, the highest hill in Dorset, lived in by an American gin-drinking couple who I had met at Lady Pinney's tea party. Mrs J, shivering in the freezing dining room, wrapped in a large mink coat, chain smoking, had complained about the 'awesome English winters'.

The highlight of every spring on the farm was the day the cows were put out to grass. This year the unusual dry but mild weather had delayed the grass from growing and the cows had become restless and dissatisfied with the winter feed. The last few days had brought warm rain and the grass had grown. Brilliant sunshine and a clear blue sky started the day of 13th April 1952, when Tom decided the cows could go out at last, it also happened to be his birthday.

The warm rain had made all spring promises come true. It had thrown a white veil over the hawthorns and released the tiny candle-like flower from the tight and sticky grip of the brown bud of the chestnuts. Young leaves on shrubs and trees nurtured by the recent rain had visibly increased in size. An earthy vapour rose from the damp warm soil and the cows picked up the scent of fresh grass as they stood at the gate of the farmyard, sniffing the air with their heads raised and champing to get out. Their mooing became louder and more demanding as they pushed against the gate, which could have broken had Tom not let them out in time. Everybody watching, for it was a sight not to be missed, stood well back from the cows as they charged out of the yard and raced down the lane, shuffling and pushing each other to get there first, their udders swinging from side to side. As soon as they reached the field they cavorted across it with their tails in the air, bellowing and farting loudly, and kicking with their hind legs like frisky horses. Some knelt on the grass and greedily tore at it, others rubbed their heads from side to side on the fresh grass. It took some time before they settled and grazed more peacefully.

Now the cows were out to grass spring had definitely arrived. I had heard the cuckoo twice and the moorhen was sitting on her usual safe and hidden place amongst the bulrushes of the farm pond, and the swallows had returned to their old nests in the stables. My newly acquired Muscovy ducks had produced several large broods which they took down to the stream every morning, and every evening I went to collect a few little ducklings which got left behind, too weak and exhausted to waddle up the long hill back to the farm.

The lovely weather had lasted all day. After supper I left my sleeping children in Marion's care and walked through the archway to my favourite field, the Barton, where Tom was helping the first Ayrshire heifer from Scotland to calve. I could see him and the cow standing under the two large oak trees halfway down the field, but, not wanting to disturb the calving, I sat down on a hillock and watched.

A gentle wind was turning the thin green blades of the summer barley in the next field into silvery streamers. I heard the farmer from across the valley calling his cows in for a late milking, his voice set off bleatings from lambs and their mothers in hope of an extra feed. Clumps of bright yellow dandelions on fat milky stems were waiting to run to seed so that the wind could play with their fluffy seed heads and scatter them to multiply. At the bottom of the field, where the ground was wet, pale blue Ladies Smock, or cuckoo spit flowers as children liked to call them, and cowslips grew, and I could smell the wild garlic with its white round feathery flowers which thrived in the shade of the alders near the stream.

The rooks, who returned every evening at the same time to their nests on top of the tall pine trees at the edge of the wood, had already settled down for the night, the wood pigeons cooed softly not to disturb them, but the blackbird sang its heart-rending song as loud as it pleased him. Lambert's castle stood in various greens on the hill to the south, and to the east Pilsdon Pen and the devil's three jumps appeared like silhouettes on the horizon.

Five years had passed since I came to England. Today it felt as if I had always been here. I looked up to the farm buildings behind me. I never failed to admire their solidness, and I loved every stone of the strong structures. Beyond the high archway stood our cosy farmhouse in the farmyard. My heart was filled with happiness and thankfulness. It had taken a bit of time to separate what had once made me happy from my new life in a foreign country. I was at last able to put my happy memories into a compartment of their own, so that I could fully enjoy my new happiness. It had not been easy to adapt to the different ways and customs of another country, but the constant love and patience of my husband and the support from his family, and the acceptance and help from friends and the villagers had enabled me to take roots like my little oak tree from Germany, which I had planted at the entrance to the farm and which was thriving.

I got up and joined Tom, and the cow, which had just given birth. The calf was lying, wet and helpless, beside its mother. Tom pushed a blade of grass up its nose to clear it so it could breath more freely. The mother started to lick the bloodstained and slimy coat of the calf and soon it made an effort to stand up. Tom helped it onto its wobbly legs and gently pushed it towards the mother's teats to suck. The mother's name was Beauty but because the calf, the first Ayrshire pedigree heifer calf of the new herd, was born on Tom's birthday, we called it Thomasina.

A stillness lay by now over the wood and fields, and the grass felt damp from the evening dew. A thin mist rose from the stream at the bottom of the field. The setting sun had made way to the sickle of a new moon. Tom put his arm around my shoulders, and happily and slowly we walked up the hill to the farm and our two sleeping children.

Drawing and book cover by Maria Greenshields-Ziman

ACKNOWLEDGEMENTS

I would like to thank my friend Diana Souhami for editing 'A Bit of Time', Jean Wellings for typing my manuscript, and also my children for their support and critical advice.

Renate and Tom Greenshields were married for 47 years and lived with their 5 children on the family farm on the Devon-Dorset border. After 35 years of farming Tom handed over the farm to his eldest son and devoted his time to painting and sculpture. Tom died in 1994. Renate still lives in the old farmhouse which remains a focal point for her children and grandchildren.

Her parents moved to England in 1970 and lived in the 'Old Dairy' on Westhay Farm until the end of their lives.

Renate's brother, Gewi, went to live in America in 1957 and managed his uncle's farm in New York State.

He never married and is now retired. He stays in constant touch with Renate and her family.